D1284747

Bruce Roberts-Goodson

METAL BOATS
STEEL . ALUMINUM . COPPER-NICKEL

Bruce Roberts-Goodson
METAL BOATS
STEEL . Aluminum . COPPER-NICKEL

COPYRIGHT 1998 R. Bruce Roberts-Goodson

ISBN 186163 031X

First Edition 1998

All rights reserved

Except for limited excerpting in a news article or review, no part of this book may be utilised in any form or by any means electrical or mechanical, including photocopying, recording, or by any information retrieval system, without explicit permission from the author.

International edition published by:
Capall Bann Publishing
Freshfields
Chieveley
Berkshire
RG20 8TF
England UK
Sales Tel and Fax + 44 (0) 1635 247050
Editorial Tel and Fax + 44 (0) 1635 248711

USA and Canadian Edition published by:
Heron House
PO Box 1086 Severna Park
MD 21146 USA
Telephone + 1 410 349 2743
Fax + 1 410 349 2744

CONTENTS

INTRODUCTION

My first and later intense interest in metal boats came about almost by accident. By 1973, I was already established as a designer of custom fiberglass sail and powerboats and fiberglass materials were inexpensive and readily available. Our building techniques were proven and widely accepted around the world; who needed any other building material. The oil embargo of the early seventies changed all of that.

Our clients still wanted to build boats, so we were forced to consider the options. Ferro cement was already thoroughly discredited as a boatbuilding material; wood/epoxy was becoming established, but the materials were expensive and did not have a wide appeal. By the process of elimination we turned our attention to metal.

In 1973, excluding the Dutch, there were relatively few designers and builders of metal pleasure boats, so we felt free to develop our own techniques, but where to start? That was easy; the Dutch had been building metal, particularly steel, boats for almost a century so I spent several weeks visiting many boatbuilding yards in Holland. Fortunately the Dutch are friendly people and I was able to study the building techniques and discuss construction methods with several established builders.

Our first plan designed for steel construction, was the Mauritius 43 sailboat; over the following 20 years 800 of this design were built by individuals and another 150 by professional yards around the world. This first plan designed especially for steel was quickly followed by several other sailboat designs for steel construction including the Roberts 34, Offshore 44 and Roberts 53. Early steel powerboat plans included the Coastworker 30, Waverunner 34, Waverunner 40/42, and Waverunner 45. As of now over 15,000 steel sail and powerboats have been successfully built to our designs.

Up until 1984 although a few boats were constructed in round bilge hull form, (these were built to modified versions of the fiberglass lines), most of the steel and aluminum boats built to our plans were constructed using the double chine technique. In 1985 we switched to computer design and this made it possible to draw radius chine designs that were easy to build and had all the beauty of a round bilge hull. At last we could offer metal hull shapes that rivalled their fiberglass sisters. These radius chine hulls can be built by anyone with some welding experience and are as simple to build as any hard chine boat.

We were introduced to Aluminum in 1974 when a client requested a design to be constructed in that material. Since that time many boats have been built using our plans that were especially prepared with aluminum in mind. As my preferences will no doubt become obvious as this text develops; I may as well state, that when considering a cruising boat, I prefer the use of aluminum to be restricted to decks and superstructures. Fortunately for the sake of variety, not all builders agree with me and we do prepare plans for aluminum-hulled vessels as well as steel and more recently copper-nickel.

Copper-Nickel has been used to build several commercial vessels and a few pleasure craft. With the greater interest in ecology, higher cost and restriction on types of antifouling available; you will find this material has a lot of advantages if you can manage the higher basic material cost.

As I spend more or less equal time on both sides of the Atlantic you may, depending on your location, note some variation in the spelling of certain words. Please excuse this omission on my part; perhaps one day the English language will be standardised to the joy of all writers who are fortunate enough to have their books and articles published on both sides of the Atlantic.

ACKNOWLEDGEMENTS

My sincere thanks go to all of those European metal boatbuilders, especially those in Holland who back in 1973 gave me such good advice when I needed it most. To Grahame Shannon, the developer of 'Auto Yacht', and other yacht design computer programs that have changed yacht design forever. To Carol A. Powell, a gracious lady, consultant metallurgist and Copper-Nickel expert, who provided me with copious quantities of information about the history, properties and handling of copper-nickel. To the Copper Development Association (CDA) and the Nickel Development Institute (NIDI) groups and their various consultants and experts for their help in furthering my knowledge of Copper-nickel. To Max Pille and all of the engineers at Heart Interface who provided me with additional information on things electrical.

To the many hundreds of builders of metal boats constructed from my plans who have sent photographs, asked intelligent questions and offered valuable suggestions; these builders have made a great contribution to the development of our metal building techniques. Special thanks are due to my wife Gwenda, who has supported me in my work for over thirty years; she has not hesitated to impose *the women's view* when it came to designing items in which she was particularly interested. As a very active first mate, these items were not restricted to the galley or other stereotype areas of design.

My thanks to Andrew Slorach, my long time partner and associate who is always ready to offer constructive advice, to George Love my boat building mentor, to Philip Sheaf my UK agent and finally to all those in the boating industry who over the past 30 years, have helped me to chart a course through the shoals that have claimed so many who have tried to turn their hobby into a business.

Spray 40 built
by Ulrich Kronberg in Germany

Chapter 1
WHY METAL?

History of metal boatbuilding. Examples of successful metal boats. Advantages and disadvantages of the various metals. Costs verses other materials.

HISTORY

It took an oil crisis, to extend the popularity of metal pleasure boats from parts of Europe to the rest of the world. Metal boats have a long and distinguished heritage stretching back 200 years. The first recorded instance of a small metal boat was a 12 ft / 3.66 M iron hull built on the banks of the River Fosse in England in 1777. Ten years later the next known example, a 70 ft / 21.33 M iron canal boat, was built using 5/8" / 13 mm riveted plates laid over a timber frame. In 1818 the first all metal commercial boat was built in Scotland. The 'Vulcan' was 63 ft / 19.20 M LOA and 13 FT/ 3.96 M beam. This boat was built using flat bar frames and riveted iron plates and was the forerunner to hundreds of boats and ships built using similar techniques.

As suitable timber boatbuilding materials become increasingly hard to find, more and more designers and ship builders turned to metal. There were many owners who continued to insist on traditional wooden boats. As recently as the late 1960's one could hear comments like 'If god wanted metal (or later fiberglass) boats he would have made fish out of those materials'. Sounds stupid now!

The year 1834 was an important milestone for metal boats; in that year a violent storm drove hundreds of wooden boats and ships ashore in England. Most of these were totally destroyed, but one exception to this universal disaster, was the 125 ft / 38.10 M all metal 'Gary Owen'. This boat was also driven ashore but the hull was able to withstand the severe pounding until she was refloated after the storm subsided. It did not go unnoticed that the 'Gary Owen' suffered only a few scrapes and scratches and that she returned to port under her own power.

Another boost for metal ships occurred when the first all metal liner 'Great Britain' came to grief on the Irish coast and was later refloated and resumed active service. These incidents did much to popularise all-metal vessels so that gradual acceptance turned into a flood of orders for builders of metal ships.

Ship owners soon found that metal ships were more resistant to the stresses of all weather conditions imposed on vessels required go to sea and keep schedules. Many wooden ships had been lost with all hands when the some of the fastenings let go under extreme weather conditions. Ship owners found that although fire can occur in boats and ships constructed out of any material, metal vessels are better able to stay afloat, giving the crew additional time to bring the fire under control.

As far back as 1853, a survey of sailing ships operating in the Far East trade, revealed that metal ships cost as much as 20 percent less to build and operate. Comparing equal sized vessels, it was proven that metal ships were able to carry up to 25 per cent more cargo that an otherwise identical wooden vessel. When the results of this extensive survey were published, it gave a great boost to metal shipbuilding and no doubt played a part, in the fact that Great Britain became the largest builder of commercial shipping and remained so until the Second World War.

In 1858, the all metal 'Great Eastern' was built in UK and at the time this 700 ft / 213 M LOA and 85 ft / 25.91 M beam vessel, was the worlds largest ship. To a world where trade was increasing at a great rate, this proved that there was virtually no limit to the size ship that could be built using metal. It is interesting to compare this early metal ship against the longest wooden ship ever built the 'Dunderberg' which was a mere 377 ft / 114.91 M LOA.

STEEL

Up to the early 1860's all metal ships were built of wrought iron, however about this time, a new material become available. Steel was lighter than iron but this new wonder material had one major drawback; it cost four times as much as the iron it would soon replace. Economy of scale soon prevailed and as steel became affordable, this together with the availability of large sheets soon established this material as the premium ship building material.

Today, we are familiar with the giant liners of the past, including 'France' which was 1,035 ft / 315 M LOA and displaced over 70,000 tons. The liner 'United States', holds the fastest passage time for an

Atlantic passenger ship making the trip in only 3 days and 10 hours and averaging 35.59 knots for the crossing. More recently the preponderance of new giant size liners entering the charter trade has spawned a great revival of steel shipbuilding.

Steel warships and oil tankers dwarf the famous passenger ships of the past. The aircraft carrier 'USS Nimitz' displaces 95,000 tons and the 'Seawise Giant' measures 1,504 ft / 458.52 M LOA, 225 ft / 68.58 M beam and weighs in at 564,763 tons.

While this revolution in large shipbuilding moved almost all construction of commercial shipping out of the timber era and into steel, small boats (except in Europe - mainly Holland) continued to be built in wood.

This situation remained until the early 1960's when the advent of fiberglass changed the pleasure boat scene forever.

ALUMINUM OR ALUMINIUM

This metal is refined from the natural material bauxite. Although discovered early in the Nineteenth century, it was not until 1886 that the first practical refining methods were developed in France. As early as 1894 an aluminum alloy was used in Switzerland to build the power yacht Alumina for Prince Wilhelm zu Wied.

The designers and builders of the liner United States made extensive use of this metal with a weight saving of over 27,000 tons compared to a similar sized all steel vessel. No matter how you spell it, aluminum or aluminium, this is one of today's premier boatbuilding materials and is used to build sail and power yachts from the smallest to the largest craft.

COPPER-NICKEL

Copper is one of the most noble metals in common use and has excellent resistance to corrosion in the atmosphere and in salt water. The Royal Navy introduced copper cladding of wooden warships in the 18th century to prevent the hulls being eaten by marine borers and fouled by other marine growth. The hull of the 'Cutty Sark' and other famous clipper ships were clad with copper. These vessels were required to make fast passages and the protection by the copper ensured that the ship bottoms remained clean and free from marine growth. In 1893 the America Cup defenders 'Vigilant' and 'Enterprise' and other cup defenders of the period had hulls of Tobin Bronze fastened with rivets of the same alloy.

The practice of copper cladding wooden ships and pleasure craft hulls was common up until the mid 1950's, when modern antifouling paints came into common usage. Copper cladding was the forerunner of modern Copper- Nickel alloys that have superior resistance to corrosion together with excellent antifouling properties. Today copper-nickel can be used to clad the underwater sections of both commercial and pleasure boats of all types.

In 1938 a 45 ft / 13.72 M motor cruiser 'Miss Revere' was built in USA using 70-30 copper-nickel welded over 70-30 framing and fitted with aluminum bulkheads. Between 1938 and 1965 many US Coast Guard motor whale boats were sheathed at the waterline in copper- nickel. In 1968 the pleasure yacht 'Asperida' was built using 70-30 copper-nickel hull plating, over framing of the same material; this boat is still in service today.

The first of several copper-nickel commercial-fishing boats was built in 1971. The hull of the 67 ft / 20 42 M 'Copper Mariner' was constructed from 1/4" / 6 mm 90-10 welded copper-nickel plate, installed over steel framing. More recently several other trawlers and general-purpose fishing boats have been built using copper- nickel alloys.

One interesting example is the 18 year old sailboat Pretty Penny. I recently inspected this boat in Faversham UK and was most impressed with her condition. This all copper-nickel boat, had not been slipped for 16 years and required only a wooden scraper to remove the layer of grass from the hull. See also chapter 16.

SMALL BOATS

Although there is a long history of metal being used to build large ships, it is only in more recent times that steel, aluminum and more recently copper-nickel have been considered as 'mainline' boatbuilding materials. Metal boatbuilding has come a long way in a few years and even as recently as 1965 very few small craft were built from these materials.

In the early 1960ís at the start of my own career in Brisbane Australia, I knew every small craft in the area and out of some 200 boats, only 3 were built of steel. By 1973 when I started to design in metal there were still less than 10 steel boats in the area. What a difference today, when metal boats are widely accepted as the optimum for serious offshore cruising. It is common for our office to receive letters from cruising people that read ' We are anchored in (any popular cruising area) and there are 20 boats

The Tom Thumb 26 is ideal for building in either Steel, Aluminium or Copper-Nickel and would make a great first project for a your metal boatbuilder.

here....12 are built from steel... a rare dash of modesty prevents me quoting the percentage of these boats that are to my design!

STEEL

This is the most commonly used boatbuilding metal and it has many advantages including great strength, low cost and ease of fabrication. There are great numbers of experienced welders available in all parts of the world. Add to this, the ease of repair and the availability of a wide selection of suitable plans designed especially for building in steel. It is easy to see why steel has become so popular with the cruising fraternity. Successful steel cruising boats can, and have been, built from as small as 25ft / 7.62 M LOA. The Dutch build steel dinghies of around 15 ft / 4.57 M and use these as tenders on their barges and other commercial craft.

One claimed disadvantage is the fact that steel is heavier than other materials, however this has proven not to be a disadvantage in cruising sail or power craft. Steel needs care and attention to prevent rust, (not a problem with modern coatings). As the owner of several steel boats I must confess I am finding it hard to find any serious disadvantages in building, owning and maintaining a steel boat.

ALUMINIUM

Now widely accepted as a boatbuilding material, aluminum has the advantage of being about one-third the weight of steel, (this is partly offset by the fact that for boatbuilding, a thicker material is necessary). Aluminum is easy to work and hand tools, including some woodworking ones, can be used on this material.

This metal is ideal for decks and superstructures where its lightweight and easy forming characteristics can be used to advantage. In some areas of the world, aluminum has become extremely popular for building commercial craft and fishing boats. The popularity with some commercial fishermen is due to the fact, that when the correct marine grades are used, the entire boat can be left unpainted.

The disadvantages include greater cost and relatively greater susceptibility to corrosion. Aluminum requires expert fabricators and experienced welders who are used to handling this material. Aluminum has less impact strength than other metals (on a dark and stormy night, think about those containers floating around in the ocean). When and if repairs are required, then aluminum also needs welders who are used to handling this material...not a problem if you have 'built your own'.

COPPER-NICKEL

This material has all of the advantages of steel, with additional benefits that it has natural corrosion resistance and antifouling elements. This material is inherently more corrosion resistant than steel. Copper-nickel requires no painting or anodes in that it has a natural anti-fouling element. These benefits may make it the choice of those that can afford the initial extra material cost. Another advantage is that you will never be short of conversation amongst your peers if you choose this material.

Disadvantages include the shortage of experienced boatbuilders used to handling this metal, greater cost and the sense of being a 'pioneer' when you decide to build a copper-nickel boat.

COST OF METAL BOATS VERSES OTHER MATERIALS

Steel is the least expensive of the metals suitable for boatbuilding and is considerably cheaper than either fiberglass or the materials used in wood/epoxy construction. Steel is definitely today's bargain boatbuilding material. Aluminum costs a few percentage points less than fiberglass or wood/epoxy and Copper-nickel is a little more expensive than the latter.

The hull costs (meaning hull, deck and super-structure) represent only 25 to 33 per cent of the overall cost of the vessel. A good argument can be made for ignoring the cost factor of the hull. If your budget allows this, then choose the material that is most suitable for your needs. After you have examined the building techniques explained in later chapters, then you will be in a better position to make an informed decision.

This tidy Pilot House would look equally attractive on either a power or sailboat

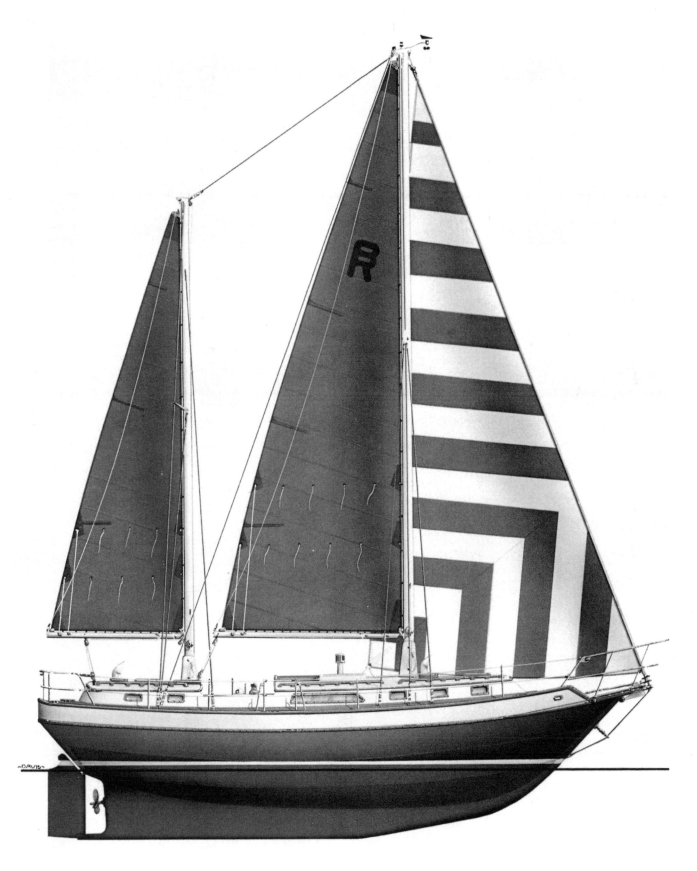

The Spray 38 is a very popular choice for those who prefer a traditional boat incorporating a center cockpit layout. Othe r versions of this design have been built incorporating a pilot house and poop stern.

Chapter 2
GETTING STARTED

Involving the family. Live-a-board or weekend cruiser? Buying new or Custom building. Buying Secondhand. Starting from a Hull and deck. Starting from a pre-cut kit. Starting from scratch. Building sites. Finance or pay as you build.

INVOLVING THE FAMILY

Before your decision making process gets into top gear, you will be well advised to get your partner and family involved. Over the past thirty odd years I have seen many boating projects come to grief because the senior family member failed to consult with, or listen to, the wishes of the others. You will have to forgive me if I repeat this advice elsewhere; I feel it is worth the telling!

Do not buy or build a boat that is larger than you need. Reaching this decision is harder than you may imagine. If you have children whom you expect to accompany you throughout your boating adventure, make sure that you think through the options. For instance if you have teenagers, the chances are that within a few years they will be 'doing their own thing' and not interested in accomp-anying their parents. It is a fact that many families cruise with young children, correspondence schooling and other provisions made especially to cater for your young crew, can turn cruising into a wonderful experience for the entire family.

Power or sail or a 50/50; that is a decision that you may have already reached before you discuss the options with your spouse or other family members. Age has a bearing on this decision; if you are under 40 then you will most probably opt for sail, up to 55 it may be a toss up and over 60 power may be your choice. There are many exceptions to the above but it is my experience that the happiest boaters fall into the age/sail/power categories outlined above.

Most female partners enjoy the comfort, convenience, 'level playing field', and perceived safety of power boats as opposed to trying to prepare meals and generally 'keep house' at varying degrees of heel. If more males chose semi displacement power boats or at least comfortable sailboats like the Spray type, then their female partners would be (and remain) more enthusiastic about the project.

The above represents my view of the comfortable cruising lifestyle. In the many years I have spent designing and supervising the construction of hundreds of boats of all types, I have met many of the families before, during, and after their boating adventure. My suggestion is that you give the above comments some serious consideration when you are making a decision as to which boat will suit you and your families needs.

LIVE-ABOARD OR WEEKEND CRUISER

If this is your first boating experience, then you should consider a boat that is suitable for weekend and holiday cruising as opposed to jumping in at the deep end and acquiring a fully equipped live-aboard cruiser. Again your age will have a bearing on your decision; the younger you are, the more time you will have to correct any mistakes of judgement you may make when choosing your next boat. Most people, who enjoy their boating experience, will own more than two or three boats in their lifetime. You will need to consider if this boat is truly 'the boat' or just a stepping stone in that direction.

A metal weekend cruiser can be as small as 25 ft / 7.62 M or as large as you can afford or handle with the available family crew. It is my advice, that one should never own a boat that can not be handled by a crew of two. Most boats that are used regularly, as opposed to those that languish in the local marina are crewed by a couple who can easily operate the boat without the assistance of outside help. How big is too big? We have many Roberts 53 sailboats successfully cruised by healthy and active couples. Neither crew is required to have an outstanding physique. Modern equipment makes it possible for persons of smaller statue, to comfortably handle the sails and associated gear.

Before deciding on size and type of vessel that will best suit your needs, you may wish to read more on the subject; see appendix 1 for a list of books that can help you to make an informed decision.

BUYING NEW

If you are considering a powerboat and you live in Europe then you will have a wide choice of metal boats to choose from. There are many builders of fine steel cruisers in Holland, UK and elsewhere in the EU. The off the shelf motor cruisers built by the Dutch are mainly intended for coastal and canal work. The quality of hull construction, interior joinery and general finish is first class.

In the USA and Canada, there are a few builders of stock metal boats, and most of these companies build fine boats. Fortunately the shoddy builders soon disappear; make sure you are not one of their customers before they quit the scene. Because of the wide circulation of this book and taking into account the time between writing, publication and today, you may wish to contact one of our offices for a list of builders and kit manufacturers in your area.

BUYING A USED BOAT

Buying a used metal boat is another option but the purchase of a second hand boat can be fraught with traps for the unwary. The term buyer beware is never more apt than when buying a used boat. With any boat age has its potential problems and for that matter any manufactured item, so the younger the better. Naturally there are cases where a well built and maintained older metal boat is superior to a jerry built near new vessel, but never-the-less try and consider boats that are less than 5 years old. As mentioned above this advice applies to any boat no matter what material is used to build the hull.

Older boats with teak decks are to be viewed with suspicion, assume you may have to replace or extensively repair the decks and factor this into your offer. Remember that a boat that needs extensive repairs and renovation will cost you nearly as much as building a new one and the result will still be an older boat with a doubtful resale value.

Now having painted that picture of doom and gloom, let me say that there are some fine used metal boats out there but you have not only to find them but you will have to sort through a considerable number of undesirable examples before you find your dream boat. We have owned many boats, mostly new, but the last two were used steel boats. Both these boats were and only lightly used and under 5 years old when we purchased them. With K*I*S*S we were able to recover all of our investment after two years use.

If you are able to deal directly with the owner you may avoid some of the pit-falls associated with this type of purchase. You must make sure you are absolutely satisfied BEFORE you hand over your money. ALWAYS hire a qualified surveyor to check out your boat purchase before you part with any substantial amounts of cash.

In the USA boats are often documented which is a similar arrangement to the UK Part 1 Register. For British residents, the UK Part 1 certificate will be a good way to prove ownership. Make sure you call the Registrar Generals office in Cardiff to check that the document is current. The certificate issued by the Small Ships Register is not a proof of ownership but it will be a start. Another way to check ownership is to contact the yacht insurers and the harbour master where the boat is kept. It is well to remember that at least in the UK, if you buy a boat from a person who does not have legal title to the vessel and it is later reclaimed by its lawful owner, you will most likely be out of pocket and lose your boat and your money. The boat you are considering buying may be subject to a hire purchase agreement, it may form part of a legal dispute or there may be some other impediment in the title. Make sure you carefully check builders certificates, bills of sale and any other documentation that is offered to prove the current ownership.

SURVEYS ARE A MUST

You will often have to pay for the boat to be hauled before it is in a position to allow for a full survey. To cut your potential costs, why not conduct a very detailed inspection of the interior, galley equipment, pumps, heating, batteries as well as mast(s), rigging, sails, dinghy and electronic equipment before you commit yourself to a full survey. Do not be rushed, do not be afraid of being a nuisance, take your time. If you have trusted and knowledgeable friends who have a proven knowledge of things boating, ask their help and advice at this early stage. Do not ignore advice because you have fallen in love with the boat. Assemble your facts and on no account part with your cash before you are in possession of all the information as to the boat's condition.

CUSTOM BUILDING

Many of you will be considering either having your metal boat fully or partially custom-built. Most owners of metal boats are better informed than owners of vessels built from other materials and many are capable of building or supervising the construction of their new vessel.

If you opt for a custom built metal boat, then you will need the services of a competent naval architect / boat designer who is familiar with your chosen material. Fortunately there are several designers who have either specialised in or had experience in designing metal boats in steel, aluminum and more recently copper-nickel.

A custom built boat need cost you no more than an off the shelf equivalent. One way to save money is to act as your own contractor. You rent the building space and then hire local workmen to do the work. This is another advantage of building in metal; any competent person with suitable welding experience that is appropriate to the particular metal, and equipped with a detailed plan, can build a metal boat. All of the materials and equipment, engines, electrical gear and in fact everything that goes into building and equipping your vessel can be purchased locally. If you go about this in the right way and buy most items at trade prices, you can save a great deal of money; perhaps this will enable you to afford a larger boat. A letterhead with your 'Boatbuilding Company' name and address will go a long way to convincing suppliers to give you trade discounts; make no mistake they want your order, so make it easy for them to supply you at trade or discount prices!

STARTING FROM A PRE-CUT KIT

In some areas it is possible to purchase a kit of parts that have been cut from plate and your job is to assemble these into a hull deck and superstructure. Now it is difficult to say if the additional cost is warranted. Most designers including ourselves have the capacity to prepare a special computer disk and with the parts 'nested' to allow economical cutting of the parts. It is necessary for the company producing these kits to have the automatic computerised cutting devices and be able to take the disk supplied by the designer and produce your kit. This service introduces additional costs on top of the plans and the metal materials however you may find this a practical and economical way of getting your project off to a quick start.

You will decide if the additional cost is justified; discuss these matters with the designer and with the company who are supplying the kit. It is worth noting that the Dutch are very experienced in producing these pre-cut kits and the primer they use is a specially formulated 'weld primer' so it does not give off fumes when you are welding. Another benefit of the 'weld primer' is that you do not have to grind of the seams before you weld and there is minimal clean up after welding.

HULL AND DECK OPTION

Many metal boat owners start with a hull (hull deck and superstructure) that has been built to their order and delivered to a suitable site for owner completion. Again the owner purchases all of the equipment and

Starting with a pre-cut kit can get your building project off to a good start. These kits are pre-shot blasted and primed.

Tack and weld kits allow you to form up a hull in days rather than weeks. The special weld primer used on many kits has many desirable features; see text.

This Roberts 43 hull and deck was built by Custom Steel Boats of Merritt North Carolina USA

Mr Ozannes built this steel Roberts 36 from scratch

finishing materials and then undertakes as much of the labour as they wish. See note above about buying at 'trade' prices.

There are many books written for those who want to build or partially build their own boat, see appendix 1. If you do not want to do these jobs yourself, local electricians, mechanics and other tradesmen can be hired to undertake parts of the work. You are in charge, you decide just how much or how little you want to do yourself.

One thing is for sure; you will save a great deal of money and end up with a boat that you can easily maintain. If you plan any extensive cruising, it is imperative that you are familiar with every aspect of your vessel. What better way to know your boat than to have worked on the construction? After studying all of the options you can personally select all the equipment required to complete your vessel.

BUILDING FROM SCRATCH

Many thousands of owners have built their metal boats from scratch. These determined individuals have selected a design, purchased plans and basic materials and built their own hull deck and superstructure. Depending on the size of your boat and whether you are building part or full time, this

process will add from 3 to 12 months to the overall building time.

There are many of you who have some welding experience. If you feel you would like to build from the ground up, do not be put off by the enormity of the project. Choose a design that has been especially drawn for the less experienced builder; there are many designers who can provide you with suitable plans. Some designers including ourselves provide full size patterns for the frames and other parts of the hull structure.

I am often asked how long it takes to build your own boat; here are a couple of extremes. One Roberts 53 steel sailboat including the hull deck and superstructure, was built and equipped ready for sailing, by one Australian man and an occasional helper, in the unbelievable time of 10 months. One has to assume that this person purchased many items ready made.

Another builder of the same design took ten years part time, however he made everything himself including the sails. This tenacious builder even made patterns to have his winches cast and then finished them himself. The builder was recently sailing his 53 ft / 16.15 M boat off the Australian coast. The photos

Radius chine Roberts 64 built by Richard White and family of Quebec Canada

they sent me show a happy couple enjoying their boat and cruising far from home. This builder has now completed his circumnavigation and is now back home in Germany. In our records there are hundreds of letters from builders who fall between these two extremes.

FINANCE OR PAY AS YOU BUILD

Unless you are financially independent, you will have to consider how you are going to pay for your new boat. If you decide to purchase a new or fully equipped used vessel, then you may decide to finance part or most of the purchase. There are many finance houses that will be pleased to offer you a loan. This involves many additional costs including interest and loan set up fees etc.

A more favourable interest rate is usually available if you obtain a 'marine mortgage' as opposed to a simple bank or finance company loan. In the USA there are many Banks, Saving and Loans and other similar lenders who make 10, 15 and twenty-year loans available to purchase a new boat. Before you sign any finance agreement make sure you are aware of all the interest and other expenses involved.

Paying as you build will mean that not only will you save on the overall cost of the boat, but you will also avoid interest and other associated charges. I have seen thousands of fine boats built or completed by their owners who on launching day have the extra thrill of knowing that their pride and joy was dept free. Some builders have it both ways, they build as much as they can afford paying cash and then raise a loan, using the part built boat as security.

BUILDING SITES

If you decide to custom build from a hull and deck package, or from scratch, you will need a suitable building site. Depending on where you live you may have many, or a limited number or choices. If you live in a warmer area, then a simple shelter will suffice. If your boat is to be built or completed in a cold climate, then you will to need to consider a heated structure. In any case you will need some form of secure building, in which to house your tools and more valuable supplies. Fortunately when building a metal boat the need for security is relatively less than if you were building in fiberglass or plywood, this benefit only extends until you start on the interior and fitting out stage. Even if working outside, it is a good idea to keep the more valuable items out of sight or maybe in more secure storage, until they can be properly secured to, or installed in the boat.

Part of the advantages of having your boatbuilding project located in a secure, comfortable and weather proof building, is purely psychological; it will be easier to make the effort to go and work on the boat. Also if you are paying rent on a building, you are more likely to 'get on with the job'. If you are building totally outside and exposed to the elements then you will often have to stop work due to inclement weather conditions. All of the disadvantages of building outside can add months to your building program.

To determine how much space you will need to house your boatbuilding project, simply plan for a space 50 percent longer and 100 percent wider than the finished boat. For instance if you are building a 40 ft / 12.19 M by 13 ft / 3.96 M boat your space should ideally be 60 ft / 18.29 M long by say 26 ft / 7.92 M wide. This is the minimum area required. When it comes to handling plate and other construction members, you will need s-p-a-c-e! You will need room for tools, materials storage as well as space to move around.

To provide yourself with an efficient working environment, plan your building site so that the minimum time is spent walking from one area to another. The siting of benches and frequently used tools, will play a part in making a comfortable and productive workplace.

Your boatbuilding project should not be too far from home and this is even more important, if you are only working part time on the project. Travelling time can eat into valuable work time and distance can be a deterrent to getting started evenings and weekends. Make sure that your work site is accessible to the large trucks needed to deliver long lengths of plate and other necessary supplies. If you are working outside be sure you have a flat level site. Carrying tools and building materials up even the smallest gradient, can soon become a tiring exercise..... Exercise, yes, you will get plenty of that!

One obvious choice is to build your boat beside your house. Many fine boats of 65 ft / 19.81 M, have been built to my design beside the owners home. To make this a practical proposition, you need to live on a large lot or in an isolated area.

Many local authorities have building ordinances that may govern just what you can do in your own back yard. Check these before you start building a shelter or erecting boat frames beside your house.

Steel. 'Boatbuilding' steel specifications. Stainless

This steel Spray 40 shows several attractive and sensible features including substantial pipe guardrails, (stainless would have been nice), a nicely laid teak deck, note wider covering board around edge, a sturdy pair of stainless bollards on the foredeck, a timber rubbing strip "stood off" the hull, a pair of stainless bow fairleads and a well laid out fore-cabin top.

"Bellavia". Built in the UK, this steel Spray 33 has now crossed the Atlantic and is currently sailing somewhere in US waters.

Generally speaking, the further you live from the centre of town, the better chance you have of being able to build or complete a boat on your own property. If you are not committed to a mortgage, you may consider renting a suitable house away from the town centre and building you boat in the grounds of your rented property. Best check with the landlord first and get permission in writing, before you sign the lease.

If you start with a hull and deck, then all you may need is a tool shed; the hull can be heated and the outside work can be completed in fine weather. Another advantage of starting with a ready built shell is that this may make it possible to complete the boat in your own yard. Metalworking is noisy especially when building the hull and deck. If your boatbuilding project is sited in a residential area, then make sure that the noise that can be heard outside the boat is kept to a minimum.

Here are a few suggestions as to possible boat-building locations: in your own yard, unused corners of marinas and boat yards, fenced in but unused industrial sites, beside or in an engineering business, inside old warehouses, inside or beside an old storage barn. These are just a few of the many possibilities and these locations can often be rented at a low monthly cost.

Make sure you think ahead to the day that the boat is completed and ready for launching. Can a low loader and lifting crane get to your location and move your boat to the launching site? Have you surveyed the route? Check for low overhead wires, sharp corners in narrow streets. We have seen it all; there are hundreds of stories about boats being lifted over houses, lifted from mountain sites by large helicopters and boats that were literally dragged through villages by willing helpers.

Build carefully if you wish to emulate this spray 40 sailed to the antartic by her owner builder Alan Sendall

Chapter 3
THE MATERIALS

steel. Aluminium. Copper. Aluminum and Copper-Nickel. Miscellaneous metals used in building a boat.

STEEL

As mentioned earlier, steel is the today's bargain boatbuilding material. If possible chooses pre-shot blasted primed materials. The terms sand blasting, grit blasting and shot blasting all have a similar meaning as is explained elsewhere. If you are building outside then you will lose some of the pre-coating. The benefits are so positive that pre-prime coating is worth your consideration and it not only provides a cleaner working environment, but it will encourage you to arrange a temporary cover. When welding prime coated steel, you should wear a protective mask. Avoid inhaling the fumes released as the prime coating is burnt off around the weld.

One of the main benefits of using pre-shot blasted and primed materials, is that when you have completed the hull and deck you should not need to shot or grit blast the interior. This part of the blasting process is the most time consuming and expensive. If it can be avoided by using pre-primed, painted steel, it is worth the cost and effort of obtaining this material. You may wish to consider pre-shot blasting and priming your metal before you start construction. Make sure you use 'weld primer' that is specially formulated for use on plate that will later be welded. One brand is Sigma weld primer; other manufacturers should have similar products.

In previous times, I was of the opinion that building outside and using unprepared steel was a good idea, the theory being that the weather removed some of the mill scale and other surface impurities. As you can see by the above text, I have changed my mind. You may take longer to build your boat than you originally planned, and the wastage of metal through rusting, could be a sizeable factor, in the life expectancy of the boat.

STEEL PLATE

When ordering the plate, make sure you specify 'Plate mill' and not 'Strip mill' plate. Plate mill stock is plate that has never been coiled. Strip mill is plate that after manufacture has been rolled into large coils; later this steel is unrolled and sold as flat plate. The Strip mill plate has a 'memory' so it will not be as neutral before you start to bend it. If you are forced to use Strip mill material, try and ascertain the natural curve of the plate and use it to your advantage.

Chart # 3. Mild steel in LBS and Kilos etc.

MILD STEEL PLATE IN LBS PR SQ FT AND KILOS PER METRE		
THICKNESS	POUNDS PER SQ FT.	KILOS PER SQ METRE
3mm	-	24.5
1/8"	5.10	-
10 Gauge	5.52	-
9 Gauge	6.10	-
5/32"	6.37	-
4mm	-	33.5
8 Gauge	6.75	-
7 Gauge	7.30	-
3/16"	7.65	-
6 Gauge	7.97	-
5 mm	-	30.5
5 Gauge	8.70	-
7/32"	8.92	-
4 Gauge	9.14	-
6mm	-	48.5
3 Gauge	9.77	-
1/4"	10.2	-

My choice for steel boatbuilding is low carbon plate. You will find there are many different grades of steel available, but we recommend LOW CARBON steel with a carbon content of less than 0.15 percent, or MILD steel that has a carbon content of between 0.15 and 0.23 percent. The highest carbon content acceptable to most classification authorities, is 0.23 percent, so it is recommended you stay below that figure. Both low carbon and mild steel are available in various shapes, strips and plate and offer good welding characteristics. As code numbers vary from country to country, you should seek advice from your steel supplier, to ensure that you receive the correct materials as suggested above.

The plate thickness will be specified in your plans but remember that it is harder to avoid distortion, when welding materials thinner that are thinner than 1/8"/ 3 mm. Even this thickness should be restricted to decks and cabins, and hulls on boats, under 35 ft / 10.66 M. Your designer will specify the plate thickness recommended for your boat. When building steel boats in the smaller sizes, it is better to reduce the amount of framing, than reduce the plate thickness

Some builders increase the plate thickness without consulting the designer. In a steel boat, this can have disastrous results. If you are unable to obtain plating as specified in your plans, always contact the designer for advice. Changing the plating thickness may require rescheduling the spacing and sizes of the framing.

DEFECTS IN STEEL

As you may be responsible for the quality of the steel being used in your boat you should be aware of the common defects that may be present. Check for 'wavy' areas in the sheet, this can appear as small uneven areas of a 'wavy' appearance. Another defect that may show up is 'rolled in mill scale' and this problem is caused when scale already on the sheet is rolled into the surface. Buckled or kinks in the plate can be caused by improper handling after manufacture. You may find thin areas in the centre and ends of pipe.

COR-TEN

Avoid materials such as Cor-ten or high tensile steels. These steels have limited, or no boatbuilding applications. Some designers have previously recommended Cor-ten, however this steel contains traces of copper and rather than inhibit corrosion in salt water. Cor-ten was developed for use in industrial applications such as water tanks on farm properties, and other uses where it would receive little or no protection from the weather. Cor-ten is intended for atmospheric structural applications. It does not have good corrosion resistance when immersed in any water especially seawater.

Cor-ten is also more expensive than mild steel and it works well when used for the purpose for which it was developed, but not for boatbuilding. Another disadvantage of this material is that it needs to be welded using copper clad continuous feed electrodes and Argon arc shielding. We do NOT recommend Cor-ten or other speciality steels for boatbuilding. Occasionally we are asked about the possibility of building a boat in stainless steel; simple answer don't! Elsewhere I will detail the uses of stainless steel.

BUYING PLATE

The price of steel plate varies from supplier to supplier, so shop around. Generally speaking the more you buy, the lower the price per pound / kilo / tonne. It is recommended that you order all of the plate, stringer materials and other flat bar and angle at the one time. Many designers supply a material list with the plans. It is wise to compare this list against the plans, as this will give you a better understanding of the drawings than any other method. Use your material list to obtain quotes from as many suppliers as possible. In most cases, 15 percent should be allowed for wastage.

Stock sizes of sheet are 8 ft by 4 ft / 2.50 x 1.25 M and 6 ft x 3 ft / 2.00 x 1.00 M however some stockist's can supply sheets 10 ft or 12 ft / 3.00 x 3.50 M long. Note metric sizes are rounded out to the most likely available sizes. Another consideration is that the steel supplier may make additional charges for the larger or unusual sizes of plate and the delivery costs may also be higher. The size of your boat and the steel handling equipment you have available may decide the sheet sizes for your project.

It is better to weld your plates into as long a length as practical, before installing them on the hull. You will achieve a much fairer hull by following this practice. The same advice applies to stringers and other longitudinal framing.

STEEL FRAMING

Framing includes the transverse frames, stringers, stem and backbone. For small to medium sized boats, these can be fabricated from flat bar stock. For deck and cabin top beams it is preferable to use L angle or T bar (flange down) as this provides a suitable cavity for the insulation material. It allows the lining materials to be fastened to the underside of the flange.

Hull frames may be flat bar or L angle. My objections to angle used to be that it was more difficult to keep the rust out of the angle. More recently we recommend that all hulls have spray in foam insulation. Where the spray-in-place foam is installed, there is much less chance of rust forming around the frames. Weight is another consideration, and for this reason alone I would not recommend angle frames in boats under 40 ft / 12.19 M. Heavy displacement boats and larger vessels can carry the extra weight and also will benefit from the extra strength of the angle frames. We have just completed plans for a new Spray Pilot House 40, and in this case I have suggested angle L or T frames as an option. The presence of the flange will assist in the lining and fitting out process. On flat bar frames timber " strips are screwed to the frames to accept the lining materials.

As mentioned above the stringers, stem and backbone will almost always be fabricated from flat bar stock. Occasionally solid round bar is used for the chines; there will be more on this subject elsewhere in this text. Web floors or otherwise known as 'solid floors' (gussets at the bottom of the frames), are best-formed using plate that is the same thickness as the frames.

STAINLESS STEEL

This material has no place below the waterline on most boats. The problem is ëshieldingí corrosion caused by oxygen starvation, which in turn will promote crevice corrosion. The important factor is the amount of oxygen over the surface of the steel; one part of the steel must not be starved of oxygen while another part has it available. This phenomenon is known as 'oxygen differential' and this condition will set up an electrochemical cell and it will lead to rapid deterioration of the stainless member.

Stainless steel is ideal for deck fittings, chain plates and stanchions. Stainless is also required as a liner in areas where dock and anchor lines, would soon wear off the paint. Always paint 2" / 50 mm onto the stainless to prevent galvanic action between any defects in the painted mild steel and the un-coated stainless fitting.

The types of stainless steel most commonly used in boatbuilding fall into the 300 series, namely 302, 304 and 316. The 316 grade is considered the best for marine use and should be used wherever ultimate strength and freedom from corrosion are required.

When the quoted number is followed by the letter L this indicates a low carbon content; this feature facilitates welds having good corrosion resistance by avoiding loss of chromium at the grain boundaries. The free machining grades, type 303 or 303e, should never be used in seawater. They are often used for fasteners and corrode as they contain sulphate particles to facilitate the machining operation. The particles create a surface with numerous built-in alloys to particle galvanic cells. See 'Corrosion Gremlins' in later chapter.

BRONZE

This material is formed from copper, tin and varying small amounts of other elements. This is a fine metal and it has been used in marine applications from time immemorial. In Roman times, bronze was a prized alloy and had multiple uses, including those in the marine field. The exact combination of metals used to make the bronze alloy will depend on the intended use of the material. Copper is the main ingredient and tin usually occupies 5 to 10 percent of the mix.

Bronze will often take its name from the third metal in the alloy, for instance Phosphor bronze contains about 5 percent tin and only 0.5 percent phosphorus and it is suitable for use in the marine environment. There are several other instances where bronze takes its name from the third most prolific component, for example, aluminum bronze or nickel aluminum bronze often used for propellers.

ALUMINUM (USA) ALUMINIUM (UK and Elsewhere)

Aluminum has been available for over a century, but it is only in the past 40 years, that it has been widely used in boatbuilding applications. Pure aluminum is a soft metal and not suitable for most commercial applications, let alone boatbuilding. There are many aluminum alloys developed and produced for various applications however there are only a few that are suitable for marine use.

Some of the metals used in varying quantities to turn pure aluminum in to a useful material, are chromium, copper, iron, manganese, magnesium, and zinc. Small amounts of these metals are used together with the industrially pure aluminium, to form the final product. For marine use, the main addition to the pure aluminum is magnesium when, depending on the grade, 4 to 5 percent is added.

Because there is no universal worldwide standard grading system for aluminium, you should check you local suppliers for advice in this area. Below are some type numbers and their recommended usage. I have grouped these into UK and US areas and most of the rest of the world follows one or the other system.

The 5000 series and in particular material with the 5086 designation is the metal most commonly used for boatbuilding. There are several different numbers in the 5000 series and it is worth checking with the aluminum MANUFACTURER in your country so you get first hand advice. Do not be fobbed off by an unscrupulous supplier or merchant, who may try to sell you what they have in stock.

The 5000 series has excellent resistance to salt water, is ductile and retains a high strength when welded. In some cases you may choose aluminum with one

```
UK    Hull Plate . . . . . . . . . . . . . . BS 1477 NP8
      Frames and Stringers . . . . . BS 1476 NE8
      Superstructures. . . . . . . . . BS 1470 NS6


USA   Hull Plate . . . . . . . . . . . . . 5086 H116
      Frames and Stringers . . . . . 5086 H116
      Superstructures. . . . . . . . . 5086-32
```

Weights of aluminium plate in pounds per sq. Ft

```
1/16" . . . . . . . . . . . . . . . . . . . . . . . . . . . . . .0.90
1/8" . . . . . . . . . . . . . . . . . . . . . . . . . . . . . .1.76
3/16" . . . . . . . . . . . . . . . . . . . . . . . . . . . . . .2.64
1/4" . . . . . . . . . . . . . . . . . . . . . . . . . . . . . .3.52
5/16" . . . . . . . . . . . . . . . . . . . . . . . . . . . . . .4.53
3/8" . . . . . . . . . . . . . . . . . . . . . . . . . . . . . .5.44
```

CHART # 2. Weights of aluminium plate etc.

designation for hull plate, another for framing and still another for decks and superstructure.

When you are ready to order your aluminum materials, it is always recommended that you make one bulk purchase. As with other metals and indeed all your boatbuilding requirements, it is always best to buy in bulk. If you can find another builder with similar requirements, then a group order is recommended.

At the same time as you are ordering your aluminum plate and framing materials, you should order the filler wire for your MIG welder. The most common wire is 5356, which is compatible with most aluminum alloys used in boatbuilding including 5052, 5086, 6061 and 6063. The 5386 wire can be used to weld these alloys to themselves or to dissimilar alloys. See notes about spool sizes in welding chapter. It is most important to keep your welding wire clean and to use the spool as soon as it is opened. Store the wire in a dry area, and discard any dirty or contaminated material.

We will mainly consider welded aluminium, as this covers most of the boats built from this material. There are exceptions, including the small boats pressed out of a single sheet; these small boats are popular in Australia where they are affectionately known as 'Tinnies'. Riveted construction is still used to build some smaller aluminum boats. Aluminum boats have been formed by explosive techniques however this and other offbeat methods are outside the scope of this book.

For transverse frames you may choose either flat bar, L angle bar, T bar or flat/round top bar. The latter is

sometimes used for longitudinal stringers. For longitudinal framing, stringers and chine bars (if fitted) I prefer flat bar, but the final choice of scantling sections should be left to the designer of your particular boat.

COPPER-NICKEL

Copper, one of the most noble of metals and on its own, has an excellent resistance to corrosion in the atmosphere and in fresh water. When combined with nickel to form 'copper-nickel', it has superior resistance to salt water corrosion. These features, coupled with its excellent anti fouling properties, make it an ideal hull building material.

This material is readily available in sheet form and generally is produced in two main grades. The two copper-nickel alloys that have a good track record for boatbuilding applications are 90-10, an alloy of 90 percent copper and 10 percent nickel and 70-30, which contains 70 percent copper and 30 percent nickel. Both these alloys include small amounts of iron and manganese. Generally these alloys are non-magnetic but in the 90-10 alloy, some magnetic response may be detected depending on how the alloy is processed by the manufacturer. For most marine applications including framing and plating the 90-10 alloy is recommended.

Copper-nickels are ductile and have excellent resistance to fracture under impact loading conditions. Both the above mentioned alloys are single-phase solid solution alloys which cannot be hardened with heat treatment; they can be strengthened by work hardening. Both alloys are easily fabricated and welded. When welding, a 70-30 consumable is preferred for the 90-10 alloy and provides a weld that is galvanically more noble than the base metal. Copper-Nickel can be welded to steel and in that case a 65 percent NICKEL and 35 percent COPPER alloy consumable, is preferred.

Because copper-nickel has good corrosion resistance, angle frames and deck beams are recommended and as mentioned earlier, this makes it simple to fasten the interior linings. These and other framing members can be easily formed out of sheet material that has been cut into suitably sized strips. By adjusting the frame spacing, it is often possible to use the same thickness of sheet material for the plating and forming the frames.

The protective surface film that forms naturally and quickly on exposure to this element obtains the excellent corrosion resistance to seawater. This feature, together with the anti-fouling properties, means that no painting or coatings are required below the waterline.

Although more expensive than other metal boatbuilding materials, copper-nickel is worth your consideration if you are planning extended cruising in areas where fouling is prevalent. If you consider the ease of working, the low maintenance costs and other desirable features of this material, you may find that it suits your requirements.

BRASS

Brass has no place as a structural member on any boat and should never be used in place of bronze. You may have a few decorative items, lamps and the like, that are made of brass. You will know which they are because you will be continually polishing them to remove the tarnish that quickly forms in the marine environment. Brass is a copper/zinc alloy.

If you use 60/40 brass in a saltwater system you can find that it suffers from de-zincification that will soon remove all of the zinc from the surface of the fitting and reduce it to a useless mess. If this item is used in the wrong place you can create a dangerous situation. Beware of cheap fittings imported from the 'Far East', they may be sold as bronze, look like bronze but more often, they aren't bronze!

MONEL METAL

The ultimate marine metal! Not cheap, in fact rather expensive, otherwise it would be more widely used. Not used for building complete boats but for various fittings where ultimate strength and machinability is required. There are two main variants, including the regular version that contains 67 percent nickel and 28 percent copper. This alloy is ideal for shafting where its corrosion resistance and hardwearing qualities are best appreciated. There may be some doubt about the use of MONEL shafting in steel boats and it may be

better to use 316 stainless for your shafting requirements.

The variant 'K' is non-magnetic and is often used for special purposes where this feature is required. Often MONEL is used as main shafting on minesweepers, they can afford it, and to shield compasses on boats and aircraft. When more boats were built of timber and before the wood/epoxy technique was developed, MONEL screws were sometimes used on the finest craft either to fasten the hull planking or in other important parts of the structure. The alloy contains aluminium, titanium as well as the usual nickel and copper. A great metal but not so important to the builders of metal boats.

MAGNESIUM

This metal is used for fresh water anodes. It may surprise many to learn that protection from galvanic and other corrosion is necessary in all types of water including salt free environments. Zinc anodes are not as effective as magnesium ones in fresh water. Conversely, if you move your boat from fresh to salt water for more than two to three weeks, then you will need to change to zinc anodes; the magnesium ones will rapidly disappear. Copper-nickel hulls do not require galvanic protection in fresh or seawater. Maximum fouling resistance is achieved in the complete absence of galvanic protection.

ZINC

This material in its pure form is used for anodes and in salt water and is the ideal material for this use. In fresh water another metal is preferred, see magnesium. A small quantity of Zinc is present in many metals. Zinc is also used in paint primers, paints and other coatings.

LEAD

This dense metal has a very low melting point and has many uses for the boat owner. The most obvious use

	Steel	Aluminium	Copper-nickel	Fiberglass	Wood
Yield Strength in pSI	36-42,000	18-40,000	15,000	10-15,000	12-20,000
Tensile Strength in PSI	60-70,000	23-47,000	40-78,000	15-34,000	16-27,000
Compression Strength in PSI	60,000	32,000	45,000	Fair	2-13,000
Shear Strength in PSI	23,000	17,000	20,000	Low	0.7-3,000
Modulus of Elasticity (x10 6)	30	10	19.6-22	2.8	0.7-2.3
Hardness (Moh's Scale)	7	4	5.5 approx	1	1-3

Chart # 4 Comparative strengths of different materials.

for this material is for the ballast. Do not be tempted to simply pour molten lead into the keel of your metal boat. Even heavy steel keels can buckle if lead is installed in this manner. The method of installing ballast will be discussed later under its own heading.

Two young fellows who were looking for adventure built this steel Roberts 38 in New Zealand. The interior and deck details are as well built and finished as the exterior.

The Roberts 28 design is a shortened version of the Roberts 34. By shortening the ends we were able to maintain a roomy accomodation arrangement while reducing the overall length

Chapter 4
HULL SHAPES AND CHOOSING THE DESIGN

Prismatic coefficients. Single chine. Double or multiple chine. Radius chine. Round bilge. Transom shapes. Bow shapes Sail, Power or Motor Sailer. How small? How large for two person crew? Selecting the hull form.

PRISMATIC COEFFICIENT

This important hull calculation is often quoted, so I will include some explanation here. If you wish to expand your knowledge of hull characteristics, performance prediction and fuel economy etc., then refer to recommended reading in appendix 1. In this appendix we have listed books on both power and sailboats. These books contain formulas, detailed hull analysis of various hull types and other information that will extend your knowledge on these subjects.

Usually indicated as PC or CP, this is a figure that represents the underwater portion of the hull. If you take a block of wood that has the maximum length, width and depth of the hull, with the shape of the midsection carved throughout its length and then carve the underwater shape of the hull from this block; the CP is the relationship of the volume of the finished block as opposed to the block originally carved to the midsection shape throughout. The number represents the fullness of the ends of the hull. The more you carve away the ends the smaller the PC number. In sailboats PCs can range from just below 0.50 for a fine racing hull, through to 0.60 for a motor sailer type. Most cruising Sailboats will have PCs that fall between 0.53 and 0.59. In powerboats, the figure will range from 0.60 to 0.75.

SINGLE CHINE

This hull form is best employed in planing or semi-displacement powerboats. It is also recommended for some displacement hulled trawler types where it can be used to advantage. Single chine sailboats are crude in appearance and inefficient in performance and not recommended by the writer. Trawler type motor sailers can sometimes benefit from using this hull form. This seems a good time to mention the US term of Powerboat verses the UK term of Motorboat; these terms at least in this book mean exactly the same thing. A powerboat or a motorboat at least in this text, can be a motor driven vessel of any length.

PLANING POWERBOAT HULLS

Almost all planing powerboat hulls are of single chine configuration; most have 'chine flats' or 'planing chines' and occasionally 'planing strakes' that assist with getting onto, and maintaining the planing attitude. It is my opinion that chine flats are desirable on all planing craft. Intermediate planing strakes are not worthwhile on boats intended to perform at less than 30 knots.

Planing chines will start with a small or no flat, at, or near the bow and the width of the flat will gradually increase, until it reaches its widest point somewhere just aft of amidships; it maintains this width through to the stern. The efficiency of the 'chine flatí may be improved by canting it downward by say 2 to 4 degrees throughout its length.

SEMI-DISPLACEMENT HULLS

Semi displacement powerboat hulls are usually of single chine configuration and these may have chine flats that start from nothing at the bow and disappear soon after the chine enters the water. The purpose of this chine flat in the forward sections of the hull is to deflect the spray generated by the bow wave. It also improves the appearance of the forward sections of the hull, by giving it a more finished look. A single line of weld where the topsides and the bottom hull

This steel Waverunner 44 built in Oman as a fisheries patrol vessel illustrates the planing flat at the chine

This Waverunner 24/26 features an external bow spray rail, which could have been carried a little further forward, nearer to the stem.

plating meet usually has a crude appearance. A similar effect can be achieved by incorporating an 'outside chine stringerí or spray rail in the same area, as described for the partial chine flat. The outside spray rail should be canted downward by 3 to 5 degrees for best affect and appearance, also you should 'snape' off the forward end, so it ends gracefully at, or near the bow, see photo.

DEVELOPED HULL SURFACE

In single chine hulls, some 'round' will naturally be incorporated when the hull is built. In the days before computer design, it was necessary to develop the hull by 'triangulation' or by 'conic development'. These processes were needed to ensure that the flat plating would indeed conform to any compound curves in the hull. This involved considerable calculation on the part of the designer or loftsman. The alternative was a very 'boxy' hull without any compound curves! Computer design and lofting has changed all that. Now it takes just a few minutes to transform a set of straight sections into a beautifully faired 'developed' hull that will accept the plating with ease. My favourite expression is; the plating simply drapes over the structure that is formed by the frames and stringers. This assumes that you are building the hull up side down.

DOUBLE CHINE HULLS

This configuration is often used as the basic shape for sailboats and displacement powerboat hulls. One of the main attractions of this hull form is that, compared to single chine, it allows superior hull shapes to be built in metal, without resorting to rolling the plate. Generally these double chine hulls take on a 'developed' hull form and have considerable round in the sections up towards the bow. Double chine hulls have their own beauty and as 'beauty is in the eye of the beholder', you either love or hate this hull form.

This steel Roberts 43 was built in Germany by Willi Janssen and sailed to USA. Sequana is currently cruising in the Caribbean.

RADIUS CHINE

Metal boatbuilding especially in sailboats, changed forever when many designers switched to computer aided yacht design. One of the first benefits, was the development of the radius chine technique. This construction method could not be practically achieved without the aid of computer software and special training. I am forever in the dept of Grahame Shannon who developed the 'Auto Yachtí computer yacht design programs that made this technique possible. While radius chine methods can be used to build fiberglass or wood epoxy hulls; its biggest impact is in the ease of constructing beautiful rounded metal sailboat hulls. These hulls are usually impossible to distinguish from their fiberglass counterparts.

This beautiful Roberts 434 Radius chine hull was built in the UK. The superb interior of this boat matches the perfect exterior hull finish. Philip Sheaf photo.

The secret of this method, is computer fairing that provides a constant radius from the stern through to the bow. This allows plate that has been pre rolled to a predetermined radius, to be installed without fuss or the degree of difficulty, associated with round bilge hulls. The secret of radius chine is that it fairs the radius through the bow. Previous attempts at this type of hull form have tried to fade out the chine before it reaches the bow. This can result in an unfair or flat spot in the forward area of the hull.

The radius chine as developed by Grahame Shannon is the perfect metal boat hull building technique, particularly suited to but not restricted to sailboats. Excellent results can and have been achieved by any person with minimum metal working experience. Full details on building hulls using this and other hull building methods will appear in later chapters.

OTHER CHINE CONFIGURATIONS

Before the advent of 'radius chine', builders had sought to 'soften' the double chine hull by the addition of mini chine panels, or by introducing rounded sections of split pipe at the chine. These 'softening' techniques required a considerable increase in the amount of welding. Not to be confused with the foregoing, is the alternative to use solid round bar of 1 in / 25 mm diameter in place of the flat bar chine

This round bilge steel hull was built from the fiberglass lines, which feature a 'hollow heel'. This is difficult to build in metal and this type of hull/keel intersection should be avoided by all but the most experienced builders.

An experienced metal worker with the minimum of boatbuilding experience can build the round bilge Spray 34.

stringer. The solid round can 'soften' the chine, but it makes it more difficult to obtain a perfectly fair chine line. The round bar also needs special attention to prevent water lying on top of the chine bar inside the hull.

Some designers have designed multi chine hulls with several chines thus trying to approximate a round bilge form. Personally I do not favour these 'many chined' hulls; they are expensive to build and usually, at least to my eye, give a 'fussy' appearance. The popularity of double chine hulls has been somewhat eroded by the development and ease of construction of the 'radius chine' hull form.

ROUND BILGE METAL HULLS

This method is best suited to sailboats and full displacement long-range powerboat hulls. This hull building method requires previous metal working experience. It is possible for a competent metal worker, with little or no boatbuilding experience, to produce a fair and attractive round bilge metal hull.

There are 'easy' round bilge hull shapes and there are relatively 'impossible' shapes and everything in between. Unless you are an experienced metal boatbuilder, avoid the difficult shapes, such as rounded 'golf ball' sterns, hollow heel garboards and the like. There are simpler shapes that will provide you with an easy to build, seaworthy and attractive round bilge metal hull.

STERNS AND TRANSOMS

There are many different types of sterns gracing the aft ends of sail and power craft and each has its benefits and drawbacks. Although not strictly accurate in nautical terminology, the termís stern and transom are often used to describe the aft end of the hull. Not all sterns have transoms. In fact, not all transoms are at the stern! You will hear terms like, canoe stern, transom stern, rounded stern, poop stern, cruiser stern, chevron stern and more recently sugar scoop stern. The shapes of and names of the after end of the hull have changed over the past years. Some changes are caused through racing rules, others through fashion. Many sterns have been developed through experience and these are the ones that concern us here.

Most sailboats today have either a traditional transom or reverse transom stern. One relatively recent development is the advent of the *Sugar scoop* stern, which incorporates a vertical transom within a reverse angle ending to the hull. This arrangement usually features steps for re-boarding from the water or when the boat is moored stern-to. The reverse transom is also often fitted with steps that are built into the transom itself. The above comments have been included, as steps are one of the most important benefits of the reverse transom.

On powerboats, the underwater section of the hull may be carried aft to form a boarding or swim platform. The underwater area is sometimes used for holding tanks or for storing other liquids. If you wish to extend the underwater section of a powerboat hull in this way, consult the designer first. You may upset the fore and aft trim of the hull. The tankage may only partially offset the extra buoyancy provided by the extended underwater section.

Rounded or ball shaped sterns are difficult to build in metal, so this feature is best left to the professional builder. If you are planning to build you own metal boat, then make sure you select a design that has a 'buildable' stern or transom.

BOW SHAPES

Before the advent of computer developed and faired hulls, we often designed bows on metal powerboat hulls that were a 'fair cow' to build. During the 1960's and 1970's flared bows were the norm on fiberglass hulls so that is what our clients wanted on their powerboats too. Today most builders are more enlightened and appreciate the beauty of a hull with properly developed forward sections. These bows, when combined with spray chines have the same effect of keeping the boat dry. They are also much easier to build.

The Waverunner 342 features a modest conical bow that is easy to build and improves the overall appearance of the finished boat

Conical bows are suitable for powerboat and to a lesser extent sailboat hulls. In the powerboat, the cone starts at little or nothing at the forward end of the chine and ends at the deck. This gives an attractive rounded shape to the bow, especially when seen in plan view. The resulting shape plays a part in keeping

This photograph of a large round bilge steel sailboat clearly illustrates how a conical bow can be formed

The PCF 40 is based on a trawler hull and is a true motor sailer. The deckhouse could be lowered into the hull to give a more balanced appearance. Many of these boats have been built and one sailed from Australia to Ireland, not a recommended use for this type of vessel.

The owners of this Waverunner 24 stretched to 26 feet and fitted with a Dutch style superstructure, are delighted with this mini cruiser.

Roberts 53 - "Henrike". This boat was built as a training ship for the sea scouts of Finland who are happy with the 9 knot performance of this steel hull yacht.

the foredeck dry, adds some extra buoyancy and increases the available deck space up forward. This extra deck space is often most appreciated, when handling anchors and ground tackle in adverse conditions. Not strictly part of the bow, a short 'anchor handling' U shaped pipe bowsprit is an asset on any sail or powerboat.

SAILBOAT BOWS

Sailboat bows come in all varieties; fortunately the few designs (not ours), that featured flared bows have long since disappeared. Overhangs come and go out of fashion and bow profiles vary from clipper, through straight, to convex. The bow on the design you decide to buy or build will have already been carefully styled by the designer and my advice is not to try and improve on their efforts.

Considering sailboat bow sections, from station two forward, be very wary of boats that are too full or have large flats in this area; they may pound excessively. Some fullness is required in the bow sections, but it must be moderate. This is a good time to say that if you are considering a wholesome and perhaps fast cruising boat, then you should avoid the excesses, fashions and the rule bending of the racing fraternity. Nothing looks more dated and is harder to sell, than a boat that is 'dated' because it was built to a race-boat fashion or rule, that has long since passed into obscurity.

SAIL OR POWER

Before buying, or building your metal boat, you should re-examine your desires, needs and intended usage. If ever there was an argument for 'his and hers', this is it! In the course of working in the marine industry, I have found that the great majority of women would prefer a powerboat and about seventy five percent of males prefer sail.

With a few exceptions, such as out and out racing, boating should be a family activity or at least one where the couple enjoys the activity together. Please, please, Mr macho boatman, consult your partner before you buy, build or order your next boat.

The above paragraphs mainly represent the philosophy of sail verses power. Now to some practical information that may help you to choose wisely once you have made that basic decision, also please refer to appendix 1.

The Pacific Coast Fisherman 40, best expresses my interpretation of the term motor sailer. The PCF 40 is a motorboat (displacement fishing boat hull) that has been fitted with a modest, but effective sail plan (one recently sailed from Australia to Ireland). The Spray type hulls while being good performers under sail, also make excellent motor sailers and are noted for their precise handling under power.

MOTOR SAILERS

What is a motor sailer? This is one term that has been used to describe a variety of vessels, from a regular sailboat that happens to be fitted with an oversize engine, to a powerboat that has a small steadying sail. The term motor sailer, used to mean a boat best described as a 50/50, that is 50% motor and 50% sail.

Waverunner 65. An active couple can handle this boat

Occasionally one would hear boats referred to as 60/40 or by some similar definition.

More recently you are likely to hear the term motor sailer applied to a variety of sail boats equipped with varying sizes of auxiliary power. Considering the term motor sailer in its more recent usage, I would say that a boat fitted with an engine with a capacity of more than 2.5-horse power per 1,000 lbs displacement, (1.82 Kw per 454 kg) might be termed a motor sailer.

You will need to consider the hull form rather than the general terminology, when you are making your decision as to which hull is most suitable for your type of cruising. If you are considering cruising in the canals of Europe with the odd foray into the Mediterranean, then a motor sailer in its true context could be the right choice.

HOW SMALL
If you are building in aluminum, then you can build as small as you wish. When you choose steel or copper-nickel as your basic building material then I feel the 24 ft LOD / 7.31 M is the practical minimum for both power and sail designs.

TWO PERSON CREW - SAIL
As mentioned elsewhere, you should only build as large a boat as you need. You may have good reasons for building a large vessel and if the crew is to be limited to two persons then my experience and those of others is as follows:

A well-equipped sailboat of 55 ft / 16.76 M (LOD), can be handled by a male and female without the need to hire crew or accept outside assistance. There are many examples of sailboats of this size sailing the world with two persons, thoroughly enjoying the cruising experience. In my opinion, this is the upper size limit that any couple or small family should consider. My advice, a boat between 40 ft / 12.19 M and 46 ft / 14.02 M is the perfect size if you can afford it.

TWO PERSON CREW - POWER
Large powerboats require different skills and handling techniques, but the size factors are about the same. Most craft up to 55 ft / 16.76 M can be handled by a couple. Again my advice, regarding practical size, cost and maintenance requirements is the same; if possible keep the size below 46 ft / 14.02 M. If you are considering undertaking some serious long distance cruising, that is a boat with a minimum of a 3,000 mile / 4,828 Km range, then the 46 ft boat can meet these requirements, but for various reasons you may want to go to 50 ft / 15.24 M and beyond.

SELECTING THE HULL FORM - SAIL
Once you have decided on the type and overall length of your new boat, you can make a decision as to which is the best hull form. There are several factors to consider, including the use you have in mind, ease and cost of construction and estimated resale value.

Roberts 53 radius chine steel sailboat built by Terry Erskine in the UK.

This Roberts 434 clearly shows the beauty of radius chine construction

Many hull types, especially the modern computer designed variety, can be matched with either long or short keels. To be effective, a sailboat with a short or medium length keel needs a skeg/rudder combination.

The older so called 'long keel' boats, where the rudder was hung off the aft end of a moderate length 'long keel', are no longer acceptable. These boats all featured excessive weather helm. Make sure you are selecting a design that has been not only proven, but also proven to be a satisfactory all-round performer. The smaller the crew in relation to the size of the boat, the more important it is to have a well-balanced hull, keel and rig combination.

With our own cruising sailboat designs, we have updated some; for example the Roberts 53 was first designed in 1969 and now is more popular than ever. I doubt the owners of the original boats would recognise the design as it is today. Other updated designs include the Roberts 43, 'Mauritius 43' and others of the same family. These were replaced by the now well-proven and popular Roberts 432. Other designs have been left out of some catalogues and lists simply because they just were not popular enough to warrant their inclusion.

I give you these examples because you must be careful not to build or buy a metal boat, (any boat for that matter), until you are sure of its design history and the designers current opinions. Most naval architects and yacht designers are very frank about the merits and shortcomings of their boats. The well-established designers can afford to be frank; they have many great boats to balance any less than successful designs.

SELECTING THE HULL FORM - POWER

Potential speed will have a great bearing on which hull form you choose for your metal powerboat. If you want a boat that will achieve speeds of over 14 knots / 25 kph then you will need to consider a planing hull. Some larger semi-displacement powerboats, with water lines of over 45 ft / 13.72 M can be made to perform at speeds of 16 knots / 29 kph but they do so at a great increase in fuel consumption. You will find more on this subject in chapter 18 and see appendix one, Choosing a Cruising Powerboat.

Metal boats including properly designed steel vessels can plane. The misnamed (length-wise) Waverunner 342 evidences this. This all-steel boat which is a 36 ft / 11.00 M LOD and weighs about 24,000 lbs / 10,886 kg is powered by two 200 hp Volvo stern drives. With these engines, the Waverunner 342 cruises happily at 23 knots.

For economical cruising, consider the Waverunner 38, a semi-displacement hull that cruises at 6.8 knots / 12.6 km/hr and only burns 1.5 gallons / 7.0 litres per hour. At 8 knots / 14.8 km the fuel usage rises sharply to 5.5 gallons / 25 litres per hour. As you see, quite a price to pay for an increase in performance.

The Waverunner 38 is a popular design for building in metal. This boat has been successfully built in both planing and semi-displacement hull versions.

For myself I would choose radius chine. This hull form has all of the advantages and no minus points, in other words the perfect sailboat hull configuration. There is one exception to this, the Spray designs are not suitable for building in this technique; I am a great admirer of the Spray and her derivatives and they can only be built with multi chine or round bilge hulls.

This Roberts COASTWORKER 30 (MK1) was built in Canada where it operates as a general-purpose workboat.

This steel Coastworker 30 (MK2) was built in UK where it is used in the fishing industry.

ROBERTS SPRAY 36A

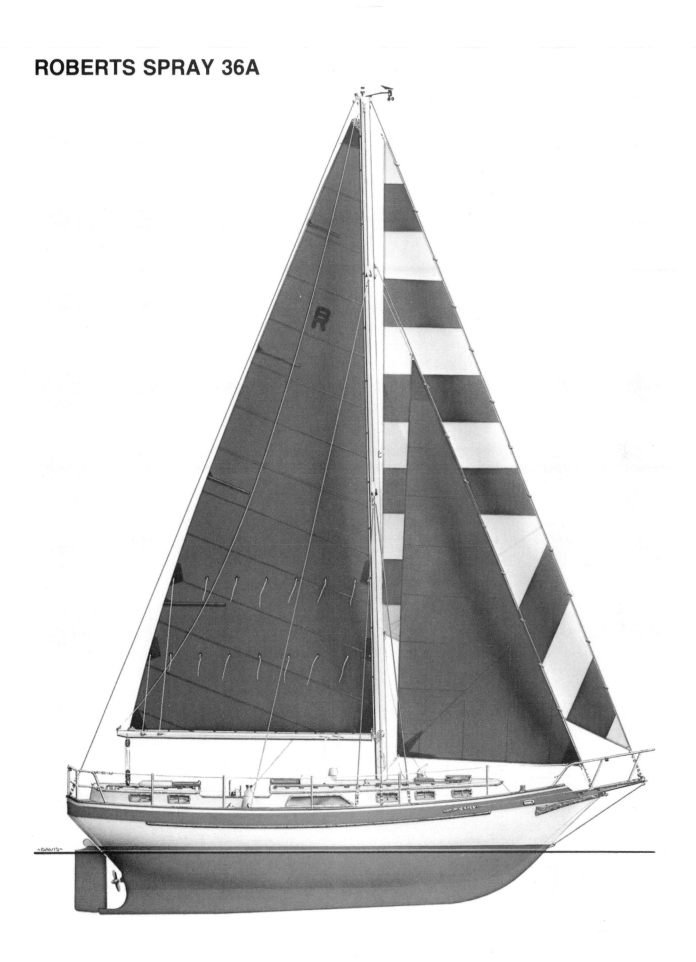

This Spray 36 is about the smallest sized sailboat where a Centre cockpit is practical. Beware of "chopping up" the interior of your boat, you may end up with an uncomfortable accommodation arrangement.

Chapter 5
TOOLS AND SAFETY EQUIPMENT

Safety equipment. Plate cutting devices. Rolling devices. Hand tools. Specialised tools. Metal handling equipment.

Today we give more thought to safety. This is a good place to start when considering what tools and equipment you will need to build, maintain or repair your metal boat. One of the best and least expensive safety items is a clean work area. Avoid leaving anything lying about that is not in use or needed in the immediate future. These are the things that can trip you up, slash yourself with or otherwise cause bodily injury. All the operations necessary when working with metal produces hazards of varying degrees. You can easily protect yourself by having the correct safety equipment. Under no circumstances sell yourself short in this area. You will need to protect the various parts of your body so give the following list of equipment your undivided attention.

PROTECTIVE CLOTHING

Starting with your head, always wear a proper industrial safety helmet. You never know when something may fall or be dropped, that could injure this most vulnerable part of your body. Safety goggles are a must. These should have side guards to protect you against flying metal particles that are present when you are cutting, grinding or chipping. You will need a face shield and the various lenses. Don't forget your ears and hearing, good earmuffs are essential. A respirator is required. Invest in good coveralls or a boiler suit. A leather apron and gloves with cuffs are definite requirements. One of our customers once built a steel Roberts 38 in a Florida nudist colony. We often wondered how he dealt with the weld splatter! Wear steel-toed shoes or boots and please no sneakers around your metal boatbuilding project.

Protective hand cream and an adequate first aid kit are essential. Have the first aid kit handy, you can not anticipate when it may be required in a hurry; its presence may save your life or at least prevent a minor injury developing into a major one. Make sure you have plenty of eyewash on hand. A good-sized fire extinguisher and an industrial vacuum cleaner are other essential items of safety equipment.

Arc welders are relatively safe pieces of equipment. A potentially lethal electrical AC voltage powers them so you cannot afford to treat them casually. Your electrical AC supply will be 110V, 220V, 240V or perhaps larger three phase. Make no mistake; all these voltages can be lethal.

Watching the arc with the naked eye is not recommended. Even when viewed for a short period with unprotected eyes, looking at the arc can cause 'arc-eye', which is very uncomfortable and feels like sand around the eyeballs. Assuming that you, as the welder, ALWAYS use a mask, then it must be the assistant or casual onlooker that will need protection.

TOOLS FOR STEEL BOATBUILDING

Many of the tools you will require for building in all types of metal, are those common to steel boatbuilding so I will give this list first. Later we will follow up with additional information on the different and additional tools you require for building in aluminum or copper-nickel.

If you have more than adequate funds, no doubt you will find many exotic and expensive labour saving devices to keep you happy. Fortunately for the rest of us, a modern metal boat can be built with a few inexpensive tools, most of which are readily available, in all parts of the world. The metal used to build either a steel, aluminum or copper-nickel boat is relatively thin so it can be easily handled, cut, formed and welded. Many tools are common to the three main metals. The few specialised tools required by each type, are available and familiar to those who posses the necessary skills to work with that particular material.

A check of the yellow pages of your telephone directory will provide sources for all of the tools and equipment that you need for your boatbuilding project. Another source is the 'For Sale' sections of the local newspapers. Perhaps a 'Wanted to Buy' advertisement in the correct classified section, will bear fruit. Flea markets, jumble sales and 'yard' or 'garage sales', are all good sources of reasonably priced tools.

Stem being checked against full size patterns.

Simple device for bending deck beams. stem and frames as required.

In the case of radius chine hulls we recommend that you have the relatively small amount of radius plating, rolled by a professional metal shop and this service is available in most areas. Our plans include details of tools that you can make yourself. Most builders make many of the metal handling tools, often 'inventing' new ones as required.

The bending of deck beams, stem and other smaller parts that may require to be formed, can easily be achieved by a simple tool that you can make yourself. This bending device is made up of a suitably powerful hydraulic jack and a simple H frame formed from angle bar.

Included in the list of small tools you will need, are a variety of metal working hammers and mallets, (including chipping hammers), an assortment of clamps (some you can make yourself), bolt cutters, a metal workers vice and a selection of saw horses. A good quality portable drill, a drill press, a large selection of high quality metal bits, cold chisels and metal files. Other tools include a bench grinder, crimper, power hacksaw, jig saw, straight edge and tin snips.

OXY ACETYLENE EQUIPMENT

There are several ways to cut steel and most other metals. The gas or oxygen-acetylene torch was the traditional way to cut steel and although it is still widely used, there are now available more sophisticated and affordable methods. Never the less, the Oxy acetylene torch and associated bottles and gauges although not a necessity, will find many uses around a metal boatbuilding project. The gas torch is quick, efficient and low in operating cost. With this equipment you will need a light to medium duty kit with a 90-degree angle and specialised cutting tips. The basic Oxy kit consists of the cutting torch, tips of various sizes, a set of gas regulators, flint lighter, goggles, special wrench, couplings for both oxygen and acetylene tanks and the two lengths of hose to lead from the tanks to the torch. This package could cost less than $300 / £200 as you may be able to pick up used equipment at a favourable price. A small cart to hold the bottles would be useful and you can either buy or make one yourself. The cylinders are usually leased from the gas supplier and you will only need to pay for the refills.

The Oxy-acetylene torch cuts metal through a rapid oxidisation process in two continuous steps. While the torch heats a small area of metal to a cherry red colour (about 1,500 to 1600 degrees F), a small stream of pressurised oxygen is directed from a central tip within the torch against the hot metal. The stream of oxygen causes the metal to 'burn' rapidly and the cut is produced as the torch is moved along the line of the desired cut. There are many different cutting tips available and these can be used to influence the size, speed and accuracy of the cut. A special plate cutting drag step tip can cut steel plate from 1/8" / 3 mm to 1/4" / 6 mm thickness with precision at the rate of about two feet / 0.61 M per minute. The resulting cut using this tip will be between 1/16" / 1.5 mm to 3/16" / 4.5 mm wide. Using this equipment is something of an art form and considerable experience is required to achieve the type of fine cutting that is required, when plating your hull.

The main drawback is that 'torch' cuts are rough around the edges and usually need some cleaning up before they are suitable for welding to other parts. You should avoid the disgusting habit of some low cost builders who plate the hulls oversize and simply 'torch off' the overlaps at the chine etc. The Oxy acetylene torch can be used for welding and brazing. For boatbuilding it is better to use other equipment, such as the Arc (stick), MIG or TIG welders for those operations. Reserve the Oxy equipment for cutting where precision is not required.

ANGLE GRINDER

You should buy the best quality angle grinder you can find; it will get a lot of use. This is a much used tool in boat construction and can perform a variety of jobs ranging from cutting lengths of flat and round bar to smoothing out the edges of torch-cut plate. You can use this tool to bevel thicker plates by grinding off the excess metal, prior to welding. Fitted with wire brushes, it can be used to clean off rust, mill scale and weld splatter. Another use is to smooth off the welds on the hull topsides and superstructure; (we along with most classification societies do not recommend grinding welds below the waterline). When fitted with a special cutting grinding wheel, it can be used to cut the slots in the frames to accept the stringers. Another use is to make many small cuts in metal bar; this feature is useful when making frames, 'snaping' off the ends of stringers and a multitude of other similar uses. Do not use this tool for heavy-duty cutting; the grinding/cutting wheels do not last very long. For

instance when used to cut 1/8" / 3 mm plate, you can only expect to get 12 to 15 ft / 3.66 to 4.57 M from a single blade. When used for cutting, the grinder has to be considered more as a convenience tool, rather than a fully-fledged cutting device.

You should purchase a 7 in to 9 in / 178 to 228 mm, heavy-duty commercial grade angle grinder. Make sure the chosen model has heavy-duty switches and a high efficiency-cooling fan. Do not order this item by mail order. You need to hold the grinder, see how it balances in you hands and check out the weight. You will be holding this tool for many hours so make sure it 'feels right,' as well as ensuring that will give long and trouble free service.

NIBBLER

A nibbler may be selected for cutting thinner plate. This tool is expensive, especially when considering its limited use on most boatbuilding projects. It may be hired if you find it useful enough to be considered for your project. This tool is like electric scissors and it slices through thin metal by taking small 'nibbles' at it, hence the name. The 'nibble' is an up and down punching action and makes a cut about 1/4" / 6 mm wide. When used by an experienced operator, this tool can produce a smooth cut with clean edges. The cutting rate will vary depending on the thickness of the metal but on 1/8" / 3 mm steel or copper-nickel it can cut 2 to 4 ft / 0.61 to 1.22 M per minute.

This builder of the Tom Thumb 26 found an angle grinder ideal for cutting the plates on this smaller design. Accuracy of 1/16" / 1 mm was achieved with most cuts.

PLASMA CUTTER

A plasma cutter is the ideal way to cut plate and other steel and metal sections so hire or buy the best you can afford. This device cuts without distortion and can be used to trim plates in position. In the hands of an experienced operator, this device produces a clean sharp cut without any sign of distortion. The cutting action is very fast and steel or copper-nickel (not suitable for aluminium) plate of up to 5/16" / 8 mm presents no problems for this device. The narrow cut of 1/8" / 3 mm makes for neat and efficient cutting. The plasma cutter uses a fair amount of electricity and the cutting tips do not have a particularly long life. Particularly suited to cutting plate, this tool finds angle and other shapes something of a problem, so alternative cutting methods should be used for those sections.

In the USA Hypertherm manufacture the portable Powermax 800 which it is claimed can cut all metals of up to 1/2" / 12 mm thickness, see Appendix 4.

TOOLS FOR ALUMINUM BOATBUILDING

Either sawing or shearing usually cuts aluminum. For straight cuts of material up to 1/4" / 6 mm you can use the same power guillotines used for cutting steel. Remember to replace the holding down pads with plastic ones that will not mark the softer aluminum metal. Particular attention should be paid to keeping the knifes sharp; blunt cutters will burr the edges of the metal. Nibblers can be used for cutting aluminum up to 1/4" / 6 mm thick.

BAND SAW

A deep-throated band saw, fitted with a narrow blade, say 1/2" / 12 mm, will be capable of cutting a wide range of thickness. The band saw should be set to run at 2,000 ft to 5,000 ft or 610 M to 1,500 M per minute; the slower speeds will be needed for the thicker plates. A band saw with variable speeds is preferred, but the older heavy types used for cutting timber are satisfactory.

TABLE SAW

For cutting straight lines, a regular table saw fitted with carbide tipped blades will give perfect results. It is recommended that lubrication such as a paraffin-oil mixture or suitable vegetable oil be provided, this will make the cuts easier and also increase the life of the blade. A portable jigsaw can also be very useful for making on-the-job cuts. When using most tools to cut aluminium, remember a spray of lubricant will make the cutting go easier.

POWER HAND SAW

A hand power-saw or 'Skilsaw', can be a most useful cutting device when working with aluminium. Fit your saw with a special blade designed for cutting this metal. This blade will have zero degrees tooth face rake angle. By using a guide clamped in position, it is possible to make long straight cuts using this saw. For cutting sheet or framing to length; in fact almost all shell and frame cutting, can be made using this versatile tool.

Treat the hand power saw with utmost respect; the chips thrown off the sawn material are not only hot, but also sharp. Always wear a full-face mask when working with this tool. Make sure that the remainder of your body is suitably protected from flying chips. Kneepads are recommended if you are kneeling when operating this saw.

Extra care is needed when cutting 3/16" / 4 mm or thinner plate; the blade will tend to jump out of the cut especially at the beginning. A plunge start just inside the first part of the cut is recommended, this allows the blade to enter the material along the line of cut and can avoid the kick-back.

ROUTER

A router fitted with a single flute carbide tipped cutter will be useful for cutting uniform holes such as lightening holes. You will find this tool has many uses in the building of your aluminum boat. As with all powered equipment, it has to be handled with care. A small electric router or an air powered one, is usually used for gouging out the back of welds or removing contaminated ones, prior to re-welding the part.

PLANING

This is possible with either a carpenters hand plane or an electric hand planer fitted with carbide tipped cutters. Any edge can be planed and this is a useful feature where a sawn edge would show on the finished boat and planing will provide a superior finish. A plane can also be most useful in bevelling the edges of plate.

RIGHT ANGLE BENDING

For forming aluminium, hand folders will handle the thinner gauges however for serious bending, a press brake with a bed of about 8 ft / 2.4 M would be useful. The press brake is a strong hydraulically or mechanically powered forming machine used to crease or bend metal. This machine comes in a variety of sizes and is found in most professional metal shops. The benefits in using this machine are that it can reduce the number of welds required. For instance a cockpit bottom and sides could be formed in one piece. If you are building a 'one off' aluminum boat and unless you already own this equipment, you will need to find a subcontractor to handle this work.

When building in aluminum it makes sense to take advantage of the easier handling of this material. Forming up large multi-surface parts by bending sheet into various angles can save a lot of welding and grinding

PLATE ROLLS

Bending rolls are used to form plate into a permanent curve and can be either hand or power operated. A typical roll consists of two lower power driven rolls and one adjustable upper idler roll. As the shape suggests, this type of roll is called a pyramid roll and is widely used in building round bilge boats. The method of operation is that the metal is inserted between the upper roll and the lower two rolls and by adjusting the pressure on the upper idler roll, it is possible to vary the resulting amount of curvature in the plate.

John Reid built this Centennial Spray 36 in the UK. John used a garden roller to roll the plates; no mean effort even considering John's considerable boatbuilding experience. This perfectly fair hull is being fitted out at Iron Wharf Boatyard in Faversham, Kent.

Although these rolls operate at slow speeds, remember that loose clothing or carelessly placed limbs can get caught. This could be extremely dangerous especially in the power driven versions.

EXPLOSIVE FORMING

This method has been used to form various aluminum shapes including boat hulls. Briefly the process consists of making a concrete or steel mould and using explosives to force the metal into the correct shape within the mould. This method was used in the US and far back as the 1960's and in Australia as recently as the late 1980's. As with many other exotic building methods, government money (taxpayers dollars) was used to pay for these experiments. Due to the current tightness of funds and the fact that the process was not cost effective, explosive forming has passed into history. I include it here because occasionally a client will inquire about the viability of this method.

This Roberts 434 built in Florida has a steel hull and aluminum decks and superstructure.

The Waverunner 38 has been built in many different versions; this one was built in Ireland for use in a local charter operation.

Chapter 6

WELDING EQUIPMENT AND WELDING

Arc welding. Welding equipment. Welding steel. Welding aluminium. Welding copper-nickel. MIG welding. TIG welding. Electrodes.

It is outside the scope of this text to teach you how to weld. The suggested uses of the various welding equipment and actual welding techniques are included to show what is involved rather than to teach you the art of welding. If you are not already a proficient welder and you intend to undertake this work yourself, then you should seek instruction and advice from the appropriate local source. There are many full and part time teaching institutions, where the art of welding can be learnt from experts.

ARC WELDING

This method can be used for steel or copper-nickel construction. There are many different types of arc welders available and it is difficult to decide just which one to buy. It is important to make sure that the welder has sufficient capacity for your project. Don't make the mistake of buying a welder that is too small. The difference in price between a welder of adequate capacity and one that is under powered for your job will not be great, but the aggravation certainly will be enormous, if you make a mistake and obtain an lightweight machine.

If you are building your boat on a non-industrial site then you will need a welder that will run off the normal domestic electricity supplied to the area. In the case of the most powerful machines, a higher input voltage will be required, but with good fortune on your side, you should be able to obtain a suitable machine to run off the local power source.

WELDER AMPERAGE

You must consider the output rating of the welder, which is measured in amps. The higher the amperage, the thicker the plate that can be welded by that machine. As the thickest plate you are likely to be using will be in the order of 1/4" / 10 mm then this thickness can be handled by an arc welder with an output rating of 140 amps. If you are using thicker plate, say for the bottom of the keel, then you can manage this by bevelling the edges of the thicker plate and using more than one run of weld. You may

think that because your plans call for 3/16" / 4 or 5 mm plate that you can get away with a welder that only outputs 110 amps, do not be tempted, as a minimum, choose between a 140 amp to 200 amp machine.

Arc welders of greater than 140-amp capacity can not be run from the normal 15 amp domestic supply so an alternative supply will required. If possible you should try and arrange a 30 amp input supply; this is the amount that is required by most domestic cookers in the UK. Heavier duty supply is obtainable in the US by way of the three-phase wiring supplied to domestic washing machines and electric dryers. No matter where you are planning to build or undertake a major refit on a metal boat, you will need to ensure an adequate power supply, of the correct voltage and amperage, for your particular needs.

The maximum input required can usually be obtained from the welder instruction manual and is often quoted in KVA, which equals 1,000 volt/amperes x power factor 0.8. As an example take a 140 amp welder that is shown at 4.2 KVA, so at 240 volts the calculation would look like this:

$$V \times A \times 0.8 = KVA$$
$$240 \times A \times 0.8 = 4,200$$
$$A = 22$$

So in this case a 25 or 30 amp input supply is recommended.

Some better quality welders are capable of being run at varying input voltage, this feature may be appreciated when you consider the voltage drop resulting from a supply that has to be accessed via a long lead. As part of your selection of the boat building site you should have considered this possibility and made allowances for any deficiencies in the power supply.

A voltage meter can be used to test the voltage; test it at the actual location where you will be operating your welder. A 10 percent drop in voltage could put paid to a successful welding job at that location. Input wires will need to be heavy duty and a single run of cable is best. Plug and socket joins can result in a considerable voltage drop. As mentioned above, the alternative is to equip yourself with a welder that will accept varying voltages. In UK the 'Oxford' is one make that can handle the conditions as outlined above.

LEADS AND CABLES

While on the subject of leads and cables, you will find that the output cables that are supplied with your welder will seldom be long enough for your type of work. You will most likely have to replace these with longer leads. Make sure the replacements are of good quality and thick enough to carry the loads, without an accompanying and unwelcome drop in amperage. The earth clamps are usually spring loaded, you may find it advantageous to replace these with the threaded clamp type, which have a more positive grip. Also on the same lines, your electrode holder will most likely be spring-loaded; be warned it should not be too heavy. The many hours you will spend welding can put a strain on your wrist and arm. This is especially so, if this is your first major all welded project. A little weight saved in the holder can make all the difference.

AIR OR OIL COOLED

Arc welders come in two main types, either air or oil cooled. The oil-cooled version has the advantage of being capable of long continuous usage without overheating. This advantage also means that the oil-cooled version will have a much longer working life than the air-cooled counterpart. Even if you are building only one boat you may want to take your welder with you as a means of earning additional 'cruising funds'. The oil-cooled version will also have a higher resale value. Against these advantages you will find that the oil-cooled version is much heavier and it needs to be stowed with care, as the oil can drain out of the vents if the unit is not kept upright.

The air-cooled version is about half the price of the oil-cooled welder, so you will need to make your own 'value judgement'. This in only one of many you will be making throughout your boat building project. Make sure the unit you select has some form of automatic thermal cutout so that in the event that it overheats, it will shut down before it self-destructs! Summer and winter temperatures will have an effect on the amount of time that you can use your air-cooled welder before you have to take a rest and let it cool down. If there is more than one person welding and using the same unit, then extra thought will have to be given to the selection of a suitable unit.

On some of the better air-cooled models, you will find a dial that will control the amperage setting. This works throughout the output range and this 'choke control' can be handy when tackling a variety of welding conditions. A proficient welder can 'tune' the output to suit the job in hand. Finally no matter which type of arc welder you choose, do not buy a cheap unit, it is unlikely to remain in working condition long enough for you to complete your boatbuilding project.

ELECTRODES

Although these are consumables rather than tools it seems practical to include them here together with the arc welders. There is a wide range of electrodes available in all appropriate materials. In some cases there is more than one type of rod available to suit a particular job. You will need to undertake some experimentation to find the rod that gives you the best results. The choice of electrode will be governed by the sequence of the work, your welding position, and the equipment powering the electrode and of course, the material you are welding.

The electrodes must be compatible with the base metal and the low hydrogen variety is recommended for a better quality and stronger weld. This type reduces the porosity, prevents hydrogen embrittlement, which in turn reduces ductility, and in turn causes hairline cracks. These 'low-hy' electrodes require a little more skill on the part of the operator. Electrodes that are promoted as high-speed single pass types should be avoided; these produce a weld that has low ductility and should not be used in important parts of the boat. If you are building 'To survey' or to pass US Coast Guard inspection, then certain rods may be required. Check this out if you are building to a Classification Society rule, or under similar circumstances. No matter which rods you are using, you must ensure proper storage and ensure that the rods are kept in their sealed packets, dry and free from all contaminates.

As you may be building your boat anywhere in the world, it is hard to recommend brands. For those of you who are building in Europe, the Swedish Oerlikon rods that are made in Northern Ireland have a good reputation among many steel boatbuilders. When fabricating a steel boat, you will be using mild steel rods but it may be useful to have a few 'gouging' rods on hand. The latter allow plate to be cut using an electric welder and although this will not, and should not, be your common cutting method, there may be situations where these rods and this facility will come in handy. The method of using 'gouging' rods for cutting, is to heat the plate using high amperage, the rod is then pushed through the plate and drawn along the desired line, thus effecting the cutting action. This method gives a surprisingly accurate cut.

For North American readers, here are details of a few of the more popular rods and their uses. Note that each number in the letter designation has a special meaning. For instance the E signifies electric welding, the first two numbers relate to tensile strength and next number shows welding position, one equals all positions, and the final number signifies the special manufacturers characteristics.

MILD STEEL:

E6010: A good beginnerís rod, use in all positions for general applications, good for tacks, will give good penetration, flat beads and light slag.

E6011: OK for all positions, can be used on galvanised steel, produces light slag and is a good beginnerís rod.

E6012: General purpose in all positions, moderate penetration, Medium slag, recommended where fit is poor.

E6020: Use for flat and horizontal positions, ideal for single pass deep groove welds.
All of the above 6xxx series electrodes are subject to hydrogen embrittlement.

LOW HYDROGEN MILD STEEL:

E7014: Can be used in all positions, produces medium to heavy slag and is useful for high-speed work

E7024: Especially good for down-hand welding and fillet welds. Is high speed but produces very heavy slag.

E7018 AC: This AC electrode produces little slag and can be used on either low, medium or high carbon steels.

E7028: Can produce X-ray quality welds. A very fast rod and is preferred when welding very heavy sections.

SPECIAL PURPOSE RODS:

E9018's: For high tensile steels, medium penetration, low hydrogen and porosity. Is often used for welding castings, fittings and pipes.

E308, E309, E310, E312, E316, E317, E320, E330, E347, and E410: For welding stainless steels.

METAL INERT GAS (MIG) WELDING

This method can be used to weld steel, aluminum or copper-nickel. MIG welding is fast has the lowest distortion of any method. With the availability of less expensive machines this method is becoming more popular for metal boat construction. The electrode for MIG welding consists of a thin continuous wire that is led from a spool. A shielding gas is blown over the surface during the welding process to prevent oxidation. Many welders claim that this type of welding is easier to learn, and better results can be achieved than with arc (stick) equipment. You should give this system your consideration.

MIG welding machines operate on DC current and can be adapted for use underwater. The usual output is between 200 to 300 amps and this is sufficient for most operations. The dials on the machine are used to set amperage and wire speed. An easily handled gun is used to feed the wire and deliver the current.

There are many advantages to MIG welding, these include a smaller and consequently lower heat weld puddle, low distortion and a slag free bead. The main disadvantage of the higher initial cost of the welding equipment is gradually disappearing, mainly due to less expensive machines that have recently appeared on the market. As with the better quality higher priced Arc welders, you can recoup more of your investment when and if, you decide to sell the equipment. MIG can be used to weld stainless steel to mild steel, a common requirement when building a good quality metal boat.

Generally the standard equipment as purchased has only a 12 ft / 3.66 M main lead to the gun. This can be overcome by rearranging the equipment so that you may use the gun with the machine located up to 50 ft / 15.24 M away from the main unit. With all gas shielded welding, you must ensure that the workplace is free of the movement of air, including wind. This latter requirement almost makes it mandatory, that you are in a fully enclosed workplace when using MIG equipment.

The MIG welding filler wire comes in two readily available size rolls, the smaller roll, generally about a one pound / 0.45 kg spool is designed to fit on the special gun. The larger 10 pound / 4.5 kg spool runs off the normal wire feeder. The smaller spools are much more expensive per pound / kilo however some builders consider the convenience outweighs the extra cost.

TUNGSTEN INERT GAS (TIG) WELDING

TIG welding can be used to fabricate steel, aluminum or copper-nickel. However due to various reasons, including cost and degree of difficulty, it is often the last choice for any welding jobs associated with boatbuilding.

The TIG process consists of an AC or DC arc being struck between non-consumable tungsten electrode, and the material being welded. The filler rod is fed independently and fluxes are unnecessary; the arc itself cleans the electrode and weld and the inert gas prevents re-oxidation. The operator has control of the amount of heat and wire feed and has better control of penetration, than is obtainable with MIG or other methods.

TIG is favoured for un-backed joins where welding is only possible from one side and where good penetration is required. Where complex welding is needed, it is possible to make some passes with TIG and complete the job using MIG.

WELDING STEEL

The great advantage of welding is that the weld has the potential to be stronger than the materials it joins. Make sure your welds always fall into this category. Good welding requires proper preparation, correct weld joints, careful use of welding positions and correct weld size and perfect root. Inadequate root penetration, presence of slag, porosity and cracking are common faults. When using arc or stick welding, you are more likely to have these problems and you will also find it harder to control these faults. MIG welding with its shielding gas will give you a cleaner and stronger weld.

Cracking is caused by excessive local stress, brought about by improper conditions, such as voids, not enough allowance for shrinkage and rapid cooling. This latter problem can occur in colder than usual weather. Poor or inadequate back gouging can also result in cracks appearing in an otherwise healthy weld. Preventive measures include pre-heating to slow down the cooling rate, back step welding and by the use of low-hydrogen electrodes.

Slag trapped in the weld consists of non-metallic material between the weld metal and the base metal. This condition is the result of either improper location of the weld; inadequate cleaning or chipping of slag from previous passes of weld. It is virtually impossible to totally eliminate this problem but there must only be a minimal amount of this foreign material in the finished weld.

Porosity is the result of improper welding current and length of arc. Low hydrogen electrodes require a relatively high welding current and a short arc. Porosity can be found in the base metal itself so carefully examine your materials for this and other defects.

Light steel plate of 1/8"/ 3 mm thickness should be spaced with a gap similar to the thickness. The 3/16" / 4 to 5 mm plate, will need to have the edges bevelled at around 30 degrees. In the heavier plates where the 30 degree V bevel is required, you will need to make one or more passes; one or two inside the V and one inside to complete the weld. This should not be done consecutively, but in order to avoid excessive heat and the resulting distortion, you must use intermittent welding techniques.

When welding steel plate where the edges fall on a longitudinal stringer or chine bar, these can be welded more robustly than other thin plates that butt each other. In any case, plates should be welded from both sides; as with all rules there are exceptions to this one but keep them to a minimum. Each weld must fully penetrate the join. Where plates fall on a stringer or chine bar, they should be either spaced or bevelled, depending on thickness, so that the weld achieves good penetration from the single side that is available for welding. The plate butt joints or plates to stringers and to chines should be welded using the staggered welding techniques, using short staggered passes and then returning to fill in the spaces.

We do not recommend welding the frames to the plate, as mentioned elsewhere, it may be desirable to allow the stringers to stand proud of the frames by about the thickness of the plate, then you may weld using 2" / 50 mm long welds on 8" / 200 mm centre s. Over welding the frames to the plating will surely spoil the fair line and overall appearance of the finished hull.

Where the plates butt together they should be joined vertically. Any one of several techniques can be used to keep a fair line in the plating at the join. the surest way, is to assemble and weld the plates into long lengths on the shop floor. You will have to be very careful when fitting of these long plates; you do need proper lifting equipment to handle them safely.

WELDING ALUMINIUM

This metal can only be welded using MIG or TIG equipment. In the case of MIG equipment, a special gun is required when welding aluminium. Argon or oxygen, rather than the less expensive carbon dioxide must be used as the shield when welding this material. Even if you only plan to use your MIG or TIG equipment for welding steel, it is worth considering the possibility of later using it to weld aluminium. For this reason alone, do not stint on quality, when purchasing your welding gear.

Experts, who work with aluminum on a daily basis, often tend to disagree as to which welder they prefer MIG or TIG. If you have only minimum experience in handling this metal, you should seek advice locally. If you have no previous experience in working with aluminium, then you should either build in steel or seek professional help with the welding. One solution to a lack of experience in handling aluminium could be solved by acting as your own labourer; hire an expert to undertake the welding, but act as the assistant. You could handle the cutting, fitting and patterning work as required.

In the USA, a wide range of DC inverters used to power MIG units are manufactured by PowCon and by Miller. You will most likely need equipment equal to the Miller XMT300 CC/CV that can be set at 230 V or 460 V single or three phase. This unit when used with three phase power, can weld aluminum in excess of 3/16" / 4.5 mm. As there is a wide choice of available units, you will need to investigate all possibilities, before making a final choice of welding equipment.

In the UK the Kemppi PSS 5000 AC/DC Multi-system welding machine is suitable for both MIG and TIG welding so this versatile unit is worth your consideration.

WELDING COPPER-NICKEL

Most normal cutting processes are acceptable for copper-nickel. Shearing, cutting with an abrasive disc or by use of plasma arc, these are all acceptable. Oxy acetylene cutting is not appropriate for this material.

As mentioned earlier, copper-nickel can be welded using Arc, MIG or TIG equipment. The alloys have been specified for use in seawater for over 50 years. Copper-nickel has been used in salt water pipe work and condenser service, for many of the world's navies and merchant fleets. Copper-nickel has been and is currently used, where fouling must be prevented and where longevity is of utmost importance. This metal

has the potential to be the premier boatbuilding material and it is expected that with an expanding market, copper-nickel will become more affordable. The choice of welding methods can, and often is, made on the basis of availability of existing equipment.

The arc welding process, using flux coated electrodes, is widely practised and only requires existing equipment and a suitable power source. The gas shielded processes; MIG and TIG are capable of producing welds of high quality. These processes have the advantages of greater control over all stages of the welding. In all cases the persons actually undertaking the welding of copper-nickel, should be familiarised with the special characteristics of this metal. Test pieces should be checked for weld integrity. If inspection authorities are involved, they will in any case wish to approve procedures and the competence of the welders involved in the project.

General preparation of the surfaces to be joined will include removing all dirt and other contaminants. Sources of elements such as lead, sulphur, phosphorus and residues from marking crayons, paints, cutting fluids, oil and grease, that can cause weld cracking must all be removed. Clean cloths should be used to apply fresh organic solvents to the joint area and to dry it off. If the drying cloth shows any residue, the process should be repeated until the cloth is clean. By now I am sure you get the picture, areas to be welded must be scrupulously clean!

In general, a 70-30 copper-nickel filler material is used for joining both 90-10 and 70-30 copper-nickels. Using this material ensures the weld metal is at least as corrosion resistant as the parent material and thus avoids the concentrated attack that might occur if the relatively small area of weld metal was more susceptible to corrosion that the substantially larger area of parent metal.

If copper-nickel is to be welded to steel, then these standard weld metals tend to crack when deposited, due to the effect of the steel, which is fused into the weld joining process. In this case, a nickel-copper of 65 percent nickel filler material is used; this composition remains sound when diluted by the fused steel.

Copper-nickels are relatively simple to fabricate and given the correct information and conditions, any competent welder can handle the material. This material is naturally ductile and does not undergo any significant metallurgical changes requiring special

Copper-nickels are relatively simple to fabricate and given the correct information and conditions, any competent welder can handle the material. (Photo by Amalgamated Technologies Inc)

treatment. Copper-nickel can be cold formed up to 50 percent deformation, before any stress relief heat treatment is required. The machinability of this metal is similar to that of aluminum bronze, phosphor bronze and other copper-alloys.

When welding copper-nickel it is important to consider two important requirements: cleanliness and protection of the weld from the atmosphere. The first ensures that none of a number of detrimental minor contaminates can cause cracking. The second prevents the absorption of gases and the formation of porosity in the weld metal.

It is preferable to set up a dedicated area when building in this material, as this makes it easier to avoid undesirable contact with other materials. It is essential that tools used in the fabrication and handling of copper-nickel are not contaminated with the residues of other metals.

For de-scaling, the surface oxide films on both 90-10 and 70-30 alloys can be very tenacious. Oxides and discoloration adjacent to the areas to be welded can be removed with very fine abrasive belts or discs. If pickling is required, a hot 10-15 percent sulphuric acid solution containing 2 percent sodium nitrate or dichromate is satisfactory. Before pickling, oxides can be broken up by a light grit blast. The pickled components should be rinsed thoroughly in running water, then preferably in 2 percent ammoniacal water, rinsed again and finally dried in hot air.

Joint preparation; in general it is possible to weld copper-nickel of up to 1/8"/ 3 mm thickness with a square butt preparation. Butt preparation for thicker copper-nickel involves forming bevelled edges; the angle of the V should be larger than is normally used for steel and should be 70 degrees or above. This is because the molten weld metal is less fluid and some manipulation of the electrode or torch is necessary, to ensure fusion with the sidewalls of the joint.

Whenever possible, it is desirable to weld in the down-hand position, since welding in other positions requires greater skill, if defects in the weld, particularly porosity, are to be avoided. It is worth the effort of manipulating the fabrication into the most favourable location, rather than attempting to operate in an unsuitable position. All of the foregoing, points towards building the boat hull upside down. In my opinion the upside down is recommended, no matter which metal is being used as the basic hull material.

In the case of arc welding, the flux-coated electrodes are designed to operate with direct current, electrode positive. They require no special pre-treatment unless they have been exposed to the atmosphere for some time, (not recommended in any case), when they will need to be dried in an oven; for example 1 to 2 hours at 250 degrees C. Taking into account the need for manipulation, it may be helpful to select a rod size slightly smaller than that of a carbon steel electrode that would be used under comparable conditions. Any weaving, however, should not be more than three times the electrode diameter. A long arc should be avoided, since this results in weld porosity through reaction with the surrounding atmosphere. Where start positions are found to be unsound, reversing the electrode direction to re-melt initially deposited weld metal or the crater at the end of the run can help to avoid problems. The joint temperature should not be allowed to rise excessively after successive runs; it is usual to restrict the interpass temperature to 150 degrees C.

Many consumable manufacturers offer electrodes for welding copper-nickel. The brand selected should conform to a recognised standard. Generally, coated electrodes meet the requirements of both American AWS A5.6 ECuNi specification and the German DIN 1733 EL-CuNi30Mn specification and contain the appropriate amount of deoxidisers to ensure sound welds in normal conditions (because of these, any quoted copper content will be a little less than the nominal 70 percent). The welding currents recommended by the electrode manufacturer should be followed.

TIG

This welding of copper-nickel employs similar methods used when dealing with other metals. Separate control of heat input, via the arc, and filler metal addition, gives this process a degree of flexibility which is an advantage when welding shaped joints or inserting root runs in thicker joints. It is essential, nevertheless, to ensure that filler material is incorporated and the simple fusion of the parent metal is avoided. The latter is important because substantial amounts of deoxidisers in the filler materials are necessary to prevent the formation of porosity. Bare filler wires are produced to the American AWS A5.7 ERCuNi specification and to DIN 1733 SG-CuNi30Fe and BS2901: part 3 Grade C18 in Europe. Argon or argon + 1.5 percent hydrogen is used as the shielding gas and, once again the need for short arc is emphasised. Direct current should be used and the currents should be adjusted to suit the wire size and material thickness.

MIG

The welding of copper-nickel can be operated over a range of currents to provide low heat-input dip transfer or the relatively high-heat input spray transfer, which is only suitable for thicker materials, say above 1/4" / 6 mm thickness. While dip transfer is used successfully for thinner materials, a more advanced technique, pulsed-arc transfer, provides a better combination of low overall heat input and adequate fusion of the parent material. This requires a power source designed for the purpose and these are available at different levels of sophistication and price. Pulsed-arc welding has substantial advantages for the operator and gives greater assurance of good quality welds than the dip transfer process. More advanced, synergetic welding power sources control the detachment of the droplet from the wire effectively while reducing the number of variables to be set by the welder.

Argon or a mixture of argon and helium is preferred as shielding gas and the spooled filler wire must be kept dry and not exposed to contamination. Because of the higher capital cost of equipment and the cost of buying spools of wire, this process is more appropriate when extensive welding such as when one or more complete hulls is to be built. This last condition applies no matter which material is being welded by the MIG or TIG process.

Filler wires for both tungsten-arc and gas-shielded metal arc processes are available to American, German and British standards. For reasons given earlier, the 67-30 copper-nickel alloy is preferred as a filler material for both 90-10 and 70-30 copper-nickel alloys. Wires of this alloy conform to the same specifications as for tungsten-arc welding. Because of the relative softness of the wire, it is important to feed it through low friction liners.

Because of the range of transfer conditions possible in the gas shielded metal arc process, welding parameters can vary widely. In all cases, these should be set for the equipment and position and thickness of the material by careful welding procedure trials directed towards stable transfer conditions and welds of good appearance. It is not desirable simply to reproduce published welding conditions, since indicated current not only depend on transfer mode but on the type of indicating instrument and power source in use.

Copper-nickel has been used extensively to clad large container ships, oil tankers and similar merchant vessels. This process has proved most successful in preventing corrosion and in virtually eliminating marine growth on the underwater surfaces of the hulls. The obvious advantages include the fact that these ships are able to continue to operate without the need for bottom cleaning and repainting; a valuable asset in today's competitive market. Information on this process is available from the Copper Development Association (CDA) in both the UK and USA, see appendix 4 for details.

Metal need not restrict the shapes you use when building your boat. This stern arrangement was built by the cut to size Kit Company ALMARINE.

Chapter 7
STARTING CONSTRUCTION - ALL METALS

Material lists. Building upright or upside down. Using full size patterns. Lofting. Making the frames. Preparing the bedlogs or strongback. Setting up the frames. Stem and backbone. Installing stringers.

This is a good time to mention that the professional who designed your boat may have spent many hours over some small detail believing that it will have an important bearing on the performance, appearance or resale value of your boat. Respect his (or her) efforts and please do not casually make changes without consulting the designer.

Making and erecting the frames is one of the most exciting parts of building any boat; having built a few boats myself I know the thrill of seeing the frames erected for the first time and standing back and admiring the line of the hull. Of course the addition of the chine bars (if present) and a few stringers gives a better idea of the shape of the hull but the initial thrill of seeing the frames erected is still a most memorable occasion.

MATERIAL LISTS
You will get a better price if you order in bulk so it is recommended that you order all of the basic hull materials in one combined package. Your building plans may include a material list and if so it usually consists of the main items required for building the hull deck and superstructure. On some occasions, if you calculate the total weight of the metals, you may find that there appears to be too much material. Your list should include an allowance for offcuts and other wastage. The list may also include details of the temporary bracing required to set up the hull.

Even if your plans include a material list (including the lists included in our plans), it is strongly recommended that you carefully go through the drawings and 'take off' the list for yourself. Don't forget to allow for wastage, 15 to 20 percent is about right. Some of this 'wastage' material will be used to make occasional tools including clamps and tags. The time required calculating the quantities will be a good investment; it will prove invaluable in your better understanding of the plans. 'One hour of study can save two hours of work' is an oft-quoted truism.

Most lists do not include the materials required for the interior joinery. In some cases this list is not included because there may be several alternative accommodation versions. It is better to compile a timber and plywood list after you have made a 'definite' decision as to which interior you will finally select for your boat.

BUILDING UPRIGHT OR UPSIDE DOWN
The shape of the boat, the choice of metal being used to construct the hull, or the particular building method you choose, may all contribute to your decision, as to which way up, you should build the hull. Another factor could be the space and facilities available for turning the hull. There are many simple systems for turning hulls, so this factor should not play too big a part in reaching your decision. You could decide to build two or more rings around your hull thus facilitating working on the hull and other areas of your boat.

Advocates of the upside down method prefer to build inverted because most of the important hull welding can be done in the down-hand position. In any case, some of the welding must me done from inside the hull, including tacking the intermediate stringers to the hull plating. Unfortunately this may be a bit awkward, but at least some of this welding will have to be done while the hull is still inverted.

Leaving the transom off the hull until after turnover will be of some help in gaining access to the interior of the hull. There is some justification in deciding not to install the transom, until immediately before the deck is installed.

In the case of radius chine construction, I consider it imperative that the hull be built upside down. Building inverted makes it easier to install the radius plating. In my opinion it is much simpler to lay the plate on to the framework from above, than it is to have to draw or hold up the plating from below until it is tacked in place. At the risk of repeating myself, you must always build radius chine hulls upside down. My preference to building upside down extends to round bilge hulls as well.

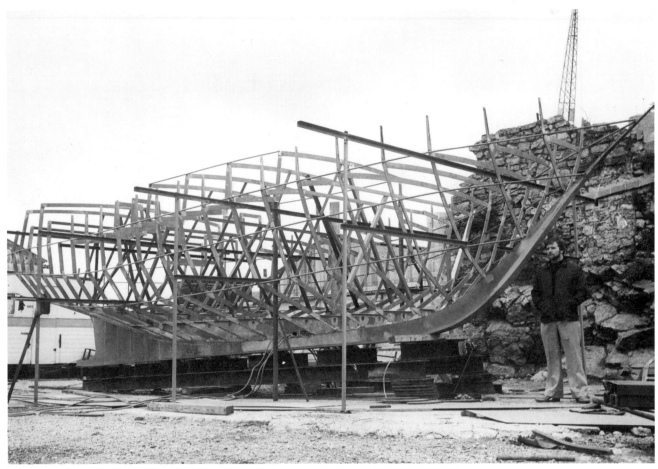

Keel and stem in place, frames erected and chine bars installed on ROBERTS SPRAY.

Photograph of the framing is typical of a hull built upside down. This is the Spray 33, which is now completed, built by John and Joan Mc Dermott in Oman.

To be fair to those who prefer to build the hull upright, the stated advantages of this method include the fact, that the hull is already in a position to complete the deck superstructure. In other words it does not have to be turned. Building the hull upright offers easy access during the entire welding operation. You can overcome some of the disadvantages of not being able to 'lay on' the plate, by employing the use of adequate scaffolding. There are also many tricks such as drilling a hole in the plating and pulling this area of the plate into position by means of chains wedges and threaded bolts. As mentioned earlier, whether you build upright or upside down, will largely depend on your circumstances and personal preference.

USING FULL SIZE PATTERNS

Let us get this straight right from the start, the only people who decry the use of full size patterns, are those who either, do not have access to this facility, or those with masochistic tendencies. Under no circumstances try and 'improve' on the patterns by using the offsets (if available) to completely re-loft the boat. Today most boats are designed, drafted, lofted and the full size patterns plotted from the computer generated offsets. You can not improve on that even by completely re-lofting the boat by hand.

The patterns you receive will most likely contain full size shapes for all of the frames for one side. This is all you will need unless you are building an asymmetrical hull (catamaran?). In addition to the frames, other full size shapes should include the stem, developed transom (the full size transom shape when the curved transom is laid out flat; the radius will be

included in the plan details) plus deck and cabin top beam cambers. Also patterns may be included for the rudder, window patterns and other items. These extra patterns are included when the designer feels that a pattern will ensure that you interpret his ideas as intended. If possible use these patterns. Usually any 'improvement' in the designerís work will result in a less attractive boat.

Paper patterns are quite satisfactory provided they are handled properly. These patterns should not be exposed to a damp atmosphere, prior to being transferred to a more durable surface. If your plans come with paper patterns, do not open or unroll the patterns until you are ready to start building the boat. The patterns that come with our plans arrive in a plastic bag. Mylar patterns are a nice luxury but they are expensive, usually about £500 to £800 / US$800 to $1,300 per boat.

You will need a suitable surface on which to layout the patterns. You can work either directly from the patterns (not recommended) or transfer the patterns to plywood or steel plate. This working area is variously known as 'the loft floor', 'the master plate' or any one of a dozen other locally inspired names. If you are transferring the frame shapes and other patterns to plywood, then you can use a 'dressmakers wheel' to mark the shapes through the patterns on to the surface of the plywood. This plywood could be later used in the fitting out process, so it will not represent an additional expense. If you are transferring to steel plate, then you will need to centre punch the main points and use a batten and straight edge to scribe in the shapes of the frames. In the case of shaped frames

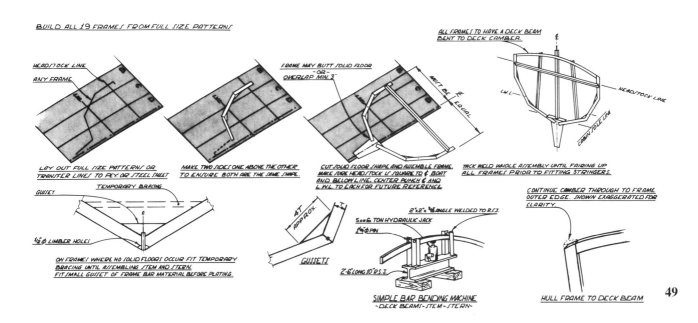

UPRIGHT METHOD
ERECT BUILDING SCAFFOLD ~ SUSPENED FRAMES FROM JOISTS ~ FIT STEM, KEEL, STERN ~ FIT STRINGERS ~ TACK WELD HULL PLATING ~ ADD REST OF STRINGERS ~ CUT AND RAISE CABIN BEAMS ~ ADD BULKHEADS ~ TACK WELD DECK AND CABIN ~ WELD UP WHOLE BOAT.

BUILD ALL 19 FRAMES FROM FULL SIZE PATTERNS

ALL FRAMES TO HAVE A DECK BEAM BENT TO DECK CAMBER.

HEADSTOCK LINE
ANY FRAME

FRAME MAY BUTT SOLID FLOOR ~OR~ OVERLAP MIN. 3"

MUST BE EQUAL

HEADSTOCK LINE

LAY OUT FULL SIZE PATTERNS OR TRANSFER LINES TO PLY OR STEEL SHEET

MAKE TWO SIDES ONE ABOVE THE OTHER TO ENSURE BOTH ARE THE SAME SHAPE.

CUT SOLID FLOOR SHAPE AND ASSEMBLE FRAME. MAKE SURE HEADSTOCK IS SQUARE TO ₵ BOAT AND BELOW LINE. CENTER PUNCH ₵ AND L.W.L. TO EACH FOR FUTURE REFERENCE.

TACK WELD WHOLE ASSEMBLY UNTIL FAIRING UP ALL FRAMES PRIOR TO FITTING STRINGERS.

GUSSET
TEMPORARY BRACING

½" ⌀ LIMBER HOLES

ON FRAMES WHERE NO SOLID FLOORS OCCUR FIT TEMPORARY BRACING UNTIL ASSEMBLING STEM AND STERN. FIT SMALL GUSSET OF FRAME BAR MATERIAL BEFORE PLATING.

45° APPROX.

GUSSETS

2"x2"x⅜" ANGLE WELDED TO R.S.J.
5 on 6 TON HYDRAULIC JACK
1½" ⌀ PIN

2'-6" LONG 10" R.S.J.

SIMPLE BAR BENDING MACHINE
~DECK BEAMS ~ STEM ~ STERN~

CONTINUE CAMBER THROUGH TO FRAME OUTER EDGE. SHOWN EXAGGERATED FOR CLARITY.

HULL FRAME TO DECK BEAM

and the stem, you will need to centre punch several points along the curve and then join the marks with the aid of a batten and 'drafting ducks'. Personally, I find the plywood surface has many advantages.

The above applies to multi-chine sailboats, single chine powerboats and round bilge boats of all types. In the case of radius chine hulls you will not need to transfer the radius sections from the patterns; only transfer the straight sections. You should have the radius frame parts bent to the radius as specified on your plans and the length as measured around each radius that will be needed to match up to the straight sections of the frames. Allow a little extra for trimming.

LOFTING

If the plans for the boat that you decide to build are not available with full size patterns, you will need to arrange for the hull to be computer lofted or lofted by hand. To enable the hull to be computer lofted you will need to supply lines and offsets so that these can be entered, faired, and then plotted as full size patterns. The computer lofting service is available from several design offices including our own.

Lofting by hand involves actually drawing out the entire hull of the boat FULL SIZE. Do not be trapped into only drawing the frames or stations, without actually drawing out the complete boat. You will need a 'loft floor' which can consist of several sheets of plywood. The sheets are laid out to form an area of say three feet / one metre longer than the overall length of the boat or longer by the amount of half the beam, if you plan to develop the transom. The floor will need to be wider than the height of the stem above the keel or baseline or half beam, which ever is the greater. You should paint this 'loft floor' with flat white paint as this will enable you to see the grid and other lines more clearly.

You will need at least one long timber batten of 3/4" x 1/2" / 20 mm x 12 mm or similar size. You will also need some smaller battens, a builders square, string or chalk-line and a set of loftsman's 'ducks' plus suitable pencils. The information included here is very basic and if you have not lofted a boat before you will need a good book containing detailed instructions on this subject.

MAKING THE FRAMES

It is normal to assemble the frames over patterns that have been lofted by the builder or supplied with the plans. As mentioned earlier you may prefer to use a plywood or steel area for this purpose. Make sure the

area is level and that it will provide a firm base on which to assemble the frames.

A boat has two basic types of framing, transverse framing generally referred to as 'THE FRAMES' and longitudinal framing usually known as 'THE STRINGERS' which also includes chine bars, deck stringers and the like. Here we are discussing 'THE FRAMES'.

In steel or copper-nickel boats, transverse-framing material may be flat bar, L angle or T bar. Your plans will most likely stipulate which is appropriate. For many years flat bar frames have been favoured in steel boats. Many designers have given this advice. The reason usually quoted is that L angle is hard to protect from corrosion and the angle portion adds unnecessary weight. More recently we have considered angle in a more favourable light.

Against the above objections, an argument can be made for angle. The flange will provide an excellent place to attach the lining material. The corrosion problems can be overcome by pre-prime coated materials and by using 'spray-in-place' foam insulation, which is now a common practice in metal boat hulls. Regarding the extra weight of angle, I believe that this is not a problem in larger and heavier displacement boats. All that has been said about angle can also be applied to T bar frames. Aluminum boats will have transverse frames made of angle, T or a proprietary extrusion that has some type of bulb or flange. Copper-nickel can have L or angle frames that are bent out of stock that has been cut from plate.

Some builders may prefer to have the deck beams included as part of the original frame construction. If you prefer this arrangement then you will find that this option is best used when you are building upright. Those building the hull inverted would find that the deck beams would interfere with access under the boat. My experience is that the deck beams are best installed after the hull is fully plated and already turned upright. It is easier to check for a 'fair' sheerline before installing the beams. In some cases, for instance if your boat has a bulwark, this last objection may not apply, To summarise, if you are building upright then you may consider installing the deck beams as part of the original frame, but if you are building inverted then do not install the beams until after the hull is upright.

After you have established how many frames you will need and which material, L angle, flat bar or T bar, it is now time to start cutting the correct lengths of material to form each frame. An angle grinder fitted with a suitable wheel can be used for cutting the frame material to the correct length and angle. Some builders prefer to use their Oxy-acetylene equipment for making these cuts and no doubt you have your own preference. Cuts made with the angle grinder are more accurate and will be preferred by many builders.

A neat trick is to make up strips of cardboard as templates for the angle joins on the frames. Use cardboard that is the same width as you frame material. Lay two cardboard strips directly over the join on your patterns ensuring that there is sufficient overlap to allow you to cut through both layers of cardboard using a straight edge that bisects the angle. You have now created a pattern that forms the angle required for both parts of the framing material. Transfer these angles to your lengths of framing material and now you can neatly cut each angle to provide the basis for a perfect join. You may prefer to use a carpenters bevel gauge or plastic protractor to obtain the correct angles. You can always clean up your angles by using the grinder, but it is preferable to make the correct cuts in the first place.

Next, tack weld your frames together and after checking against the patterns, then make the final welds. It is worth noting that an incorrect angle at the chine of only 1/8 in / 3 mm, can become as large as 1 in / 25 mm at the sheer or keel. The frames may be made up in two halves, or one half on top of another, and then opened up like a clamshell to form the frame. You must carefully check the fully assembled and welded frames against the patterns and one half against the other. Accuracy is vital at this stage. It is not a good idea to tack the various parts of the frame, on to a steel master or loft plate. Frames assembled in this manner can have in-built tension, that will cause them to change shape when released from the loft plate floor.

A good way to avoid distortion is to follow the same sequence for assembling each frame. For instance, place a tack weld at the centre of each angle join, let this cool for a few seconds before tacking either ends of the angle. Several frame sections can be done in sequence, ensuring that minimum time is lost through waiting for welds to cool, before proceeding to the next step in the assembly process. The object is to keep the job moving forward, without setting up stresses in the frames, and avoiding unnecessary delays in the work schedule.

Once you have tacked the frame together, you should be able to move it about and check the accuracy against the master patterns that have been scribed on the metal or plywood loft floor. When one side of the frame is tacked together, you should turn it over and tack the other side. Again check the accuracy against the master patterns.

You will be installing some form of headstock across the frame. This headstock may be used to support the frame on the strongback or bedlogs. Make sure you install other bracing between the headstock and the sides and bottom of the frame otherwise it will be too flexible and impossible to set in position on the strongback.

Mark all of the important reference points on all frames. Include such points as LWL (DWL), sheerline, deck line (if this is below the sheer), plus any other points indicated on your full size patterns. Finally, please follow the designerís specifications for making your frames; never overlap the ends of the frame bar where they join in the misguided belief that you are making the boat stronger. Overlapped metal can harbour corrosion also the practice ads unnecessary weight and looks unsightly as well as giving your boat an 'amateurish' appearance. On the same theme, do not add extra permanent gussets at the frame joins, these items were necessary for frames in wooden boats, but add extra unnecessary weight in a metal hull.

There are several ways to make the various cuts in the frame to accept the stringers, deck shelf and sheer stringer. One method is to divide up each area between the chines into equal spaces and using a square, mark in a notch for each stringer. These notches may then be cut while the frame is still on the loft floor. If you prefer this method then it may be better to cut the notches before tacking the frame together; cutting the notches will probably distort the frame part, so this is best corrected before you assemble the frame.

In the past we have recommended standing up the frames and then marking in all of the stringer locations on the frames by using a batten to simulate the fair curve of each stringer. Next step is to take the frames down and cut the slots. Finally check each frame for accuracy, before reinstalling it in its correct location. This method is time consuming but it does ensure that you get a fair set of stringer notches and in turn a fair set of stringers. This method also makes sure that the final frame is still the shape intended by the designer and in due course it will contribute to building an attractive and fair hull.

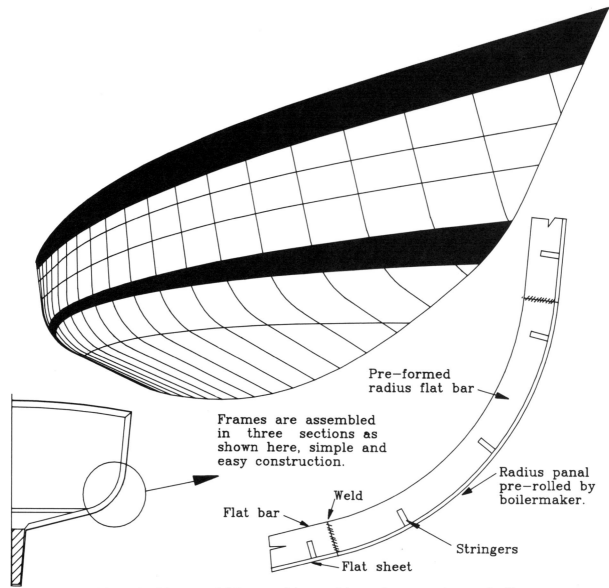

Frames are assembled in three sections as shown here, simple and easy construction.

Pre-formed radius flat bar

Radius panal pre-rolled by boilermaker.

Weld

Flat bar

Stringers

Flat sheet

At last it is possible to build a round bilge steel boat without the great time and effort, not to mention experience, required using traditional methods. Radius Chine building techniques are developed through Computer fairing which provides you the builder with Full Size Patterns of all the frames, full size stem and full size expanded transom pattern. The secret of Radius Chine depends on FAIRING THE RADIUS THROUGH TO THE BOW. Most other attempts at this type of hull form have tried to fade out the chine before it reaches the bow. This usually results in a flat spot or unfair area up forward. Previous methods have been (are) more difficult to build than Multi Chine. Our Radius Chine is very easy to build, the secret lies in the exact way in which we develop these hulls using our In-House Computer programs. The Full Size Patterns are all plotted on Milar film.

DRAINAGE

This is a good time to think about drainage in the inside of your hull. When the hull is in its correct position, there will be low points on the stringers. Careful observation will enable you to locate these at this stage. This is the area where moisture can collect inside the hull and can cause a potential corrosion problem.

If you are intending to install foam insulation especially the 'spray in place' variety then you will not have this problem because the foam should come at least to the inner edge of the stringers. The foam will provide a flush surface and leave nowhere for the moisture to collect. The insulation will go a long way towards preventing the generation of any moisture caused by condensation. In foam insulated boats, any condensation that does occur will drain into the bilge. As your boat will need insulation this is the obvious answer to a known problem.

If you are going to install 'insulation bats' instead of the spray-in-place variety, then you may wish to grind small semi-circular holes in the low point of the stringers. The holes will be arranged so they leave a drain hole between the stringer and the hull plating.

Some frames will require limber holes. There is no point in cutting limber holes in the areas of the frame or keel webs where the hole will be later filled with ballast. The forward and the aft frames will need limber holes to allow any water to flow to the lowest point. Check our plans and give some thought to this drainage situation.

AVOIDING THE 'STARVED COW LOOK'

In Europe, many designers and builders prefer to have the stringers stand proud of the frames by say 1/8 in / 3 mm to 3/16 in / 4 or 5 mm, this practice prevents the frames touching the hull and causing the 'starved cow' look that spoils the appearance of an otherwise fine metal hull. If your boat is large enough, say over 36 ft / 11.00 M, then consider using 3/16" / 5 mm hull plating as this will result in a fairer hull.

RADIUS CHINE FRAMES

Do not confuse this type of hull with one that simply has pipe chines. True radius chine hulls have a radius of between 24 in / 610 mm and 36 in / 910 mm. The radius chine hull has many benefits, including all of those attributed to a round bilge metal hull. The fact is, the radius chine hull is one of the easiest hull forms to build in metal. This ease of construction

applies from making the frames, right through to the final plating.

All true radius chine hulls are designed; faired and lofted in the computer so you will almost certainly have accurate full size patterns. Naturally it is most important to have accurate patterns from which to make your frames, and computer lofting is the most accurate way to achieve this end. As the radius sections are all the same radius it is only the amount of arc measured around the curve, that will vary. This means that you will not need to transfer all of the radius curves to your loft floor. Transfer only the straight frame sections. Make sure that the ends of these lines are clearly defined; use a cross check mark to give a clear definition to the ends. Next, simply cut the straight lengths of framing and place in position. Now cut the exact lengths of curved frame material that have been pre-bent to the correct radius.

You can either bend the radius frame material yourself, or had it bent by an outside metal shop. Assuming that you farm out this work, we recommend that you have the radius frame sections, stem bar, and lengths of plate all bent to the correct radius section at the same time. See details on plating the radius chine in the chapter on plating your hull. The remainder of the techniques used for assembling

For the less experienced steelworker it may be practical to build a timber framework on which to plate your frameless hull.

the frames of your radius chine hull, are virtually the same as those used for the other hull forms.

FRAMES FOR FRAMELESS HULLS

If you are building a 'Frameless' boat, that is a hull with only a few frames, or one, which has no transverse frames, then you, may use angle frames as a mould and these will not remain in the boat. When you are building the 'mould' for a frameless boat, it may be possible to eliminate every second frame when setting up the shape of the hull. When the designer prepares computer designed lines it is usual to have only 4 to 6 control sections (similar to frames) and the remainder of the hull is faired through these sections. Most light to medium displacement steel chine hulls (not radius chine), under say 40 ft / 12.19 M, are suitable for building using the frameless technique. Contact the designer of your boat, if you are interested in building using this method. Ask if some frames may be eliminated either in the finished boat or in the setting up mould. Some frameless hulls are built over a timber framework; this may be helpful if you are building a metal hull under 35 ft / 10.66 M and have limited metalworking experience. You could build the timber framework yourself, and then hire an experienced welder to weld up the hull.

PREPARING STEM, BACKBONE AND KEEL

You will find that metal boats use many different metal sections for building the stem. Some boats feature a stem that is a flat bar on edge, and this is the material specified for many of our sailboat designs. Other designers favour, solid round bar, round or rectangular tube or rolled plate. In many of our powerboat designs, we favour stems that incorporate rolled plate above the top chine. Your home-made bending machine will come into use for bending the flat bar stem if part or all or the stem is to be formed from this material. Some stems may include a conical section of rolled plate.

The aft section of the backbone may be installed on edge, without it being necessary to form it in a bending device. Some stems such as those used in the Spray designs, may be constructed using a box section and of similar construction to that used to fabricate the keel. You will need to make plywood or hardboard patterns for the sides of the 'box stem' and trial fit these before cutting any metal.

The leading edge of the KEEL will be either flat bar, split or full pipe or rolled plate. Flat bar keel leading edges are satisfactory for very small powerboats. In

most cases a rounded leading edge will not only be stronger and less liable to damage, but it will also offer a better surface to the water that will flow past the leading edge, and on around the keel. The aft end of the keel is usually formed of flat bar on edge.

PREPARING THE BEDLOGS OR STRONGBACK

For hulls built upside down, your plans should include details of preparing the base needed to set up the hull frames. This base can have one of several names including 'bedlogs' or 'strongback'. In our plans a set of bedlogs consists of a framework of suitably sized timber or steel I beams placed on a prepared surface. The surface can be cement, packed earth or other similar base. If a packed earth floor is used, then it is wise to install strategically placed cement pads capable of supporting the bedlogs and the completed hull. You are building a foundation, abet a temporary one, but one that has to support the hull until it is plated. In the case of a hull built upright, the strongback or setting up bedlogs will be required to remain true, until the boat is completed.

The strongback is a framework that is usually about 3 ft / 0.91 M off the ground or floor, and is used to support frames on a hull being built in the inverted mode. The idea of the strongback was to have the inverted hull set up far enough above the floor so the builder could easily climb underneath the hull to undertake the necessary tack welding of the stringers to the inner hull plating before the turn-over stage. More recently we have found it easier to simply extend the frames to a common headstock or upper baseline. Using this method we ensure that the hull will be far enough off the floor to clear the stem, and allow a welder to have easy access to the interior of

Overhead gantry set on simple rails will make handling of plate much easier.

the hull. In all setting up methods, a wire 'stringline' down the centre line will be an essential part of your headstock or bedlog setting up procedure.

GANTRY

You may consider installing a gantry that can be used to erect the frames, and assist in installing the plating. If you are assembling your hull inside a commercial building then you may be fortunate in having an overhead gantry already available, otherwise you will have to arrange your own. The 'track' will consist of a pair of channel rails made from some 'U' section steel and running full length, and each side of the hull. Two sets of 'A' frames set to run on wheels in the channel and an 'I' beam rigged with one or more 'chain blocks', 'chain falls' or 'chain hoist' (all the same device), will complete the arrangement. An even simpler gantry is to use a three-pole tripod

arrangement, which can have an attachment point for a chain hoist and use this to lift the plates and other large metal sections.

PREPARING TO BUILD A HULL UPRIGHT

Professional builders have many methods of setting up the frames, transom and stem, to build a metal hull upright. These methods, while they are suitable for the professional, could in some cases cause problems, when used by the less experienced builder. For instance they could allow errors to creep in resulting in a less than fair hull. It is the responsibility of the designer, especially when dealing with a less experienced builder, to ensure the method of setting up the hull is well detailed in the plans. This will make it easier for the first time builder who otherwise may be unsure of how to proceed. Experienced

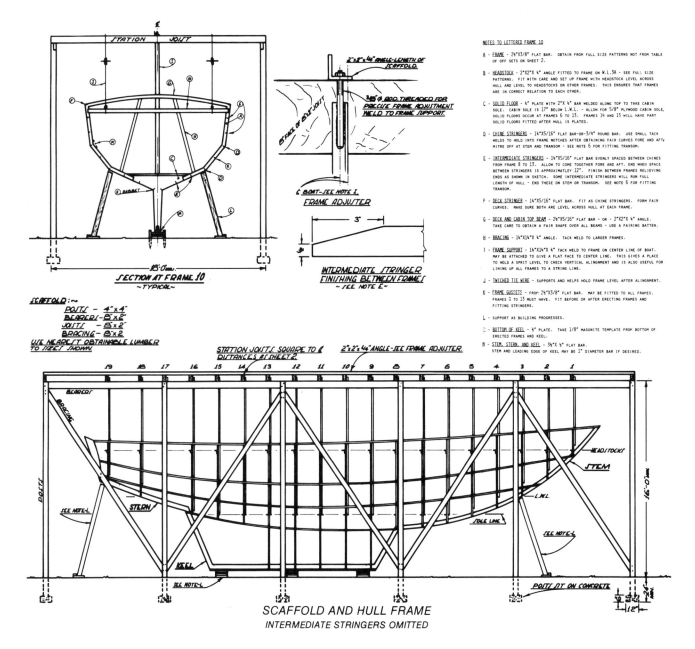

SCAFFOLD AND HULL FRAME
INTERMEDIATE STRINGERS OMITTED

Typical solid web floors on ROBERTS design

welders and metal workers and fitters who have no previous boat building experience have built many fine metal boats.

For the less experienced builder, the secret is in having a well prepared building frame, strongback or similar arrangement to allow the frames to be set up in their correct locations in and to avoid errors. One method we have used is to build a framework for a shed-like structure and support the frames from overhead rafters. Another way is to build a set of bedlogs and use pipe supports to hold the frames in position until the keel; stringers, chine bars and stem are installed. With a hull built upright, once the keel is plated, then the structure can be more or less self-supporting with the weight mostly on the keel. Additional supports should be installed under the ends and sides of the hull to avoid it sagging during construction.

SETTING UP INVERTED HULLS

By now you will have constructed and assembled all of the elements of the framework. Now you can start to install the frames on the strongback or bedlogs. A tensioned wire will mark the centre line of the building jig. This wire will remain in position until the hull is turned upright.

You will need a carpenters rule, a steel measuring tape (at least as long as you boat), a 'plum-bob', a large carpenters square, a spirit level (say 3ft / 0.91 M long), and a line spirit level. Each frame must be square off the strongback, and must be parallel with its neighbour. The plum-bob will be used to ensure the frame is vertical.

After you have marked out the strongback or bedlogs with the correct station spacing; you can start with station 5 or the mid-section frame (same frame in most cases) and install it firmly in position. Work alternatively fore and aft installing the frames until they are all in place. Needless to say you should check everything several times until you are absolutely sure the whole structure is true and fair. I have seen boats with stems that are crooked and leading edges of keels that are out of line; this really a sad sight. Your eye will be one of your best guides to fairness; use it and then check again by measuring and use of level and square and plum-bob to ensure you have everything set up true and fair.

Next install the stem and aft centre line bar and the centre line transom bar. The transom may be left off at this stage and not installed until after the plating is completed on the remainder of the hull. Generally you do not install the keel sides or the bottom of keel plate, until after the hull is plated up and has the strength, to support the heavier plating that is usually specified for the keel.

In some designs a few of the bulkheads may be included as frames; this works fine, providing you do not change your interior plan after the bulkheads have been installed. The bulkheads at the forward and aft end of the engine room will be metal as will the anchor locker bulkhead (sometimes called the crash bulkhead). The aft bulkhead of the main cabin and the forward bulkhead of the aft cabin (at least above the deckline), will all be metal. In my own designs I prefer to install at least some, or all of the bulkheads after the hull is turned over. In most cases the bulkheads will fall on a frame. As detailed elsewhere, it is no problem to deal with intermediate bulkheads. Some bulkheads will be metal and others are best built of plywood.

On our designs the web or solid floors form part of the frame structure, similar to a 'mini bulkhead' at each frame. These web floors generally extend up from the keel to the cabin sole and can be used to contain and divide up tanks, ballast and to support engine beds. There is no need to ring these web floors with framing bar; in fact this is a bad idea, because corrosion can form between the bar and the web. The material for the webs should be the same thickness as for the flat of the framing; this way there will be no dis-continuation of thickness where the framing and the webs are butt welded to the remainder of the frame.

Solid round chine bar and flat bar stringers notched into frames.

STRINGERS AND CHINE BARS

Longitudinal framing will play a very important part in maintaining the strength of your hull. After you have set up the frames, it is time to install the stringers and chine bars. As a designer I prefer flat bar for stringers. For chine bars both solid round bar and flat bar have advantages and disadvantages; the choices in this area are covered elsewhere. We do not recommend closed pipe for chine bars. Steel pipe can rust inside and it is difficult, if not impossible, to paint or otherwise protect the interior of the pipe. When used in the leading edge of the keel, the pipe can be filled with lead.

Many designers and builders prefer to have the stringers stand proud of the frames by 1/8 in / 3 mm to 3/16 in / 4.5 mm thus avoiding every frame showing through the plated surface. Obviously if the stringers are not touching the plating then it will be impossible to weld the plating to the frames; in my opinion this is not a problem especially in boats under say 45 ft / 13.72 M. Using this method, the stringers are welded to the frames and the plating is welded to stringers and this ties the structure together providing adequate overall strength.

If the frames are away from the plating then it is possible to paint behind them during the painting of the interior; as most hulls now have spray in insulation this benefit may be academic. The main benefit is to keep the hull fair and not allow any frame show-through on to the plating.

Check with the designer of your particular boat, before welding or not welding frames to the hull skin; his calculations may require one or the other practice. In any case the frames should have been set up in such a way as to avoid the frames showing through the plating; frames '0' through 5 (mid section) are set so forward edge is on station mark and frames 6 to the stern are installed so the aft edge of the frame is on the mark.

When installing the stringers, only tack weld them into the slots. In most designs the plating will take a fair curve and the stringers may need to be 'relieved' so that they will make contact with the plating throughout the hull. It is a fine judgement whether to pull the plate into the stringers or let the stringers out to lie neatly against the plating. By now your eye should be developed sufficiently, to make it obvious

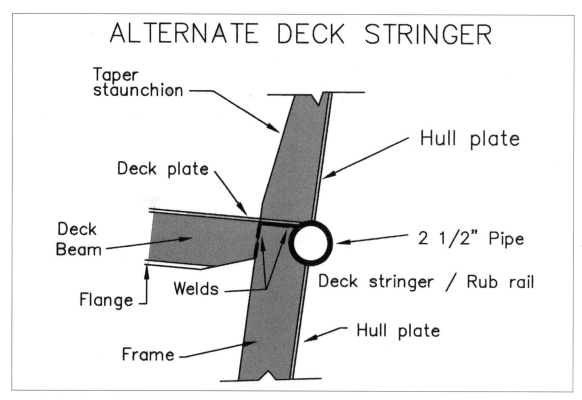

ALTERNATE DECK STRINGER

Taper staunchion

Hull plate

Deck plate

Deck Beam

2 1/2" Pipe

Flange

Welds

Deck stringer / Rub rail

Hull plate

Frame

The alternate deck stringer shown in this sketch with double as a rubbing strake.

which course to follow. In some places the stringers will need to 'take the strainí while the plating is pulled into place; again your eye will help you to make the right decision.

The order of installing the stringers and chine bars (if present) can be as follows. Firstly install the sheer or deck stringer, making sure that you keep the ends of the frames equally spaced and square off the centre line. Next, in the case of a chine or radius chine hull, install the chine stringers (chine bars). As mentioned elsewhere, there is room for discussion as to whether you should fit flat bar, round bar or have no chine stringers at all; follow the recommendations as shown in your plans.

RADIUS CHINE STRINGERS

In a radius chine hull, fit the two stringers one each side of the radius. These should be just a little inside or outside of the radius/flat join as you will need to be able to weld the plates from inside as well as outside so the stringer must be a small distance from the intersection of the radius/flat line. One reason for having these two stringers, one each side of the radius/flat intersection, is to provide a fair guide of the radius/flat intersection. See your plans or full size patterns where this line should be clearly marked.

Some builders may prefer to have the radius chine stringers right on the line that intersects the flat and radius section. If you choose this last method, then

This stern tube arrangement will allow adequate flow of water to the propeller.

you will need to make sure that the plate to stringer weld attains full penetration from outside. A few short welds either side of the stringer from inside the hull, may be advisable.

ADDING INTERMEDIATE STRINGERS

After you have installed the sheer, deck stringer, (if present as a separate item), and chine stringers, then give your hull a check for fairness. Again using your eye, and perhaps the eyes of other more experienced builders, to help ensure that the hull is progressing without being pulled out of line. Now proceed to install the intermediate stringers. The number of intermediate stringers in each chine panel will depend on the size of the hull and the particular metal being used. In most cases a spacing of 12 in / 305 mm will be adequate. Under no circumstances finally weld the intermediate stringers into their slots at this time. You may want to release them later, to allow the stringers to take up the same line as the plate.

When all the chine bars and stringers are in position, the next job is to again check over the structure to ensure that it is 'fair' in all aspects. A timber batten sized approximately 1"x 1/2" / 25 x 12 mm and about 6 ft / 2 M long, can be laid diagonally across the hull at various locations and your eye will probably give the best indication of the overall fairness up to this point. Check over the whole structure and make sure there are no unfair areas. On a round bilge hull a longer batten will be needed to achieve the same results.

STERN AND RUDDER TUBES

Before you commence plating you will need to decide if you are going to install these items at this stage. It is reasonable to install the rudder tube(s) before the plating is in place. The stern tube(s) for the propeller(s) are more difficult to place correctly at this stage. If your hull is upside down you need some very accurate calculations and measurements to get the correct angle and position for the stern tube. It may be better to leave the installation of this tube until you have completed the plating and turned the hull. In hulls built upright, it is easier to figure out where the engine beds are located and where you should install the stern tube.

Just a note on stern bars. If your plans call for a stern bar that is say 2" to 4" / 50 to 100 mm wide then you may be better served by using a flat bar placed in the fore and aft plane and cutting this to take the tube, When you plate the hull, the plating will have a half oval shape around the stern tube and the water flow to the propeller will be much cleaner and less turbulent, than with a wide stern bar. These sketches show a simple way to build a 'heel' to support the rudder and incorporate the tube for the transmission shaft in such a way as to allow the maximum amount of water to reach the propeller

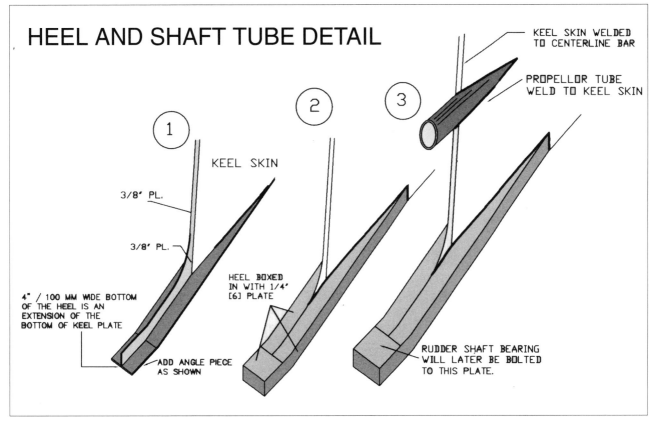

HEEL AND SHAFT TUBE DETAIL

KEEL SKIN WELDED TO CENTERLINE BAR

PROPELLOR TUBE WELD TO KEEL SKIN

KEEL SKIN

3/8' PL.

3/8' PL.

HEEL BOXED IN WITH 1/4' [6] PLATE

4" / 100 MM WIDE BOTTOM OF THE HEEL IS AN EXTENSION OF THE BOTTOM OF KEEL PLATE

ADD ANGLE PIECE AS SHOWN

RUDDER SHAFT BEARING WILL LATER BE BOLTED TO THIS PLATE.

Chapter 8
PLATING THE HULL

Plating single and multi chine hulls. Plating radius chine hulls. Plating round bilge hulls. Handling the plates. Welding plates. Plating the keel. Plating the transom. Rubbing rails. Turning hulls upright.

REVIEWING YOUR HULL

On a well designed metal boat, many of the potential problems associated with plating multi chine, radius chine or round bilge hulls have been eliminated by the naval architect preparing your plans. If the plans and patterns for your hull have been computer faired, conically developed or especially prepared for round bilge construction, then the plating will lay on or can be pulled or raised into position without undue problems. The curvature in all directions should be such that it is gradual to allow the bending of the plate by simple bending methods and devices employing simple mechanical advantages.

This also a good time to review your safety procedures, especially important in the case of steel and copper-nickel, where you may be handling heavy plate. Make sure of the integrity of the weld when using various pad eyes, lifting eyes, 'dogs' and other devices, where you will be lifting heavy plate and other sections, using these attachments.

Considering the keel; if you are building upright then plating the keel and installing part of the ballast may be one of the first operations you will consider before plating the hull. If you are building the hull inverted, then you should leave the plating of the keel until you have plated the remainder of the hull and built up sufficient strength in the structure, to support the heavy keel.

SPECIAL TOOLS

You will need a variety of special tools and devices to assist in the plating of the hull. Fortunately most of these labour-saving tools are simple in nature, and can be made by the builder from scrap plate and bar. As mentioned earlier, a simple gantry from which to suspend your chain block-lifting device will save you many hours of lifting plate and other materials by cruder methods. In the case of steel and copper-nickel, while the material is still on the shop floor, the heavier plates can be moved about with the assistance of pipe rollers. Aluminum being a softer and lighter

material will need to be handled more carefully to avoid scratching the face of the plate. Lifting eyes can be tack welded to the plates, making sure there is sufficient strength in the weld to take the load.

Plate can be moved sideways using a 'come along' or pipe lever. Every time that plate has to be moved there is a mechanical device or aid that can achieve the result with the minimum of effort. The use of these simple devices multiplies your 'muscle power' many times and will take much effort out of installing the plating and other heavy parts of your boat. In metal boatbuilding you should try and work smart rather than hard! Here is an example of what can be achieved by a little forward thinking and preparation. We have on our records the case one builder with no previous metal boatbuilding experience, who with the assistance of a simple tackle and gantry, successfully installed full length plates on a 53 ft / 16.15 M sailboat, that he built to our design.

PLATING THE KEEL

One of the many advantages of a metal sailboat is that the keel will almost certainly be of the 'envelope' type and your ballast will be fully enclosed and protected within the hull. Needless to say there are no keel bolts to worry about. If you are building upright then you may plate the keel first.

It is recommended that you install a percentage of the recommended amount of the ballast, during the construction of the keel (this only applies to boats built upright). It is much easier to install a fair proportion of the ballast in the keel now, while you simply have to lift it into the partially plated keel. This is a good time to remind you that the sides and bottom of the keel form part of the ballast; remember to deduct the weight of the keel structure from the overall recommended ballast before proceeding further. In our designs we recommend you install 75 percent of the total ballast (including the weight of the keel structure) before launching. The remaining 25 per cent can be installed as 'trim ballast' after launching and trimming and preliminary sailing trials are completed.

You can use inexpensive plywood or hardboard to make patterns for the sides of the keel. The leading and trailing edges plus the keel webs will already be installed. It will depend on the actual type and design of your keel as to whether you can plate the sides in one piece. In a deep keel you may have a problem reaching down far enough, to weld the lower ends of the webs and the inside side-to-bottom intersection. In this case you may prefer to have a longitudinal join say 12 in / 305 mm (or other suitable distance) above the bottom of the keel. On occasions it may be necessary to cut slots in the keel side plating so you can plug-weld through to the webs. Your plans should give you some guidance in these areas. If you are building the hull inverted, then you will follow similar procedures for building the keel, but you will undertake this work after the other parts of the hull are fully plated.

PLATING CHINE HULLS

After you have carefully checked over your hull to ensure that it is fair, you may now start to prepare patterns for the plating. The plating patterns or templates are made from a number of 6 in / 150 mm strips of inexpensive 1/4" / 6 mm plywood or hardboard. The outer edges of the templates represent the outer edges of the plate. Seldom is it necessary to use a complete sheet of plywood or hardboard for a template. Usually these patterns are made up of straight strips and corner gussets like a frame and made to fit the particular area to be plated. To strengthen large areas, cross brace your templates by nailing reinforcing pieces as necessary. The templates are built right on the hull by clamping the strips in place in between the chines. The length of each panel may vary; you want the patterns as long as possible but not so long as to be unmanageable. Do not end a template on a frame otherwise your plate will have a bulge in that area; always end a pattern between two frames. The ends of the patterns are always vertical; this helps in getting one pattern to join to the next with the minimum of error.

Your plating pattern should lie flat on the plate; this is a test of its ability to lay evenly on the hull framing.

After you have formed the outline of the pattern you can trim it to exact shape with a grinder or jig saw in fact any tool that will help you achieve a perfect pattern. Check and double-check the template to ensure that it is a neat fit. After you are satisfied with the pattern, you can mark in the frame locations and use these as a guide when positioning the section of plate. See welding details to decide on the welding gaps between the various plate edges. After you are satisfied that you have an accurate template, lay it in the floor; it should lay flat if the plating is to lay on your hull in a fair manner. Successive sections of patterning templates can be joined to make a pattern for one long plate. The longer the section of plate you intend to have in one length, the more accurate must be your patterns; small discrepancies are greatly magnified over the length of a long plate. The patterns can contain other information including stringer locations and any other information that you feel will help you to match the plate precisely to you hull framework.

It is usually best to pattern the largest panel first and then the pattern can be trimmed and used for the next section simply by trimming off the excess, this will save on patterning material. You should start at the keel and work either down or upwards depending on the aspect of your hull. Make the patterns as sturdy as you can and they will serve you well.

PREPARING THE PLATE

You must decide how long each plate will be before it is installed on the hull. Some builders prefer a plate as long as possible, the actual length will depend on the size of your hull, your previous experience and the capacity of your scaffolding and lifting gear. Panels that are welded to full length on the shop floor where it will lay flat will be easier to install in a fair curve. This helps in eliminating any humps and hollows in the finished hull plating. On smaller boats say under 30 ft / 9.10 M you should be able to plate 'full length' in one operation. Larger boats will require more sections. For instance, one man with a helper plated a 75 ft / 22.86 M hull using three 25 ft / 7.62 M panels. For your hull, use the longest sections you can comfortably handle. Builders of aluminum hulls will have some advantage here, as the material weighs only about one third that of steel or copper-nickel and is therefore much easier to handle in this respect. You can transfer the outline of the template to the steel plate by laying the pattern on the plate, (it must lay flat), clamping it in position and then carefully scribing around the edge. Mark in the frame and other pertinent locations on the plate.

Start plating at the keel and work either up or down making sure that you work from side to side on the hull, that is never plate up one side completely before plating the other; keep the plating 'balanced' so that undue stresses are not placed on your hull framework by the plating 'pulling' one way or the other. This can result in a twisted or otherwise deformed hull. The transom is best installed after the remainder of the plating is completed. The open transom will provide access inside the hull for the welders as well as allowing the passage of light. Once you have marked the template outline on to the plate, you can proceed to cut it to shape. The method of cutting will depend on the hull material and is covered in detail elsewhere.

Once you have cut the plate you will want to serve the panel up to the correct area. Using the alignment marks you have previously marked on the boat, pattern and plate, clamp the piece in position. If there are any discrepancies in the fit take the panel down and make the necessary adjustments before reinstalling the plate. It is worth noting that professional boatbuilders often find it necessary to 'serve up' the plate several times before they achieve the desired fit. It is obviously easier to trim off excess than to put back areas that are over trimmed! Keep this in mind when making patterns and cutting the plate.

Under no account try the sloppy practice of installing an oversize plate and then trimming it by simply 'torching' off the excess. If you plate your hull in this manner it will clearly show in the finished job. Buckles, hollows and other large imperfections will tell all who care to look at your boat, that you were indeed a sloppy builder. Always remember that one day you may (will) want to sell your boat and an unfair hull is one of the greatest factors in reducing the value of any used boat.

Before the plates are finally installed in place, make sure you have ground off any imperfections on the edges. Unless your plate is shot blasted and pre-primed (recommended), then make sure to clean up the face of the plate as well. It easier to clean the plate before installation, than when it is in place as in the case of the interior surface, partly obscured by the frames and stringers.

For steel there are several ways to clean the faces of the plates prior to installation. Grit blasting or sandblasting is the easiest and best method but in the case of steel it must be immediately followed by prime coating to protect the sandblasted surface. You can use a disc grinder, a power driven wire brush, or one of any number of similar methods. These techniques are very noisy, and are only for 'tidying up' the plate, rather than preparing it for painting.

You should remove any mill scale and any other foreign matter, so you can make sure the panel of plate has no imperfections before you install it as part of the hull. Before you paint the hull, you must bring the surface back to bare white metal; you must paint this within a very short time, minutes rather than hours, to ensure a rust free surface in the future. Finishing techniques are discussed in a later chapter.

The edges of the plate will need to be bevelled prior to installation; the amount of bevel will depend on the thickness of the plate and the metal being used for plating. Aluminum and copper-nickel need to be prepared in a different manner to steel and these preparations are covered elsewhere in this text.

Before hoisting the plate, you will need to ensure you have made provision for it to be supported while you are fitting it into position and later welding it to the chines and stringers. One method is to tack weld a few lengths of angle to a chine bar, frame and stringer to support the bottom of the plate. Support the chine bar with another piece of angle that extends to the shop floor thus transferring the load, so that the weight of the plate does not deform the fair line of the chine. The 'plate holders' should be tilted inboard so that the plate will naturally slip into the correct location and also not slip out of the 'holder' as it is moved side to side to get the exact alignment required for a perfect fit.

You can use a selection of home made 'C' type clamps to draw the upper edge of the plate to the chine, centre line bar and the stem. As you tighten the clamps you will be drawing the steel plate into position in all planes. In a well-designed chine hull, you will find that the plating will naturally conform to the shape provided by the framework of chine bars, frames and stringers. Most plating is between 1/8" / 3 mm and 3/16" / 5 mm so it will lie in place without you having to resort to extreme bending methods.

In cases where more pressure is required there are several techniques that will help you achieve the desired result. A popular method is to tack weld lengths of threaded rod in the area where you need assistance in making the plate lay in the correct position. You can judge the length of the pieces of rod needed for the job. Use 3/8" / 8 mm diameter rod which is tacked at a 90 degree angle to the inside of the plate and use a prepared section of 2" x 2" x 1/4" / 50x50x6 mm L angle which is placed behind the stringers and chine bars and received the inboard ends of the threaded rod. By tightening up on the rod, you will be able to coax the plate into its correct location. Another method is to weld U shaped eyes on to the inside of the plate and then attach a 'come-along' or other suitable device, such as a Spanish windlass to pull the plate into position.

As you have no doubt only tacked the stringers and chine bars into the slots as we advised earlier, then do not forget that it is permissible and often advisable to 'relieve' the stringers and even the chine bars by allowing them to come out of the slots so as to meet the plating. It takes some judgement to know when to let out the longitudinal, verses pulling harder in the plate to make it take up the desired location.

You will find many ways to make the plating take up its correct shape and fit. Do not hesitate to weld eyes, U shaped round bar and threaded rod to your plate, to help achieve the desired results. These temporary protrusions can be simply knocked off when you have fully welded the plate in position. Do not compromise on a good fit. Follow the guidelines, given in the chapter on welding the particular metal, that you are using to plate your hull.

Butt joins (where two sections of plate meet on a vertical plane) can be drawn together through the use of bolts and large washers. The butt joins must be in near perfect alignment for you to achieve a smooth hull surface. Butt seams can be fitted together through the use of bolts and washers. The seams must be in alignment to achieve a smooth and fair hull. Unless the butt joins are perfectly fitted together, they will show as bulges or uneven patches in what may be an otherwise perfectly plated hull. The problem of fitting the butts can be solved by drilling several holes in the bevelled seams between the plates and inserting bolts fitted with large washers and a nuts. When you take up on the nuts, you will be exerting great pressure up and down the vertical butt join and you will even out any bulges or other irregularities in the join. After you tack weld the plates along the bevels, you can take out the bolts and close the holes with weld.

As you install the various plates, making sure to work from one side to the other and keeping the plating evenly balanced. Be sure to achieve a good fit. A little grinding here and there can make all the difference in making the plates fit as perfectly as possible. The plates may need to be slid back and forth to correctly position them.

A 'come-along' or a tap with a hammer using a wooden block to protect the ends of the plate can work wonders. The fore going is another reason to ensure that you have the plate held securely, but with some freedom of movement, as you prepare to tack it into place.

Do not rush, you will be looking at your hull for a long time! Do not fully weld any plate into position until you have installed all of the hull plating. Do not forget to work side to side along your hull, never get more than one plate ahead on one side, and keep the plating 'balanced'. Once you have tacked a few plates into position you will notice a considerable stiffening up of the hull structure. Sight along the hull as each plate is installed to ensure that you are maintaining a fair curve and no plate looks out of line. If you find you have incorrectly installed any one plate, take it off and correct the problem before proceeding further. The first plates will be the hardest to install so make sure you get these right and you will find that the plating process gets easier as you proceed. Most builders are able after some practice to pattern, fit and install one or two plates per day. If you are achieving more than that you may be working too fast at the expense of quality.

Any boat hull has to look absolutely perfect before painting, for it to look reasonable when it is painted. If in doubt, apply some water to your hull and bring up a shine and then judge how well you are doing. Another trick is to take torchlight and examine your hull at night. When you shine the torch along the hull all the imperfections become more apparent. Aim for perfection, you may not achieve it, but if you aim high, then you should finish up with an attractive and fair hull.

PLATING RADIUS CHINE HULLS

In the case of radius chine hulls, we recommend that you plate the radius section first. Unless you have experience in rolling plate to an accurate radius, then we suggest that you give this job to a local metal shop. Choose a metal shop that has the knowledge and the necessary equipment to undertake the work. A look in the 'yellow pages' will provide many possibilities. Steel, aluminum or copper-nickel are all easy to roll to a constant radius, if you have the correct equipment and are used to this type of work. Perhaps the supplier of your metal plate will have these facilities; if not, he will certainly be able to point you in the right direction.

To ascertain the arc of radius you will need for the largest (widest) plate, simply measure around this arc

Radius Chine 1. Frames are stood up starting at station 5 or midstation of hull

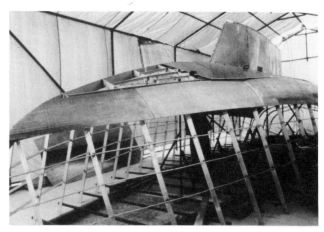

Radius Chine 2. Once all the stringers are located then plate radius section first.

Radius Chine 3. Radius panels around the centre of the hull are split lengthwise and fitted in place.

Radius Chine 4. After both radius chines plated then proceed to install bottom & side plate working

Radius Chine 5. Hull ready for turnover.

Radius Chine 6. Hull has been turned upright ready for bulkheads & deckbeams etc.

on your full size patterns. Usually the largest arc is at the stern or just ahead of the transom. It may be cheaper to have all of the plates the same width even though the arc (not the radius) will get smaller as the plating progresses towards the bow. You will simply trim off the access and use the offcuts for scrap. Needless to say if you do measure each plate, then make sure there is enough width to allow for trimming.

The radius plating should be ordered in about 10 ft / 3.00 M lengths. The centre of the hull will almost always involve some compound curvature and it will be necessary to split the centre plate at least once, maybe twice lengthwise. The plate either side of the centre one may also need splitting, but the plates near the bow and stern should be able to be fitted in one piece. Especially in a sailboat with the greater beam to length ratio, the more plates you will have to split lengthwise, to get a perfect fit. When the plates are split, the two halves are served up to the hull and allowed to overlap; the excessive material is removed, before tacking the radius panel into place. As with all plating, keep the ends of each plate exactly vertical as this will assist in obtaining a good fit for the butt joins, at the ends of each section of plate. As mentioned you will generally find that the largest arc of radius is at, or near the stern of the vessel. You should install the radius plates first, starting at the aft end of the hull and keep the edges neat. Trim to a fair line using a batten to strike a line where the radius panels meet the straight panels of the bottom and the topsides. You should have previously clearly indicated where the radius and straight sections meet on each frame.

Do not let the above explanation frighten you off the radius chine technique. Hundreds of builders have used this method to build beautiful metal hulls. Many have taken the time to write, telephone and seek me out at Boatshows to report their entire satisfaction, with this metal building technique. The flat or the non-radius areas of a radius chine boat are usually simpler to install than a regular chine hull. Simply lift on the bottom and or side plate, mark the join from underneath, and trim the plate to shape. Of course all of the plating, including the radius and straight sections are only tack welded at this stage.

PLATING ROUND BILGE HULLS

Building a round bilge metal hull is the most difficult hull building method and should not be undertaken lightly. You must know that you can produce a fair hull or you should choose to build using either the chine or radius chine techniques. If you can find a professional, who can plate your hull to your entire satisfaction, that can be the solution.

It has been known for some round bilge hulls to be plated lengthwise using strips of varying widths, but allowing the strips to overlap. This technique is similar to that used to build timber clinker hulls. Although the famous 'Joshua' class is built in this way and these are proven boats, it is my contention that corrosion must occur where the plates overlap. My advice is to avoid overlapping plates of other metal sections wherever possible. The foregoing applies especially to steel hulls; as for aluminum and copper-nickel, we are conducting research in this area. A copper-nickel clinker hull could be a possibility, as they say, watch this space!

How you go about plating a round bilge hull will depend on the shape of the hull. There are easy shapes, difficult shapes and near impossible shapes. Starting at the bottom of the keel, you will find that the lower portion of the keel in a round bilge hull will be similar in most, if not all respects to one fitted to a similar style of multi-chine hull. If the hull features a 'hollow heel' then this will definitely be a job for a professional metal boatbuilder. If the hull and keel meet either near, or at right angles, then the plating the keel of the round bilge hull will not present any undue problems.

Now you must examine the overall shape of the 'canoe body'. For instance the traditional Spray design has a very full 'golf ball' shaped bow that makes it a difficult plating job even for any experienced metal boat builder. In our round bilge versions, (also in the chine hulls), of the Spray we have 'drawn out' the bow to make the hull easier to plate. In the case of the Spray this also improves the performance and comfort of the vessel in that it cuts through short steep waves, rather than pounding over them. Some metal hulls may have been designed full-bodied rounded sterns or other features that will make them difficult to plate. A careful study of the plans can give you some hints as to the 'plateability' of the hull in question.

Once you are confident that the design you have chosen features a hull shape that is within your plating capabilities, then you should consider the best technique for fitting the plate. The three ways you can lay plate on a round bilge hull are longitudinally, in multi shaped sections or in diagonal strips. If the hull has a suitable shape then the diagonal method may suit the less experienced builder.

FINAL WELDING

Do not attempt any of the finish welding; until the hull plating is all tack welded in position. Before starting the final welding give your hull a final check for any irregularities; these will be easier to correct before the welding is completed. Bumps can be removed by any one of several metal working techniques including using a rubber mallet on one side, while a helper holds a suitably shaped timber backing piece on the other. Hollows on the hull are most unsightly and must be removed. Small wrinkles along the chine can be removed from inside with the careful use of a large plastic faced mallet and a person holding a suitable backing piece from outside the hull.

Final welding consists of short welds executed in the proper sequence that is suitable for the particular plating. As mentioned in the chapter on welding, different techniques are required to weld steel, aluminum and copper-nickel. You must be fully conversant with the method best suited to the plating of your hull.

Much of the work up until the running of the finish welds is capable of being handled by a person with minimum welding experience. The final welding of the plating is another matter. If you are not a fully experienced welder, then this may be the time to hire a professional, to run the final welds. If you plan to take this route, then we recommend that you seek help before you start the project. Discuss with the professional how much you can do yourself, and when and where, you will be needing his (or perhaps her!) assistance.

If you are going to seek outside assistance, make sure the person understands the vagaries of welding a pleasure boat. Welding a boat is quite different to commercial welding. In commercial welding strength is important but laying down a considerable amount of weld per hour, also has a high priority. To the commercial welder a fine finish may not be considered to be so important. Explain your expectations to the professional before you enter into a firm agreement. If you find that the person you have chosen does not come up to your expectations, make other arrangements before the job gets out of hand.

When the welding of the plating is completed, you will need to grind off some of your welds from the outside of the hull. If you have laid good quality welds with good penetration, then you will have the minimum of chipping and grinding, before repairing or re-welding any unsatisfactory joins in the plate. It is normal practice to only grind the welds above the waterline. Most classification societies insist that the welds below the waterline are left un-ground and therefore will retain all of the strength of the original weld. Do not over grind the welded seams above the waterline otherwise you may weaken them to such an extent that you are compromising the strength of the vessel.

KEEL PLATING

If you have built your hull upside down, now will be the time you will plate the keel. The keel leading edge, usually complete or split pipe, the webs, and the aft end of the keel will already be in place. Your plans will instruct you as to which order to plate the sides and the bottom. In the past we have usually specified 1/4" / 6 mm for the sides and 1/2" / 12 mm for the bottom plate. Today I would be happy to have the whole structure built of 1/4" / 6 mm plate; this means on the sides/bottom intersection you will be welding the same thickness material. Also in the case of boats built inverted you will not have to struggle with the heavier 1/2" / 12 mm plate BOK.

Chester Lemon fitting rubbing strip to his ROBERTS 44.

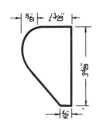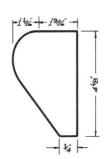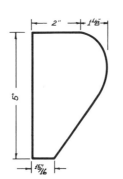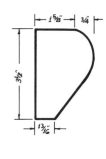

PROPORTIONAL SECTIONS FOR RUBBING STRIP MOLDINGS. MAKE PATTERN TO SUIT. SIZES GIVEN ARE FOR VESSELS 35 TO 45 FEET.

FORMING AND PLATING THE TRANSOM

You may be fortunate in that your plans and full size patterns contain an expanded pattern for the transom. If you do not have this pattern then it is a simple matter to make up some transom formers to the correct camber and then using inexpensive plywood or hardboard, simply make up a pattern to fill in the transom cavity.

Make sure that you do not allow a 'fish-tail' effect to creep into the aft end of your hull; this is caused by making the transom too large, usually too wide, and preventing the side and bottom plating from taking on its fair line. Do not forget to allow for the deck or transom camber when making the pattern and cutting the plate for the transom.

Once you are convinced that the transom plate is the right size and shape, then you can install this in position. It is usual to have a centre line bar extending from the bottom of the hull to the top of the transom and you can 'hang' the transom plate on this while positioning the plate. The remainder of the transom stiffeners, usually vertical and transverse stringers, can be installed from inside, once the transom plate is fully welded from the outside.

RUB RAILS

Rub rails, rubbing strips or rubbing strakes can be made in a variety of ways and out of either the same metal as the hull or one of a variety of other materials. The selection includes, but is not restricted to, 'D' section rubber mounted on a suitable metal structure; timber bolted in place or rope mounted in a channel or other arrangement.

A half round pipe as described in the text is fitted to this Waverunner 52.

Many builders have fabricated various turning over devices. The sophisticated turning wheels shown here are ideal if you are building more than one boat.

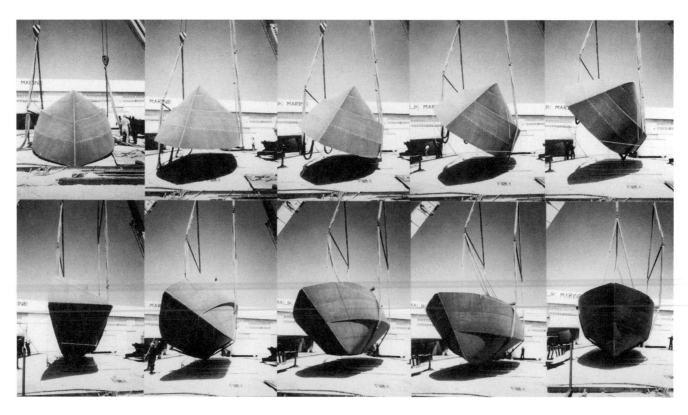

This Waverunner 44 built in Oman was turned using one crane, two spreader bars and two slings.

Considering timber first, this material should best be hardwood. Timbers similar to teak or softer timbers can be satisfactory when fitted with a stainless protective strip. For the ultimate timber rubbing strake, Australian spotted gum has the advantage of being durable, takes a bend, and will wear well without the need of any additional metal protective strip. In general timber, is easily replaceable, can be attractive and is 'kind' to other boats and structures.

A metal half round split pipe of suitable dimensions makes an ideal rub rail on a metal boat and this is what we show on all of our metal sailboat designs. If you take the correct length of pipe and split it lengthwise, the two portions required one for each side.

The aft end can be 'snaped' and plugged with an appropriately shaped piece of hull material; it will finish either at the transom or at 6" / 150 mm ahead of that structure. The other end is tapered so that it will bend around the forward end of the hull, usually ending at or about station '0' or above the forward end of the waterline.

The problem with this pipe rub rail is that you cannot repaint the inside. Even if you are very careful to give the inside a superior paint job before it is installed, the welding will undo at least part of your work. The pipe itself will have sufficient wall thickness to withstand many years of interior corrosion however the plating underneath may not be so long lasting.

One solution would be to have a thicker base plate, say three times wider than the pipe, inserted in to the hull plating but not over the regular hull plating, or you can have problems between the two plates. Skegs and other appendages are covered in a later chapter. If there is a skeg involved in your hull design, then you may prefer installing this after the turnover operation.

Some hulls take a little more effort to move than others do. This is clearly illustrated with the moving of this Roberts 53 hull from Marine Park Brisbane Australia.

TURNING THE HULL UPRIGHT

If you have built your hull in the upside down manner, then now is the time to consider the turnover. When the plating is competed and all of the final outer welds are run, now you can decide on the best method for turning your hull and setting it in the upright position. No matter if yours is a large or small hull, give considerable thought to safety factors when considering how you will effect the turnover. Plan the setting up of the hull, and levelling it ready for completion. The last thing you need at this stage is an injury to yourself, a friend or hired assistant, so take care.

There are several methods that have been used successfully to turn large boat hulls. The method you choose will be in some part decided by the size of your boat, the location and accessibility of your building site. Boats up to say 25 ft / 7.62 M, can be rolled over without the use of mechanical assistance. For smaller hulls a few friends to help and a few bottles of cheer supplied after the operation is completed, should be all that is required to effect a smooth turnover.

If you are building in a large substantial commercial building then you may have the advantage of the availability of overhead track fitted with chain blocks. It may be possible to set up strong points in the building that are capable of taking the load. You can arrange two overhead chain blocks that can support two endless slings that are capable of lifting the hull. Now the structure can to be rolled over in its own width. The two slings are placed one in at about 20 percent from each end of the hull. You will need restraining lines to control the hull during the turning over operation.

It may be preferable to remove the hull from the building and effect the turnover outside where there is more room and less obstruction to hinder the operation. See also the paragraph regarding moving hulls. You may have already built hoops around your hull so that it can simply be rolled over. The hoops will later be used to tilt the hull to various angles; thus allowing easier access to the job at all times. You may wish to build a 'turnover cradle' shaped something like a crate, around your hull and turn it over one side at a time.

My choice would be to hire a crane fitted with a spreader bar and two endless slings. The slings are placed in about 20 percent from the bow and stern and the crane lifts the hull sufficiently to allow it to be rotated in the slings. Make sure you determine the balance fore and aft before the serious lifting begins. You will need restraining lines attached to a winch or other suitably strong device, to control the hull as it reaches the up and over stages.

When you have turned the hull then it will need to be set up level in all directions. Use the waterline locations that you have previously marked on the outside of the hull as a guide. The simple clear tube water level will make it easy for you to set up the hull true and level in all planes.

MOVING HULLS

You can move large bulky and heavy items such as boat hulls using the simplest of tools. A few 2 in / 50 mm diameter pipe rollers about 9 in / 230 mm long can be used to roll your hull. Simply lay planks for the rollers to run on and keep taking the rollers from the back and reinstalling at the front as the hull moves along the desired path. If you use either 4 in x 2 in / 100 x 50 mm timber or 2 in / 50 mm pipe levers say 5 ft / 1.50 M long, these will multiply the strength of one man many times when it comes to lifting or shifting heavy weights. When lifting the hull or frame to insert the rollers, you will find the levers are much quicker to use than a lifting jack.

Record breaker "Omani". This radius chine R434 was sailed single handed around the World by Major Pat Garnett in only 218 days.

Chapter 9
DECKS AND SUPERSTRUCTURE

Planning. Grit blasting. Bulkheads. Making a camber board. Bending and installing the deck beams. Setting up the cabin structure. Installing cabin top beams. Patterning and installing cabin sides. Installing decks and cabin top plating. Bulwarks and toenails. Building or adding a pilot house. Hatches, companionways and doors. Portlights. Building cockpits. Fly-bridge. Teak decks. Other deck coverings. Plywood and timber decks and superstructure. Aluminum decks and superstructure.

PLANNING

Some thought will need to be given to the sequence you will use to complete the various steps needed to finish the deck and superstructure. The sequence of events will include grit blasting, insulating the hull and fitting out the interior. Some of these steps will be undertaken before you build the decks and superstructure. You will need to plan your own work schedule and be prepared to make minor changes as you proceed with the work. You may be considering if you will build the decks and or the superstructure in a different material to the hull. As most of you will be building the entire boat is one metal; I will leave detailed discussion on alternative deck and superstructure materials until near the end of this chapter.

Before you start to build the decks and superstructure, you should consider installing all bulky items that will need to be in the hull and which may be difficult if not impossible to install after the deck and cabin are in place. The engine, large tanks, bulkhead panels, the plywood sole and similar items need to be in position before the hull is 'closed up' by addition of the superstructure.

If you hull is large enough, say over 35 ft / 10.67 M then you may plan to set up a mini workshop inside the hull where you can manufacture much of the joinery on the spot. This is worthwhile if you can fit a small bench, a table saw and a band saw, otherwise it may be better to consider one of the other alternatives. If you boat is smaller or if you prefer to work outside the hull, then consider setting up a work area at the sheer or deck level, then you will only have to climb a few steps to saw, plane, rout, sand or temporarily assemble a piece of joinery. This can save a great deal of time and effort. Up and over and out of the boat to make each cut can soon become very tiring, so a better plan is needed.

You may find that some of the cabinets and joinery can be set up inside the hull and then taken out to a nearby bench for sanding, painting and so forth, before being reinstalled in the hull. It is better to undertake as much preparation as possible before the deck goes on.

GRIT BLASTING AND PRIMING

This brings us to the grit blasting that is necessary in steel boats; when is the best time to undertake this work. In my opinion the best time is before the boat is started, yes this means pre-grit blasting and priming all of the materials. If you opt to work with untreated steel then you will have some problems with working out the sequence of fitting out. You can not install the insulation, engine and other large items until after you have grit blasted and primed the inside of the hull. You certainly can not grit blast the interior once these items are in place! You can see that if you work with untreated steel, then you will create work-scheduling difficulties. Builders, who choose steel as their building material, should avoid these problems by either purchasing the steel already pre-blasted and

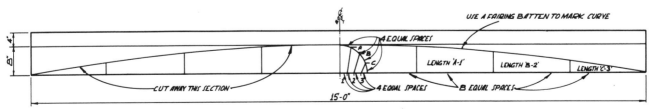

MARKING OUT A CAMBER BOARD

primed or doing the job themselves before they start construction. See chapter on painting.

MAKING A CAMBER BOARD

Your plans and patterns may include either the measurement for or an actual full size pattern for deck and cabin top cambers. Using this pattern it is a simple matter to cut a hard pattern from plywood or suitable timber. If you get the balance right, you can cut a male and female pattern from the one plank. The pattern will be used to obtain the correct camber when you are bending the deck and cabin beams.

On sailboats, the cabin top and perhaps the pilothouse top will usually have more camber than the decks. On powerboats the opposite is sometimes the case, although quite often the same camber is used throughout. If your plans do not include full size camber patterns, then using the designers recommended cambers, you can create patterns as shown below.

BULKHEADS

If you are building upright then you may have included some of the bulkheads as you were setting up the initial frames. It would also be possible to include bulkheads when setting up an inverted hull but this may involve raising the whole structure so far off the floor, that it would be impractical. Any setting up method that causes you to have to climb or walk more than is absolutely necessary is not recommended. In all cases my preference is to wait until the hull is plated and upright, before considering the installation of any bulkheads. Waiting until the hull shell is plated and upright, has the advantage of allowing you to have an overview of the hull. You can take stock of the available space, before making firm decisions about bulkhead placement that will affect the layout of the interior accommodation.

You will need to decide which bulkheads will be metal and which will be constructed from plywood. The bulkheads that will be exposed to the elements should all be metal and these include the aft bulkhead of the cabin and the bulkhead located at forward end of the aft cabin. If you have a pilothouse, then the aft bulkhead should be metal. In Dutch style powerboats, the aft end of the saloon or pilothouse is sometimes made partially of timber. This is acceptable if there is some awning or shelter over this bulkhead to protect it from the elements. Bulkheads will usually be constructed from metal that is the same thickness as is used for the decks. In boats under 40 ft / 12.19 M, try and keep the number of metal bulkheads to a minimum and use plywood where practical.

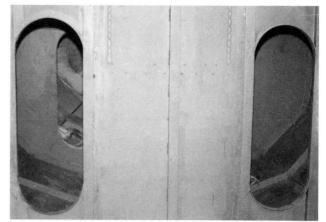

Steel bulkhead in ROBERTS 44 hull. Note rounded doorways and stiffening on bulkhead.

METAL BULKHEADS

The bulkheads at the forward and aft ends of the engine room in both sail and powerboats should be constructed from the same metal as the decks. As was demonstrated in the 'Falklands war' aluminum can burn! For this reason particular attention should be paid to insulating any aluminum bulkheads located where a fire risk is present with fireproof material. The bulkheads that enclose the engine space will need special attention.

It is common practice to make the bulkhead adjacent to station 'O' from the same metal as the hull. This 'crash' bulkhead is usually located at the forward end of the waterline. Some classification societies and authorities including boats built to US Coast Guard survey, require this first bulkhead to be located 5 percent of the LWL aft of the forward end of the waterline. This is a sensible rule, but it sometimes takes up valuable space. Boats built to Coast Guard survey will need the accommodation to be moved further aft than would otherwise be necessary.

Some bulkheads may need stiffeners. This will depend on the size of the vessel, the metal used in constructing the bulkheads and the size of the particular bulkhead. These vertical L angle stiffeners are spaced at approximately 12 to 18 in / 305 to 457 mm centre s and are installed with base of the L inwards thus making an excellent base for installing the cabin lining material. Some transverse stiffening may also be required. Check with the designer of your boat regarding the requirements in this area. The cavity formed by the L angle can also be used to install the insulation.

Concerning those bulkheads that you are installing before the deck and superstructure are in place, make sure that the height above the sheer or deck will allow you to later cut the correct cabin top camber. We always recommend that you do not try and cut the shape for the cambered decks, cabin sides and top camber at this stage; simply allow the top of the bulkhead to stand up square from the sheer. This latter advice applies to all metal and plywood bulkheads. Later you can mark out the deck camber, lay-in of the cabin sides and the cambers for the cabin and/or wheelhouse top. These cuts may be more difficult to make with the bulkhead in an upright position but they will be much easier to mark out with all of the bulkheads in place, rather than one at a time before the bulkheads are erected. More experienced builders may prefer to mark and cut the bulkhead tops as they install each one.

Bulkheads will need trim strips around edges and, exposed areas of hull should be lined.

Bulkhead need only be faced with fancy plywood where it is visible.

If you are building upright and if many of the bulkheads are on a frame location, then it may be worthwhile to include the basic bulkheads as part of the frame construction. My advice is still leave the tops square as mentioned above. If you prefer you may carefully work out the measurements and cabin side angles of each bulkhead and cut these to shape before installation.

PLYWOOD BULKHEADS

Intermediate and partial bulkheads can be best built from plywood. You can use any suitable grade that has a 'marine glue-line'. One way to test the durability of any plywood is to boil it for a number of hours. This widely used 8 hour boiling test for plywood will give you a clear indication of the quality of any plywood that you may want to use in your boat. This material provides stiffening and strength in many directions and will assist in keeping the weight of the interior down to reasonable proportions. The plywood bulkheads should be installed with the tops left square so the areas above the deck can be marked and shaped at the same time as the metal bulkheads. If your plans do not state the thickness for the plywood bulkheads, keep in mind that the adjacent furniture and joinery will add stiffness and strength.

The transverse plywood bulkheads will need to be bolted either to existing metal frames or to short sections of framing material commonly knows as 'tags'. The tags are 6 in to 12 in / 150 to 300 mm long and spaced at the same intervals as their length and are welded to the hull to accept the bulkhead. The tags become necessary if the location of a transverse bulkhead falls between or adjacent to but not at the exact location of the frame. It may be possible to alter the bulkhead location by a small amount by bolting it on to one side or other of the frame. Be careful not to create a space such as a berth, that is too small or over long, better to install the tags which provide more than adequate strength for the bulkhead attachment. Do not forget to pre-drill the tags at 4 in to 6 in / 100 to 150 mm centre s, to accept the bolts, which will be used to attach the bulkheads.

As you are unlikely to be able to purchase plywood sheets that are large enough to make the complete bulkheads in one piece, some form of laminating or joining of the sheets will be required. The thickness of the plywood bulkheads will vary depending on the size of the vessel as well as the purpose and location of the bulkhead. Transverse plywood bulkheads are generally thicker than longitudinal ones. The designer of your boat may have specified the thickness required.

To form one complete bulkhead, you can use plywood of the specified total thickness and either have this scarphed to the correct sheet size or you can scharph or half lap the sheets yourself. My preferred method is to divide the thickness into two or more parts and then laminate two or more sheets face to face. For maximum strength the joins can be widely staggered by alternating the joins in each layer. Plywood bulkheads excepting those in the area of the mast in a sailboat will not be exposed to great strains. The bulkhead adjacent to the mast can be strengthened by the addition of framing as required.

CORED BULKHEADS

If you are weight conscious, then you can consider one or more cored bulkheads. These can be used in dividing the accommodation longitudinally, or used to construct half bulkheads such as those that may form the one end of a hanging locker or similar piece of joinery. The core material can be structural sheet foam, or a light timber framing or other suitable material that is both light and fire resistant. The face plywood can be either 3/16" / 4 or 5 mm and could be veneered with a teak or similar surface. The fiberglass ' bats' used in house insulation are unsuitable as they will soon 'shake down' into a floppy mess when exposed to marine conditions.

BENDING AND INSTALLING THE DECK BEAMS

The material for the deck beams can be either flat bar, L angle or T bar. It makes sense to use an L angle or T bar as either of these when installed with the flange down, will provide an attachment point for the interior lining material. The insulation for the deck and cabin top will fit neatly in between the angle or T beams.

The beams can be bent using the hydraulic jack and steel frame method or you may prefer to have them bent by a professional metal shop. Your plan will at least give you a camber figure for example, 6 " in 13 ft / 150 mm in 3.96 M. If you do not have a pattern but you do have the numbers for the recommended camber then you will have to make a pattern using the formula shown. If you have patterns for the various cambers then you should make a master pattern out of plywood or timber. You will use the pattern to check the beams as they are bent to the correct camber and also as a general pattern for cutting bulkhead tops.

In our designs we recommend that you install the deck beams in one piece right across the hull. This method of installing the beams is much easier than trying to support short side deck beams while

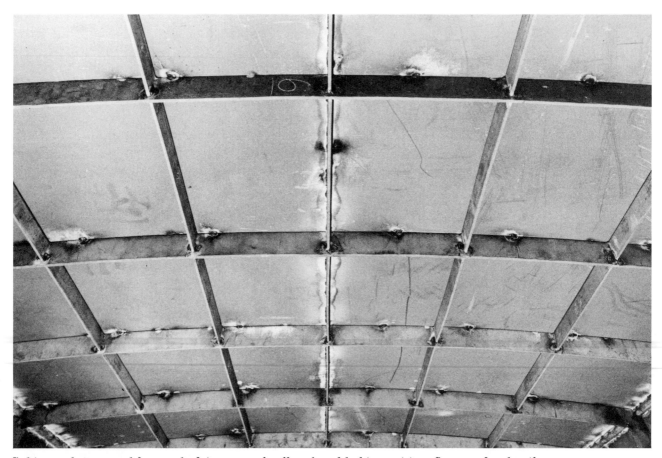

Cabin top beams and fore and aft intercostals all tack welded in position. See text for details.

maintaining the correct sheer and curve of the deck/cabins side intersection. Later you will cut out the centre of the beams and the section you remove will be re-bent to be used as cabin top beams.

You may need fore and aft intercostal deck stringers depending on the spacing of the beams and the size of your boat. The intercostal's are best cut from flat bar and should be snaped in at the ends and welded in between the deck beams as required. You could use a lighter angle for the intercostal and have the flange level with the inside to provide a base for the lining material. The depth of the intercostal should be the same as the deck beams as you may need to weld the underside of the deck plating to the intercostal as well as to the deck beams themselves.

Once all of the deck beams are in place right across the hull, then you can mark out the position where the cabin side intersects the deck and install a carlin to accept the inner edge of the side deck plating. The carlin will be a vertically located length of flat bar running around the inner edges of the cut inner ends of the deck beams.

You can at this stage, make provision for hatches in the fore and aft decks or you can cut these out later and install any extra deck framing at that time. Once you are satisfied with the framing for your deck you can go ahead and plate the foredeck, side decks and the aft deck area.

CABIN SIDE LAY-IN
At this stage you will need to consult your plans regarding the correct lay-in for the cabin and pilothouse sides. Too much lay-in will be an invitation for leaky windows and may also interfere with your interior accommodation. Too little lay-in

Flybridge decks need less camber than regular cabin tops. Note the bevelled edge of the overhang

will make the superstructure on your boat look 'boxy' and at worst can make it look as though it is actually laying outwards at the top. How much lay-in is correct? Never less than 5 and usually not more than 20 degrees. When you cut the angle for the side lay-in you may leave the tops square and cut the cambers after the cabin side is installed.

SETTING UP THE CABIN SIDES
Your plans should provide measurements for the cabin sides so that you can make a pattern of the sides and then raise the pattern into position to check the accuracy before cutting metal and welding the sides in place. If your design includes a pilothouse then this structure may be part of the cabin side or installed as a separate item.

On many occasions it is preferable to have the sides of the pilothouse set slightly inboard of the line of the cabin sides/top intersection. This latter option will 'break up' the large pilot house/cabin side area and reduce the 'apparent' height of the combined structure. Until the other parts of the superstructure are installed and to ensure that the sides remain at the correct angle and position when and they are first installed, you will need to use bracing from the sides, one to the other and to the bulkheads and other areas.

Do not make any cutouts for windows or portlights at this time. Cutting the cabin side plating before the whole structure is complete will allow the plate to buckle and spoil the fair line of the sides. You may wish to mark out the windows and ports, as this will enable you to locate the correct position for any framing required in the sides.

CABIN SIDE STIFFENERS
Depending on the size and type of boat, you may need some form of stiffeners installed in the cabin or pilothouse sides. If possible, always line up the cabin side stiffeners with deck and cabin top beams so you have in effect a 'ring frame' which will always be stronger that a framing system that is 'dis-continuous'.

You can use the same material for framing the sides of the cabin or pilothouse as you use for the deck and cabin top beams. Assuming you are using angle, then the flange of the L or T will be faced inboard and will assist in providing a ground to attach the lining. Do not forget to arrange some form of insulation in the cabin sides; failure to do this will assure that you have condensation problems in the future.

Quarter of pipe used at pilot house corners.

Rounded corners can greatly enhance the exterior appearance of any metal boat

ROUNDED CORNERS

Rounded corners where the cabin sides meet the top and where the cabin front meets the top and sides are an important consideration. Nothing screams 'amateur built' louder than the sight of sharp corners on a metal boat. This latter comment applies to the corners everywhere on the boat except the hull-sides-transom intersection, which may be fairly sharp without spoiling the appearance of the vessel. You can use sections of suitable sized pipe, say 3 in / 75 mm cut into quarters or have some plate rolled to a suitable radius.

INSTALLING CABIN TOP BEAMS

Installing the cabin top beams will follow much the same procedure as you have used for the deck beams. Hatches can be framed in now or cut out later and framed from underneath. I would recommend that the main hatchway be framed up at this stage, as you will need access to the interior when you plate the cabin top. As the surface area of the cabin and pilothouse tops will most certainly be greater than that of the

decks (except in a flush deck boat) then you will need intercostal beams in the top. The intercostal's can be installed before or after the top plating. If you install the intercostal's from inside after the plating is in place, you will have more welding to do from underneath, however installing the intercostal's after the plating will insure that you do not have any ridges in the cabin top caused by improperly aligned and installed intercostal's. The intercostal can be installed in the same manner as those for the decks. Your cabin top may receive considerable 'traffic' so make sure the framing is adequate. A relatively light closely framed cabin top will serve you better than a few widely spaced heavier beams. Follow your plans or consult the designer of your boat if you are unsure regarding the framing.

INSTALLING CABIN FRONT

The front of the cabin will most likely be rounded, about the same amount of round as was used for the deck beam camber will be about right. Cabin fronts on traditional craft can be flat. The problem with 'flat' cabin fronts or any part of a boat that is 'flat', they tend to look convex; for that reason it is recommended that you always have a slight amount of curvature in any 'flat' area on your boat.

The cabin front will always have some layback. If a truly vertical cabin front was installed then it would look as though it was leaning outwards (forwards) at the top. The line where the cabin front joins the sides must either be parallel with the centre line or be closer to the centre line at the top than where it joins the deck. If this important visual intersection is not right it will look awful. Do not forget to allow for the camber when installing the cabin front. You are dealing with many angles in this area and overlooking sufficient camber allowance in the front is not an unheard of occurrence.

INSTALLING CABIN TOP PLATING

By now you should have the cabin sides, cabin front, cabin top beams and intercostal all installed and checked over for accuracy and fairness in all planes. You will need to decide if you are going to have any overhang by the top over the sides and or front of the cabin. Many boats have these overhangs which have many advantages. While overhangs on a fiberglass or timber boat may present a potential weak point in the construction, this does not apply on a metal boat.

Check you plans regarding overhangs and 'eye brows' as the forward cabin and pilot house overhangs are sometimes called. Overhangs must have a trim to complete the edge, either pipe, solid round or flat bar

BULWARK DETAIL

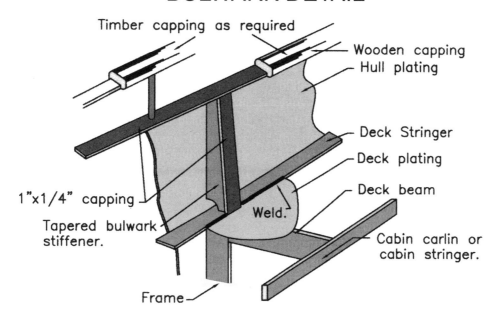

Timber capping as required

Wooden capping

Hull plating

Deck Stringer

Deck plating

Deck beam

1"x1/4" capping

Tapered bulwark stiffener.

Weld.

Cabin carlin or cabin stringer.

Frame

Steel decks and cabin on ROBERTS SPRAY built in England for BRUCE ROBERTS, U.K., Ltd.

can be used depending on the design of your superstructure. Side overhangs, especially on powerboats can carry the rainwater or spray from the top out past the windows. You can see that a careful balance of cabin side lay-in and top overhangs can improve the appearance and practicality of the design. Installing the deck plate will follow the same procedure as used for the decks.

BULWARKS AND TOERAILS

If you plan to have bulwarks on your metal sail or powerboat, then you will have fitted a deck stringer at the appropriate height. The lines plan and or the full size frame patterns may show exactly where this stringer is to be installed on each frame.

If this information is not on your plans, then you can scale off the relevant measurements and use a batten to fair in the deckline on each frame from stem to stern. Before or after the hull is plated, you can taper the inside of the frame between the deckline and the sheer. Taper the frame so that it is the right width on top to accept a flat or round bar to be installed as a cap-rail.

If your bulwarks are less than say 8 in / 200 at the highest point, and your hull is 3/16" / 5 mm plate, then the frames may finish under the deckline and it will not be necessary to have the frames extend from the deck to the sheer. You should install either a pipe, solid round of minimum 3/4" / 20 mm diameter or flat bar, to accept a wooden cap rail on the top of the hull plating. In any case you should stiffen up the cutouts, see waterways and fairleads below.

WATERWAYS AND FAIRLEADS

If your hull has a bulwark then you will need to install waterways on the frames and freeing ports to allow water to flow between the frames and also through the bulwarks and off the decks. The bulk of the freeing ports must be situated at the lowest point of the deck/bulwark intersection and the apertures must be large enough to let the water out without delay. Usually several freeing-ports spread over the lowest area are better than one large hole. All openings made in the hull plating for freeing ports fairleads or for any similar purpose must be reinforced by installing a surround of suitably sized solid round bar. If docking lines are used with fairleads, the reinforcing bar in a steel hull, should be stainless steel. The movement of docking lines and the anchor

Bevelled cockpit coaming on Roberts 53 built by A. Skjodt in Canada.

This Roberts 39 built in the UK by Terry Erskine has a typical sailboat pilothouse

rhode would soon wear away any paint applied to mild steel reinforcing.

THE BEVEL

A bevelled section makes an attractive intersection between the cabin or pilothouse sides and the top. There are other areas of the superstructure where a bevel can be an attractive alternative to a round or plain right angle.

The bevel is one of my favourite architectural features and I note that a few boat manufacturers are incorporating a bevel between the cabin sides and the top. The bevel can be any size but it is usually set at about 45 degrees to the vertical and could measure 3 to 6 in / 75 to 150 mm depending on the size of the boat. The use of the bevel is also a good way to disguise cabin height. If your design calls for a high cabin structure, then consider the bevel. For the record, the bevel when used in timberwork is often referred to as an 'arras', meaning to take a small bevel off the corner of a post or other feature. The arras or bevel does 'soften' the appearance of any area where it is used, and it is a great way to remove sharp edges from any object in your boat.

BUILDING OR ADDING A PILOT HOUSE

This one of the most likely areas you should consider if you want to improve the liveability and comfort of your existing or future sail or powerboat. You may already own, be working from plans, or purchasing an existing boat and considering how a pilothouse would improve the vessel. Pilothouses have gained in popularity over the past 30 odd years that I have been recommending these structures. Almost all of our sailboat designs feature at least one version that includes a pilothouse.

If your boat could be improved by the addition of one of these structures, then you will need to carefully consider the style and design before commencing the actual installation. It is strongly recommended that you contact the original designers of your boat and request them to prepare plans for the structure. The addition of a pilothouse can not only provide a more comfortable living environment aboard your boat, but it also can enhance its appearance and value. Conversely a poorly designed appendage can totally destroy what you have set out to achieve.

One decision you will need to make is whether you prefer forward or reverse sloping windows. Most fishing and workboats have reverse sloping forward windows; there is a good reason for this. When steering into the sun and under other difficult conditions, reverse facing windows give you the best chance of an unobstructed view. When there is only light rain, then the overhang of the top of the reverse facing windows will keep the windows clear. Reverse forward windows are practical but their appearance is not to everyone's taste. Regular forward facing windows have a more 'racy' appearance and do enhance the appearance of your boat. For best vision where you need it most, keep the slope of these windows to a reasonable angle; an extreme angle in this area will cause vision problems perhaps when you need a clear view ahead in difficult conditions.

Building a pilothouse follows a similar procedure to that used to build your regular cabin structure. You will need to make sure that supports of adequate proportion, are left between the generous sized windows often associated with this structure, Additional strength by way of side framing may be required and the window areas should be divided up in to reasonably sized areas. If your boat is capable of offshore work, then you should make provision for shuttering that could be fitted in the event of one or more of the windows being broken. In order to keep the weight of these rarely used covers to manageable proportions; you could consider fiberglass sandwich, fiberglass-covered plywood or aluminum for these storm covers.

HATCHES, COMPANIONWAYS, PORTLIGHTS AND DOORS

If your vessel was designed for offshore use then your plans should indicate the size and location of the various hatches. If you are the builder, the details of strength and suitability will lie in your hands. In the interests of safety, all hatches and companionways are best located on the centre line of the vessel. This is especially important for passage-making vessels as in the event of an unexpected knockdown; an open off the centre line hatch can admit tons of water before it can be closed.

You should take some time in deciding where and when to fit hatches. Before you start making holes in your decks, you need to have a firm idea as to the exact layout of your accommodation. You can simply plate the entire decks and superstructure leaving the main hatchway available for access and lay out your hatches at a later stage. Always keep in mind that these areas need to be carefully planned and strongly constructed, especially in long distance sail and power cruisers. The integrity of the hatches that cover the openings in your boat may be called upon to

Ready made hatches can add a professional finish to any deck arrangement

withstand tons of water being dumped on the deck. Do not treat these items lightly, they need to be as strong as the hull.

About the only places a steel boat can leak are around the hatches and other openings. It is important to construct and fit these hatches so that they are absolutely watertight. Strong hinges and closing devices are a must. There are many cases where boats have been seriously damaged and lost through the fitting of inferior hatches. Combining safety with liveability, it is best to fit hatches with hinges on both the forward and aft edges.

COMMERCIALLY MADE HATCHES

Deciding if you will make your own or use commercially made hatches may be a matter of economics. Careful shopping can often reduce the prices to an acceptable level. Professionally manufactured hatches may add a nice finishing touch to your otherwise self-built boat. Most commercially made hatches will be manufactured from marine grade aluminium.

Unless you have your decks and superstructure built out of the same material, you will need to isolate the hatches from the steel or copper-nickel. A good commercially made hatch will have a precision cast body of high tensile alloy that will not corrode in the harsh marine environment. Tinted glazing is preferred and it must be capable of taking the weight of more than one person and able to withstand the force of a breaking wave without deforming. Larger hatches should have three hinges that have been cast as part of the body of the hatch. To ensure watertightness under adverse conditions, a hatch that uses a neoprene 'O' ring seal is preferable to one that uses soft rubber strips. The neoprene is far superior to the spongy type of rubber seal and it will not deteriorate as quickly; also the 'O' ring neoprene seals are more resistant to sunlight.

BUILDING YOUR OWN HATCHES

If you decide to build your own hatches you can save a considerable amount of money. It may be possible to construct the hatches from materials that would otherwise be classified as wastage. It is recommended that you build your hatches of steel, aluminium, copper-nickel or fiberglass. Timber and plywood hatches require considerable maintenance and could, if of insufficient strength, offer a weak link in the security of your boat. On the other hand timber hatches and skylights can give a metal boat a touch of 'warmth' so if you are prepared for the additional work, both during and after installation, then timber hatches may be worth your consideration.

Metal deck hatches can be built easily with inner and outer coamings. The coamings can be welded directly to the deck, making sure you have installed either deck beams and / or intercostalís to reinforce the deck plating from below. The reinforcing beams can be

installed from underneath after you have cut the aperture for the hatchway.

METAL HATCHES

Obviously it is best if you construct the hatches out of the same material as the decks and superstructure; you are more likely to have these materials to hand and there will be no additional corrosion problems caused by miss-matched materials. Arranging rounded corners on your hatches should not present you with any problems, as all metals are capable of being formed into say a 3 in / 75 mm radius. If you build you're hatches then some of the money saved can be invested in over-thickness acrylic sheet used to admit light. Make sure your glazing is set in a suitable sealant and bolted in place using an adequate number of fastenings.

Metal hatches can be built with inner and outer coamings; this arrangement is like a box made with a fitted lid. The inner box that acts as the coaming can be welded directly to the deck around the cutout you have created in the deck or cabin top. The height of the inner coaming can be from 2 in to 6 in / 50 to 150 mm and higher in larger vessels. The hatch top can

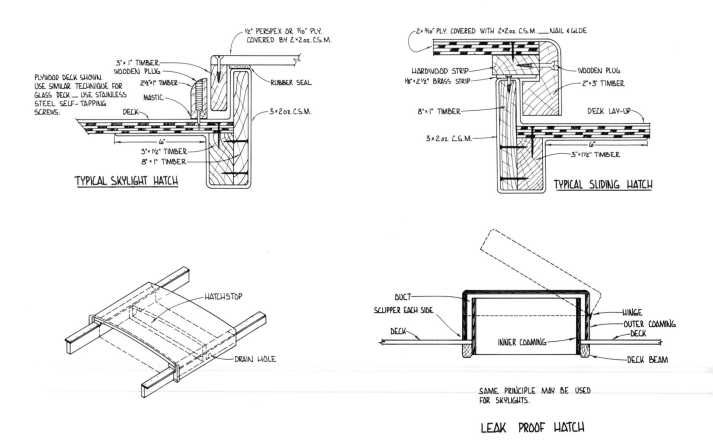

These plywood hatches can be used on timber and plywood decks and cabins or adapted for use with a metal superstructure.

have 2 in to 3in / 50 to 75 mm sides. The top will look best if it is cambered similar to the deck. This will look more professional with a cambered top but is harder to build, especially if you plan to have acrylic, lexan or similar material included in the top of the hatch.

Hinges for metal hatches are simple and easy to construct. They are basically one set of square tangs welded on the hatch cover to face a set of lugs welded at a 90-degree angle from the deck. A suitably sized rod, usually 3/8" to 3/4" / 10 to 20 mm depending on the size of the vessel and the hatch in question is inserted through the tangs and lugs and the hatch cover will pivot on the rod. The rod will need a right angle bend, a nut or similar stopper at one end and a removable retaining device at the other end. If you install hinges both fore and aft on the hatch you can have a hatch that can be forward or aft opening. At sea you should always have the hinges on the forward side but in port or sheltered waters it may be useful to be able to open any hatch in more than one direction. On our current power boat we have a hatch in the pilot house top that can open straight up or in any one of four directions; a wonderful arrangement when one is seeking relief from the heat and need to catch some breeze.

Any one of a variety of locking devices can be arranged to work with a metal hatch. In serious offshore cruisers, both sail and power, it is important that the hatch can be screwed down tight to prevent pressurised seawater from forcing its way into the interior of the vessel.

The top of the inner coaming will need to be fitted with a sealing strip, as with other types of hatches, the round neoprene 'O' shaped material is the most long lasting and properly installed gives a superior seal. A proper hatch should have a separate raised coaming of sufficient height and placed ahead and on the two sides to deflect the spray and rainwater streaming across the decks and/or cabin top. Do not underestimate the power of water and its ability for force its way into any weak areas of your deck openings.

WOODEN HATCHES

Wooden hatches are relative easy to construct but ensuring a perfect fit will take some woodworking skills. The best way to build these hatches is to build two boxes, one being the inner coaming and the other, the hatch itself. Obviously one box will fit neatly over the other. The inner box should be made of 2" / 50 mm thickness hardwood and should be 4 to 9" / 100

to 230 mm in height. Usually the larger the vessel the higher the coaming. This box will be equal in size to the inner dimensions of the hatch opening. The minimum size to allow access by the average size person is 20" x 20" / 508 x 508 mm however you should decide what size hatches are most appropriate for yourself and likely crewmembers.

It is important the upper edge of this inner box (coaming) is perfectly square and level as this is the edge that will contact the sealing material of the hatch itself. When you have constructed this basic square box for the inner coaming, you can then cut a hole in the deck or cabin top to match the inner dimensions of the box. Next add reinforcing intercostal and other beams underneath around the perimeter of the hatchway.

Next build the box that will be the hatch that will fit over the coaming. The hatch can be built out of 1 1/2" / 35 mm timber and 3" / 75 mm high is about right. This hatch will fit snugly around the coaming but will have sufficient clearance to allow the completed hinged hatch to be opened and closed. So far you have no top to your hatch. You can use 3/4" / 20 mm marine grade plywood for the top and screw and glue this to the frame. For a fancy finishes you can glue and temporally staple 1/8" / 3 mm mahogany or teak faced plywood to the top of the hatch. In any case, the edges of the plywood top will need to have an outer timber strip installed to protect the edges.

If you want a Lexan or Plexiglas top instead of plywood, simply substitute it in place of the plywood. You can have a combination of glazing and plywood for the top simply by fitting the ply top first, and then cutting out for the required amount of glazing. The glazed area should be of 1/2" lexan or Plexiglas. When buying your glazing material, check the 'yellow pages' of your telephone directory and endeavour to buy scrap material rather than specifying cut to size for which you will pay a premium price.

You will need to take some special precautions when working with the plastic glazing fitted to your hatch tops and portlights. The holes you drill in the plastic must be slightly oversize. You must allow for the different expansion and contraction rate, as opposed to the timber framing. You will most likely use tinted plastic and this will expand in hot weather and if the bolt or screw holes are too snug then the plastic will crack and need to be replaced. Usually the next size up hole verses the screw size, will be about right. The safest type of screw is one with a flat surface where it meets the plastic; self-tapping stainless steel screws are ideal. Fancy screws such as hex headed sheet metal stainless steel screws will give you a good looking and strong fastener. Sheet metal screws have larger threads than woodworking screws and therefore provide additional fastening surface.

The plastic should be bedded against the timber with as good a grade of silicone sealant as you can find. A small amount of the silicone sealant in each hole prior to screwing the glazing in place will ensure that the oversize holes remain watertight.

Hinges are fitted to the forward area of the outer coaming so that the hatch is aft opening. The hinges should be heavy duty and made of stainless steel or other non-corrosive metal. To secure the hatch from below there is a number of catches and locking devices available. One of the best is the type with screw down devices, so you can screw down the hatch firmly onto its gaskets.

When fitting the hatch, assemble it completely with gaskets and then lower it into position. The best way to make the fit between the coaming and the deck or cabin top is to firstly make sure the whole assembly is set up level. Next 'spile' the shape of the cut required allowing the coaming to make a good fit with the deck or cabin top. Now you can bolt or screw the coaming in place through the metal deck; working from underneath the deck. Make sure you bed the coaming in a suitable sealant.

Custom hatches can be made even more suitable for the rigours of cruising conditions, by a few simple additions to the basic hatch. You can add an extra coaming on the deck or cabin top, immediately adjacent to the hatch. This coaming should surround the forward edge and sides of the hatchway. This coaming or baffle will be slightly less in height than the entire hatch assembly and fitted to not interfere with the operation of the hatch. The extra coaming will help keep water away for the hatch. The top of this extra coaming could be timber or metal and if made of timber, the top is rounded off to give the best appearance. In all cases, the sides can have holes in the bottom edges of the sides to allow for drainage.

Another 'improvement' to any hatch is to install eyebolts close to either side of the hatch assembly and these can be used in extreme weather conditions to add a safety line across the hatch. The eyes need to be close by the hatch so as not to provide an obstruction on which to stub your toes. Large Plexiglas hatches can be strengthened by having timber cleats running fore and aft across the top of the hatch. These cleats

can improve the look of the hatch at the same time. These 1in x 1 in / 25 x 25 mm timber slats can be screwed into the outer frame and then screwed to the acrylic from underneath. The main purpose of the slats it to take some of the force and distribute the weight of persons standing on the hatch or the weight of a heavy breaking wave. Canvas covers can be made for all of the hatches. Not only will you need these in hot climates, but they can be an additional safety factor when included as part of the 'lashing down' arrangement.

ACCESS HATCHES

Access hatches as opposed to hatches used only for ventilation, must be of a size sufficient to allow even a large person to enter and exit the boat in an emergency. Do not make hatches unnecessarily large; remember they must be able to withstand all that the sea can offer! All hatches should be capable of being opened from both outside and inside the vessel and must have a means of locking to deter unauthorised intruders from gaining entry to your boat. Hatches located in accommodation areas should be built with some form of glazing to admit light and to assist in adding a spacious feeling to the interior.

COMPANIONWAY HATCHES

The main access hatchway can be in the form of a sliding hatch, a hinged hatch or a quadrant companionway type hatch as illustrated. Sliding hatches should not be simply a sheet of plastic running in the simplest of aluminum tracks. This is sometimes seen on production powerboats! Build or buy and install a proper seagoing hatch as your main entry and exit point.

The companionway hatch is constructed in two main elements; the runners, which fit on the cabin top, and the hatch, which slides on or in the runners. The runners and also the hatch may be constructed of timber or metal. If timber runners are used you will need 3 in high by 2 in wide / 75 x 50 mm timber. The timber runners could be deeper and could be bolted directly to a set of intercostal beams situated around the perimeter of the hatchway. The runners will need to extend beyond the opening; the length is twice the hatch length plus 3 in / 75 mm. Where they extend over the cabin top, they will need to be screwed from inside through to the timber.

The tops of the runners are faced with heavy say 1/4" x 2 in / 6 x 50 mm brass strips which act as runners for the hatch top. The brass strips are set in silicone and screwed to the runners using flathead screws that are set flush with the surface. When properly set-up the hatch must be able to run smoothly on the brass slider.

The sliding hatch is another box with the frame built of 1 1/2 in x 2 in / 35 x 50 mm hardwood and the corners can be half jointed. Considerable care is needed to ensure that the frame is a true rectangle and sits perfectly flat on the runners. Around this inner frame an outer frame is constructed from 1 1/2" x 4" / 35 x 100 mm hardwood. The outer frame is glued and screwed to the inner frame with the tops of both frames flush and the outer 4" / 100 mm deep frame acting as a guide to allow the inner frame to slide on the runners. The whole arrangement must slide smoothly. A hatch that jams is in no way desirable aboard any boat. Now you need an arrangement so that the hatch will stay on the runners and this is achieved by gluing and screwing a 1/2" x 1/2" / 12 x 12 mm cleat inside the outer frame 1/8" / 3 mm and underneath the brass runner. Now the hatch has to be slid on to the runners from the front.

The forward and aft end of the hatch is finished off with a hardwood plate. The front can have a handle or grip built into the top of the front. The bottom of this front facing will need to be shaped so it clears the cambered cabin top as it glides (we hope) forward to its fully open location. If you have the recommended garage, then the front should be large enough to cover the aft end of this arrangement. The front facing with the handgrip built into the top will also need to accommodate the hasp part of your hasp and staple locking arrangement. The top of the hatch can be finished with 1/8" / 3 mm teak plywood and the whole structure coated with epoxy and light fiberglass cloth for a long lasting life.

The top of the hatch can be three layers of 1/4" / 6 mm plywood and if you have taken our advice and made the top match the cabin top camber then you will find that the plywood will laminate into a strong and durable top. A trim strip will be required for the outer edges of the plywood top to seal these from the elements.

When building the timber/plywood-sliding hatch above a metal cabin, the hatch opening can be finished off inside with a timber trim strip or suitable width. You will need washboards that will fit in pre-installed metal channels and complete the closure of the main access companionway.

It is worth noting here that any timber elements you attach to your steel hull or superstructure should be given at least three coats of epoxy resin, which will go a long way to stabilising and protecting the timber. All timber runners, hatch coamings and the like must be set in silicone before they are either screwed or bolted in position. Space the screws or bolts at 3 in / 75 mm intervals.

A 'garage' is an essential part of any companionway-slicing hatch

If you opt for a sliding main hatchway it is advisable to provide a 'garage' to house the hatch when it is in the open position. The 'garage' is particularly important in forward facing sliding hatches as it helps to divert water away from the open companionway. The 'garage' also partly provides a neat cover for the runners and the open hatch eliminating one area where lines can snag and toes can be stubbed.

DECK PRISMS
Another form of light admitting device that is under-used is the deck prism. These wonderful devices admit much more light than their size would indicate and they can be installed to be absolutely watertight and secure from the ravages of man and the sea. Check with your local hatch manufacturer and other equipment suppliers to see what they have to offer in this area.

PORTLIGHTS
Portlights and windows can be opening or fixed and it is a fact that the opening variety, no matter how well constructed and maintained, will always be a source of leaks and worry for the crew. It is often desirable to have at least one or more windows or ports that can be opened; however it is wise to keep these to an absolute minimum. The plans for your boat will no doubt give you some indication of the size and location of the ports and windows. My advice is use only fixed portlights and relies on opening hatches to provide adequate ventilation.

If you are planning to use opening ports then these should be professionally made and of the highest quality you can afford. Most commercially made ports are manufactured from marine grade aluminum so if you boat is either steel or copper-nickel you will need to isolate the aluminum from the other metal. Neoprene is commonly used for this purpose. Do not forget to sleeve the boltholes where the ports are bolted to the hull or superstructure. Occasionally you will find steel framed professionally made ports, however they are generally made for very large vessels so may not be suitable for your requirements.

PORTS AND WINDOWS, SAIL OR POWER

To allow the installation of insulation, you have a variety of options in the way the windows can be fitted. One popular way is to set the windows back into the cabin side or into the hull. To achieve the latter result, the window aperture is framed with an inward facing, 'L' angle shaped flange, the bottom of the 'L' is where the window or fixed port light will be set in sealant and bolted in place. With this arrangement and the addition of suitable 'L' metal angle or timber furring strips as framing, we now have a cavity in which to fit our insulation and a framework on which to attach our interior lining.

Timber furring strips fitted to flat bar frames to accept the lining materials.

As you will realise, this is a more complicated procedure than simply bolting the window into a hull or cabin side cutout, however the results are worth the extra effort. Set in ports and windows give a vessel that extra touch of quality that not only enhances pride of ownership, but one day will return dividends in a better resale value. Forward facing wheelhouse windows that will be fitted with windscreen wipers, will need to be glazed with toughened glass instead of the usual acrylic favoured for most other boat windows and ports.

SIMPLE PORTS AND WINDOWS

If well executed, the simplest port light or window can have an appearance that belies its low cost. The design and method of installation is simple. You cut a hole 1 to 1 1/2" / 25 to 35 mm smaller than the overall size of your port or window and fit and bolt a larger piece of Plexiglas or similar, over the aperture. The glazing is set in silicone, the holes for the bolts are slightly oversize and the corners of the hole and the covering Plexiglas are all radiused.

The silicone may be clear but it is preferable to use silicon that matches the colour of the area of the boat into which the port or window is being installed. If the bolts have hexagon heads and/or you line-up any slots in the heads, then this will improve the appearance of the glazed area. If the ports or window is located in a high traffic area such as adjacent to the side decks, then you should have bolt heads that fit flush with the glazing and thus avoid scratching or otherwise injuring any crew who 'brush by' the window. Be careful when making counter-sunk holes to allow bolts to fit flush. acrylic can be induced to crack if handled too roughly during the shaping and assembly stage.

Make sure the windows do not have an over-large area without sufficient support in the underlying cabin or wheelhouse side. Plexiglas and similar acrylic materials come with a paper protective covering; never remove the bulk of this until the boat is completed and ready for launching. You will need to remove a strip of the paper after you have drilled for the bolts but before you install the window or port light. The thickness of the glazing will be between 3/8" / 10 mm and 3/4" / 20 mm and the actual thickness will depend on the size and area of the aperture.

For most windows and ports you can use Plexiglas or the harder and more scratch resistant Lexan. You can dress up the outer edges of these bolt on windows by using timber, stainless steel or other suitable metal frames that can be cut to say 1 to 2 in wide and bolted in place, the same time as the window is installed. If you use metal, it can act as an outer washer for the fastenings and will generally enhance the appearance of the windows and ports on your boat.

WINDOWS IN POWERBOATS

In powerboats where the boat is more or less always in an upright position and where the boat is not designed or built for extended ocean voyaging, then one can be more liberal with the expanse of glazed area. Most powerboats have at least one forward facing opening window adjacent to the inside helm position. This opening window can admit copious quantities of fresh air and when open can be used to improve vision ahead in fog or similar difficult conditions.

Even in powerboats I find that opening windows, usually of the sliding variety, are a source of problems. Sooner, rather than later the rubber or other material used in the bottom track for the glass will perish and allow water to enter the boat. In some steel powerboats it is common practice to have the large side windows fitted without any provision for insulation. Perhaps the designers and builders feel that the expanse of glass takes up so much of the available area that it is not worth insulating the remainder! The problem is that when plywood lining is attached directly to the steel cabin side, then the resulting condensation can cause problems. In one case, it was natural to mistakenly blame a leaky window for causing discoloration of the teak plywood lining. It took some time before the culprit was diagnosed as lack of insulation in the cabin side and that condensation was the problem. As it would be too expensive to remedy the situation, it was discovered that a dehumidifier could be used to solve the problem. Lesson; always insulate all areas of your accommodation.

OUTER DOORS IN POWERBOATS

If you wish to have a door opening in the side of the accommodation, usually near the helm location, make sure it is a properly designed and fitted door suitable for marine use. Marine doors are usually of a more robust construction than sliding windows and therefore are easier to maintain and keep watertight.

Side doors in a Trawler Yacht style cabin can be built of timber and may be arranged to slide or if you have a very large yacht and wide side decks, then it may be possible to have the door hinged at the forward edge or perhaps open inwards.

On smaller boats a half height side access door adjacent to the inside helm position, may be found useful. Any doors especially sliders that are either outside or inside the accommodation should have a means of securing them when in the open position, as well as when closed.

A recent report told of a boat owner receiving severe injuries to his neck caused by an unsecured aluminum sliding door. Patio style aluminum doors at the aft end of a powerboat main salon UGH! These doors, especially the sliding variety, are famous for lopping off fingers. The large glass area is vulnerable to being broken in a variety of ways.

If your powerboat is of the aft cockpit variety, then you will most likely have a metal aft bulkhead in which you can fit a pair of timber doors. The top one third of the doors can be glazed and you will have all the light you need. As the cockpit and aft deck area is usually well protected, the timber doors will need minimum maintenance.

On a similar subject, you may wish to have the capability of locking some of the interior doors; this may slow down an intruder in the event that you experience a break-in during your absence from the boat. If you are interested in learning more about additional security arrangements, please consider the relevant books listed in appendix 1.

BUILDING COCKPITS

Not all boats have this feature but most sailboats have or should have a cockpit. Most of us prefer the security; real and perceived offered by a well-

Cockpit and coamings on ROBERTS 34.

Cockpit coamings and cockpit seating.

designed self-draining cockpit. These work particularly well when combined with protective coamings and comfortable seating.

The dimensions of this arrangement are most important and can influence the safety and comfort of the boat in many ways. It is desirable, but not always possible to have the cockpit seats measure 6ft 6 ins / 2.00 M long, this allows a person to lay full length. The width is best arranged so a person can rest one or both feet on the seat opposite; this usually results in a well that is 2ft 3in / 686 mm wide. The depth is best at 1ft 6in / 457 mm. Seats should be between 1ft 3in / 381 mm and 1ft 6 in / 457 mm wide and for comfort behind your knees, rounded on the inboard edge.

The height of the seat back that usually forms part of the coaming, will vary depending on the design however about 2 ft 0 in / 610 mm seems to work out well for most people. All cockpits should be self-draining with two separate outlets of generous size, minimum 2" / 50 mm diameter. The cockpit drains should be fitted with seacocks that can be closed when required. Finally you should have a reasonable view forward when seated in the cockpit. This is easier said than achieved, especially if there is a pilothouse structure ahead of your cockpit.

The choice between centre and aft cockpit is usually governed by your choice of interior layout. This choice has become blurred with the advent of staterooms fitted beneath and around an aft cockpit.

Metal cockpits can be framed up using L angle or flat bar depending on the size of the vessel. Boats under say 30 ft / 9.14 M can use flat bar and larger boats can use L angle placed flange down. Provided the transverse framing is spaced the same as the hull, minimum of fore and aft reinforcing should be required. Most boats today, have cockpit cushions so these need to be considered when laying out the area. Self-draining arrangements for the well are obvious, but do not forget to drain the seats. Wet seats and continuously wet cushions make for very uncomfortable seating, so consider how you can best drain these areas. A teak grating in located in the well adds a nice finishing touch to any cockpit.

FLY-BRIDGE

The main thing to consider when building a flying bridge on any vessel is KEEP IT LIGHT. This structure is always high above the waterline so any unnecessary additional weight in this area is most undesirable. If you plan one of these items on your boat, then you will have made sure that the cabin top does not have excessive camber, usually the same camber as the decks would be acceptable. No matter what material is used to build your hull deck and superstructure, you can use aluminum or fiberglass for the construction of this item. Do not have the area of the flying bridge so large that more than the acceptable number of passengers can occupy this area at one time. Keeping in mind the stability of the vessel under all conditions, some restriction on the number of seats available will help in this regard.

DECK COVERINGS

Your metal deck will need some form of treatment to provide a non-slip footing as you move about the boat. The least expensive treatment to make a deck safe to walk on is to apply a special paint, which contains grit to provide the non-skid surface. Many metal boats use this paint/grit combination and provided it is installed in a proper manner it can look

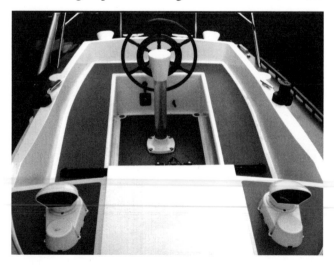

This is the finished result of the cockpit construction shown in the two previous photographs.

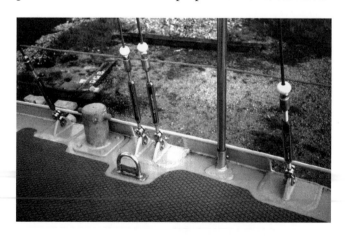

Here is an example of reinforced chain plates and deck fittings. Note how the Treadmaster deck covering is kept clear of the fittings to assist with drainage of water off the decks.

attractive and does work well in practice. When installing a painted non-skid surface you should leave small borders around various fittings and alongside the cabin and inside the bulwark etc., which do not have grit added. Be careful how you lay out these un-gritted areas, as you do not want to leave skid inducing, shiny spaces, in high traffic areas. If the un-gritted areas are no more than 1 1/4" / 320 mm wide around any feature, then you should not have a problem. You can always fill in any problem spaces with gritted paint.

The next step up in cost and appearance is to use a deck covering like ëTreadmasterí or a similar product. These coverings are composite materials formed in patterned sheets suitable for gluing to your deck. When laying out this covering you should use a similar pattern as suggested for painting decks with gritted material. Available in a range of attractive colours, these products are bonded to your deck with special glue that is complimentary to the particular product you are installing.

The diamond pattern on some of these sheet products can be hard on your bottom and other areas that may come into contact with the deck. Do not use it on cockpit seats or similar locations. There are alternative less harsh patterns that can be used where a user friendly, non-slip surface is required.

TEAK DECKS

Some of you may be surprised to learn that there are other species of timber that are suitable for using as a laid planked deck. In Australia Beech is widely used and in the USA quarter sawn Douglas Fir has been used for the same purpose. Not withstanding the above, teak is the premier material and the one you are most likely to be using to finish the decks of your metal boat in style.

After you decide that a laid deck is for you, then the next step is to determine if you are going to have a 'wannabee' teak deck or the real thing. The 'wannabee' type is usually 1/2" / 12 mm or less thick and in most cases do not do justice to your boat or to the craftsmanship needed to install any laid deck. A 'proper' laid deck should have planks of 5/8" / 15 mm and preferably 3/4" / 20 mm minimum thickness.

There are many ways to install this deck on a metal boat but all will involve setting the planks in some form of bedding compound. Again we can take a lead

This one inch / 25 mm teak deck has been in place on a steel deck for over six years with no sign of problems Note the bulwark supported by a pipe cap rail.

This diagonally laid Beech deck would be improved by the addition of a covering board around the outer edge of the planking but still leaving a waterway between the planking and bulwark or toerail

from the Dutch builders who have been successfully installing laid decks on steel and other metal boats for a long time.

The regular planks should be about 1 3/4" / 42 mm in width. The outer and inner 'covering boards', king plank and other featured planks around hatches and vents, will be wider, usually 4 in to 6 in / 100 to 150 mm, depending on the size of the boat and the way the deck is installed. The outer 'covering board' is a misnomer in this case, as there should be a space between the edge of the teak 'covering board' and the edge of the deck to create a channel for the water to run alongside the outer teak plank and on out through the scuppers.

The bulk of the fore and aft planking can be laid in several ways. It can follow the outer shape of the hull, it can follow the line of the cabin sides or it can split the difference. The main effect of these various methods is the way that the planks need to be 'nibbed' into the outer and inner covering boards and king plank. It is also possible to lay the deck in a herringbone pattern; this had been done on more than one of my own designs, however I personally prefer longitudinal planking 'that splits' the difference, naturally this is the most expensive form of planking!

ALTERNATIVE DECKS AND SUPERSTRUCTURES

Although there are arguments for building a boat using all steel, all aluminum or perhaps all copper-nickel, there are many reasons why some of you may prefer to take a different approach. For instance, having an aluminum deck and superstructure can enhance a steel-hulled boat. In the case of copper-nickel, as this material is somewhat more expensive than either steel or aluminum, it would make sense to have the hull built from copper-nickel, where the material is most beneficial; the decks and superstructure could then be built from an alternative less expensive material. If your metal working skills are limited and you have more experience with working in timber then you may consider a timber deck and superstructure. As you can see there are a considerable number of options and you have to weigh up the benefits and disadvantages for yourself.

PLYWOOD AND TIMBER DECKS AND SUPERSTRUCTURES

If your woodworking skills outweigh your metal working experience, then you may wish to consider building timber and plywood decks and super-structure on your metal hull. Another reason to install a plywood deck and superstructure would be if you are building a small steel boat and you wish to keep the weight down to reasonable proportions. If you take the timber and plywood deck option, then you will need to select a point where you make the transition from metal to timber. The choices are to have the hull built in metal and install a 'margin plate' welded to the inside or sheerline of the hull where the deck will join the hull. The margin plate will take the place and be installed in the same location as would be occupied by the deck stringer in an all-metal boat. Another alternative is to have the hull and complete decks built from metal and include an 'upstand' in metal to accept the timber superstructure and located all around the inner edge where the cabin sides will be installed. In both cases the timber and or plywood would overlap the metal so that any surface water or other moisture would be less likely to get between the metal and a timber and cause corrosion.

If you are planning a laid teak deck then this may influence your decision. A teak deck is much easier to install over a timber and plywood deck than a metal one. There is no doubt that a timber deck and superstructure is a beautiful sight from both without and within. You pay a price, at least for the beauty of the exterior. The maintenance requirements of timber and plywood used externally on any boat will be far greater than if the items were constructed from metal. This applies not only to large items as in a pilot house or cabin structure, but extends to timber hatches, handrails, cap rails and rubbing strips. These items when built in timber and finished natural do improve the appearance of any boat, but the maintenance requirements can be horrific.

After you have installed either the metal 'margin plate' to the hull or the metal 'upstand' to the inner edge of the metal decks, then you should install a timber carlin to allow you to carry on the remainder of the construction in timber. You should rebate this timber in such a way as to discourage any water from becoming trapped in the joint and later causing rot in the timber. It is imperative that you make a watertight join between the timber and the metal.

Deck beams may be timber or metal. In the case of a metal deck, then L or T metal deck beams will be used, however in the case of an all timber and plywood deck and superstructure then you may choose either metal or timber beams. If you use metal beams on a plywood deck make sure you place the flange upwards (this is opposite to what you would do for metal decks), and the flange will provide a ground and will allow you to screw the plywood to the beams from underneath. Timber beams can be laminated or sawn but laminated beams are recommended.

This is a good time to mention that you should use epoxy-based adhesives throughout the construction of any plywood decks and or superstructure. Where the plywood is attached to the metal margin plate or upstand, then a suitable bedding compound will be used rather than an epoxy adhesive. An epoxy system similar to the WEST (TM) system should be used to saturate all of the timber and plywood parts used to build your decks and superstructure, not on teak decks.

It is usually preferable to laminate the decks and cabin tops from more than one layer of plywood. If your deck calls for 1/2" / 12 mm plywood then use two layers of 1/4" / 6 mm, if the recommended thickness is 3/4" / 20 mm then use two layers of 3/8" / 10 mm or better still three layers of 1/4" / 6 mm. Use

This builder combined steel side decks with plywood cabin structure.

Laminated timber deck beams, king plank, and underside of plywood deck on ROBERTS SPRAY.

either bronze nails or staples to apply pressure to the glue-lines until the adhesive has cured.

If you are installing plywood decks, one labour saving tip is to paint the underside of the first sheet before it is installed. Make sure you do not paint the strips where the plywood will rest on and be glued to the beams. Fit the panels first, and from underneath, mark where the beams will fall and where the plywood rests on the other timber supports. Now mask off those areas on the plywood and paint the rest.

There are several methods of finishing off your plywood decks and cabin structure but no matter how you achieve this, I recommend that you give the entire area a coat of fiberglass cloth installed using epoxy resin. Do not use polyester resin to fiberglass over plywood or timber, always use epoxy resins. The only place that you should use polyester resins is as part of the construction materials used to build an all fiberglass boat.

When using Epoxy resins and adhesives, make sure that you follow all of the safety precautions recommended by the manufacturers. When handling these materials, always-protective gloves and use protective skin creams. Keep in mind that epoxy stays 'toxic' for several days while the curing process is taking place. When building timber and plywood decks and superstructures you will find the Gougeon Brothers WEST ™ system book is a good source of information. See appendix 1 for more details.

ALUMINUM DECKS AND SUPERSTRUCTURE

If you are building an all aluminum boat, then you will almost certainly install the decks and super-structure in the same material. The benefits of installing an aluminum deck and superstructure on any metal boat include the lighter weight of the material, which in the case of the decks and superstructure is where this benefit is best utilised. Aluminum is easier to form into small radius sections, such as those used on the corners of cabins, pilot house fronts, coamings, seat front/seat and seat/ back intersections and in similar areas. A little forethought and a considerable amount of welding can be saved by combining seats to backs etc.

The aluminum decks and superstructure area are somewhat more removed from the seawater elements than the hull and it is easier to avoid some of the electrolysis problems suffered by boats completely built from this material. The practice of installing

aluminum decks and superstructures of steel hulls has been well proven over the past 30 to 40 years so you can consider this as acceptable boatbuilding practice.

Aluminum decks and superstructures fitted to steel or copper-nickel hulls will need to have the different metals isolated one from the other to prevent electrolysis. There are a number of methods that can be used to achieve this isolation. The first that comes to mind is to insert a neoprene strip between the two different metals and bolt them together using bolts that are housed in nylon sleeves and nuts that are isolated with nylon washers.

The superior way to join aluminum and steel is to use the specially manufactured strip that has aluminum on one side and steel on the other. The two metals on this strip are explosively fused together so that when you weld the steel to the steel side and the aluminum to the aluminum side, no contact occurs between the two metals and the possibility of electrolysis is eliminated, or at least reduced. Careful planning will be required so that the intersection of the two dis-similar metals is located in such an area as to reduce the chance of prolonged contact through salt water.

Unfortunately these small black and white photographs can not begin to show the beauty of this teak deck fitted to a Roberts 434 Radius chine steel sailboat built in the UK.

This version of the Roberts 370 shows a style of deck that is popular with those who not only want a quick boat but one that looks fast.

Recessed ports and windows always exhibit a professional finish to any metal hull. The stern windows on this Roberts 64 add an attractive feature to this sailboat.

The steel deck on this Roberts 64 is now ready ro receive either a laid timber deck or one of the many other alternative treatments that may be used to finish this deck.

Chapter 10
PAINTING A METAL BOAT

Colours. Pre-grit blasted and primed steel. Hot metal spraying. Filing and fairing all metals. Preparing Steel. Preparing Aluminium. Prime-coating. Undercoats and fillers. Finish coatings. Boot-top. Anti-fouling.

COLOR

This subject will probably be the first thing that comes to mind when you, or at least the family, are considering the paint job for your new or used metal boat. Even a simple matter as choosing the colours has its technical side.

In metal boats, a darker colour for the hull makes good sense. The darker colour will absorb sunlight and drive off both the dew and some internal condensation. If the decks are painted then you may choose a two-tone scheme of light beige for the larger areas and cream for the trim or un-sanded areas. This arrangement will look smart and it will be easy on the eyes.

You should never paint decks white, as the reflected light will cause too much glare. Except in the coolest climate, dark coloured decks will be too hot for bare feet and will also make the interior of the cabin unbearably hot.

GRIT BLASTING AND PRIMING STEEL

Variously referred to as sand blasting and grit blasting. Employing this process is the only way your can provide a satisfactory base on which to apply your prime coating and subsequent layers of protective paint. This process is necessary to remove all of the contaminates and corrosion for the surface of the metal. The process slightly roughens the surface and provides an excellent surface for the paint. The exact roughness of the surface will in most part depend on the particular metal and the type and grade of grit used and the force at which it is applied during the blasting process.

The result is commonly referred to as the 'anchor pattern' and will vary between 1.5 mils (thousandths of one inch) and 4 mils. Four thousandths is considered a heavy and deep blast and may be satisfactory for tar epoxy finishes. For most paints,

you should aim for a 1 1/2 to 3 mil anchor pattern. Your paint manufacturer may have special recommendations in this area. Make sure you choose a warm and dry day with low humidity, when you are blasting your boat.

For blasting, you will need to use a powerful compressor for instance one that can deliver something over 350 ft per minute would be perfect. As mentioned elsewhere, you need manpower, 2 or three men plus your own presence would be adequate. There are many specifications for the blasting of steel. Here is one that sums up what is required, if you are to have a successful, corrosion free and long-lasting paint job.

NEAR WHITE BLAST CLEANING

This is a method of preparing steel surfaces which, when viewed without magnification, shall be free of all visible oil, grease, dirt, dust, mill scale, rust and paint. Generally evenly dispersed, very light shadows, streaks and discoloration caused by stain of rust, stains of mill scale, and stains of previously applied paints may remain on no more than 5 percent of the surface."

Sand is the least expensive abrasive, but due to the high silica content and the health hazard presented by the silica, you may find that your local contractor is not willing to use this material. If you are doing the job yourself and you wear the correct protective facemask, then blasting one boat with this material should not represent an undue health hazard. It is your responsibility to decide on using sand as opposed to the more expensive alternatives. This material can not be reused, so you would need more sand than slag or grit.

Grit is a little more expensive than sand and contains none of the silica that when used over a period, can cause among other things respiratory and lung problems. In the USA these products are marketed as Copper blast, Copper slag, Green diamond and Garnet. Similar products are available in UK, Australia and elsewhere.

Crushed steel shot is more expensive than either sand or grit but as it can be reused many times you may consider it to be worth the additional expense. This material is formed from crushed iron or steel and has irregular shapes with very sharp edges. This is one of the better blasting materials.

You will need to consider matching the type and roughness of the blasted surface, compared to the paint you plan to install on your boat. A surface that is too rough will allow some show through to your paint finish and a surface that is too smooth will not provide a long lasting bond for that most important element in your paint job, the primer.

If you are building in steel then you will have taken the advice given earlier in this text; you will have built your hull deck and superstructure using pre-grit blasted and primed metal. If not, then here are some suggestions about how to complete this process, once the hull deck and superstructure is complete.

Many builders have found that it saves very little in cost and takes a lot of effort to do this job themselves. By the time you hire the equipment, purchase the grit and arrange for the help needed, it can cost nearly as much as a professional job. Three people are needed for this operation; one to operate the blasting gun, one to feed the material and one to apply the primer. You need at least a three-person team otherwise the job will take much longer. For instance if the blaster has to feed his own abrasive, then he has to remove and replace his bulky helmet each time more grit is needed; a time wasting exercise.

In the case of steel hulls, the prime coating has to be applied immediately following the blasting. This means that the painter has to follow the blaster as closely as is practical. Rust can form in a surprisingly short time; the actual time depends on the weather and humidity conditions prevailing when the blasting takes place. It is usual for the owner or his employee, as opposed to one of the contractor's employees, to undertake the painting.

By doing the painting, or at least controlling this critical job yourself, you will be assured of its success. Make sure the paint is being applied to a perfectly clean and dry surface at a minimum temperature of 50 degrees F / 10 degrees C. The paint should best be applied within 30 minutes of the blasting; As well as avoiding rust, this will have the extra advantage that the steel should still be warm, as a result of the blasting process. Finally, 3 to 4 hours are the absolute maximum time lag, blasting to prime coating. This is definitely not a one-person operation.

Estimating the time it takes to blast and prime coat is difficult, given all of the variables involved, however about 50 sq ft / 4.65 sq M per hour seems about average. No grit operator or painter can operate flat out for extended periods. It is wise to divide the hull, deck and superstructure into reasonably sized segments, say quarters on a small to medium sized hull and smaller proportions on larger craft. Keeping the blasting and the painting apart will take some organising, but you will need to do this to ensure a clean and long lasting priming job.

When you purchase pre-blasted and primed steel from a specialist supplier, then these materials have most likely been 'blasted' using a wheel process rather than regular blasting. This process is most effective in plate of 1/8" / 3 mm / 10 gauge and larger thickness. The lighter plates can distort when exposed to this treatment.

Wet blasting involves using the water mixed with the grit or sand. This process is successful as a dust inhibitor but after the blasting operation is complete, it leaves a great deal of heavy wet grit or sand to be cleaned up. A rust inhibitor is used in the water, however there is also the problem of blowing the hull dry and applying the paint before the effects of the inhibitor disappear.

The interiors of the hull, under the decks and inside the superstructure will all need to be grit blasted, a difficult and messy job. Don't forget to have all of the cutouts and openings for windows, ports and hatches already completed, before you grit blast and apply the prime coat. It will probably be best to blast the outside first, that way you will not have any worry about grit coming through openings into an already prime coated hull interior.

We have now come the full circle. We have considered the alternatives and you can see that my advice to use pre-shot blasted and primed material makes more sense. Even if you are building in the open, depending on the climate and the amount of care you take in covering the hull, you may find that the pre-blasted and primed materials are worth the extra cost and effort. In the latter case, covering your hull during non-work periods will pay off. Of course you could consider the excellent alternative of installing an aluminum deck and superstructure on your steel hull and thus eliminate many of the problems of blasting above the sheerline.

If you used pre-prime coated steel then you will only need to clean up in the area of the welds and re-coat these areas before proceeding with another all-over prime coat of the entire hull deck and superstructure. The welds can be cleaned using a grinder, wire brush and similar devices to ensure a clean surface that is ready to be touched up with matching prime coat.

Be careful in using solvents and other liquids for cleaning metal; be aware of the deposits they leave behind, so that you are not faced with an ever-ending circle of clean and re-cleaning a particular area. Acids can sometimes be used to advantage to remove surface contaminates including rust. Acids tend to etch the surface and thus improve the adhesion of the paints that are subsequently installed in this area. Generally acids are only used as cleaning agents in smaller areas such as those where welding has spoilt an otherwise prepared and primed hull.

HOT METAL SPRAYING

This method is included here because we are still occasionally asked about the merits of this type of protection for a steel hull. Metal spraying was at one time popular with some steel builders. During the 1970's, when it was most popular, there were many who decried its use, on the grounds that if it chipped or otherwise failed, then water would creep underneath and cause considerable unseen corrosion problems. Time has proven these detractors correct, and the method is infrequently used today. Another drawback was that the materials used for these coatings were notoriously averse to holding paints as intended. The development of modern epoxy and urethane protective coatings has allowed 'flame spraying' or 'metallizing' as it was popularly known, to fade from the scene. In the interests of thoroughness here are the details.

Hot metal spraying is a thermal sprayed metallization process that is accomplished by melting either zinc or aluminum metal wire in a special gun that drives it at high speed in molten droplets onto the bare steel. Fuel gas and fed heat the metal by oxygen, to create the molten spray. Like surface prepared for painting, the surface must be prepared by grit blasting down to white metal. Without this etched surface, the hot metal spray will either roll off or after cooling, it will flake off.

Many advocates of this method claim those chemical bond forms between the aluminum or zinc and the steel; they claim that the metals are 'fused' together. Actually the hot metal spray forms a mechanical bond only, and depends on the correct spraying techniques as well as a grit blasted surface to maintain its grip to the steel. If you plan to metal spray your hull, you

should not use sand as the blasting agent. Commercially manufactured grit is necessary to give the correct key, to the metallization process.

If a hot spray involving aluminum or zinc is used, then a special wash should be applied to the to the aluminum coating prior to applying any paints. One example is Interlux Prime wash, which is specially formulated to adhere to bare aluminum and is a good primer for the other coats that will follow. If you are considering one of the hot metal spays for your boat, you should seek out the latest information on the subject. My advice is stick to the well-proven regular painting procedures for metal hulls.

FILLING AND FAIRING - ALL METALS

Almost all-metal boats, to achieve a perfect or near perfect finish, need some filling and fairing using a suitable compound. It is important that you do not rely on the filling compound to cover sloppy workmanship. The following advice will probably be ignored by the sloppy builder and resented as unnecessary by the perfectionist. It is to the greater proportion of you who occupy the middle ground that I address this advice. Your aim should be to make every step of the building process produce a fair and smooth hull deck and superstructure. You should strive to build a boat that will require the minimum of filler.

Now having established that all hulls and most superstructures need some filler to produce the near perfect appearance, it is simply a matter of choosing and correctly applying the right material. Automotive body putty is not the correct filler for your boat. This material will not withstand the rigours of marine use. Please let the recommendations of your paint manufacturer over-rule any advice we give here. You must choose one manufacturer and use their products exclusively. If you mix brands, you will have no protection if the product fails. Each manufacturer will all blame the competitors product as the cause of the problem.

The correct filler for your metal boat should be epoxy and not polyester based, as is usual with automotive fillers. Your fairing compound should contain inert fillers such as micro-balloons. Many of the paint manufacturers have their own fairing compounds as part of the overall paint system. Make sure you choose a brand or manufacturer where you can obtain local advice and technical assistance. This is not just a case of visiting your local marine store and taking what is on offer. You will need to undertake considerable research to ensure you end up with a long lasting and attractive paint finish on your metal boat. To quote my own experience; our current 38 ft / 11.58 M steel powerboat was originally painted in 1991 and now almost seven years later, the superstructure looks as good as new. Due to mishandling and neglect by the previous owner, the hull recently needed a 'blow-coat' to cover scuffmarks.

THE TOOLS FOR PAINTING

Before selecting the paint, you will have to consider how it will be applied. Certain finishes lend themselves better to one application method than another. Some paints can be applied using a variety of methods so this may influence your choice of paint as well as what equipment you either purchase or hire for the job in hand. No matter which method you choose for applying the various paints you will need a selection of brushes, rollers, paint trays, scrapers, sandpaper and all the usual tools one associates with painting any structure. I have seen many fine metal hulls painted using 'hand tools' including a combination of rolled and brushed finishes.

Airless or air assisted spray equipment is favoured by those experienced in painting hulls and it is possible to lay on high build paints in a way that could not be achieved by hand application methods. It is well worth considering using a professional team to at least install the prime coating on your hull immediately after the blasting process is completed. A team of say 3 or 4 professionals can blast and prime your boat in just a very few hours and thereby ensure that you get the best cover of the blasted steel before it has any chance to get the corrosion process underway.

PAINTING STEEL

The success of your paint job will depend on the care and attention you lavish on the preparation of your vessel before the first finish coat is applied. You must identify individual items than will be more prone to rust and then give these areas additional attention. One way to identify potential problem areas, is by studying other older steel boats. If you have followed our advice on layout and construction, then you will already have avoided most of these potential problems. Now all you have to do is carefully check your own boat before you start to paint.

Usually rust does not form on smooth areas of the hull. Irregular and sharp surfaces are often the culprits. For instance, we have always recommended

Good protective coatings are essential - check out this Roberts 370 built in Finland.

you avoid sharp corners on your hull or superstructure. To avoid creating rust traps and areas where paint is easily damaged, liberal use should be made of split pipe and/or rolled plate. When you eliminate the potential problem areas, you will also eliminate the corrosion problems that at best, ruin the appearance of any metal boat, and at worst, endanger the security of the vessel. No sharp edges, no sharp corners, no water traps, no overlapping plates or other bad practices, that we have already covered in earlier chapters.

Do not attempt to paint areas of high wear such as anchor fairleads, cleats, and similar fittings. These must have a stainless steel liner welded in place to accept the wear and thus avoid any corrosion problems. All welds in areas above the waterline must be ground smooth and filled. This will ensure that no jagged edges or high spots are present. Sharp corners and jagged welds prevent the layers of paint from lying on evenly and equally protecting these areas.

As mentioned elsewhere, it is not recommended that the welds below the waterline is ground smooth. This is a safety factor and means that these welds should be the most carefully executed, so as to have maximum strength and maximum smoothness, to enable them to accept a full quota of paint.

PREPARING AND PAINTING ALUMINIUM

Many aluminum workboats are left unpainted and this is not a problem when the correct grade of marine aluminum has been used to build the vessel. The metal forms an oxide on the surface and further protection is unnecessary. Even these 'unpainted' aluminum vessels need some protection below the waterline, so this area must be coated with a suitable antifouling paint. In France I have seen many aluminum hulled sail and powerboats with unpainted topsides and quite frankly, they look unfinished. Unless you want your boat to look like an untidy workboat, you should accept the fact that you will be painting your aluminum vessel.

You will need to abrade the surface of your aluminum hull by sanding, or by using abrasive pads to roughen the surface of the metal. Next, thoroughly clean the surface using the chemical preparation recommended by your particular paint manufacturer. Now etch the surface. This is usually achieved using a phosphoric acid solution. This action changes the chemical properties of the surface of the aluminum allowing better adhesion between the first coat of paint. Your paint manufacturer will recommend etching primer or

a wash. A primer coat will follow this. Needless to say this primer coat is one of the most important of the whole system; if it fails then the whole system will break down.

After you have installed the primer coat, this is followed by two or more high build barrier undercoats above the waterline. The finish coats will be applied above the waterline. A special tin-based antifouling is normally applied below the waterline. In some countries a licence is required to purchase and use these toxic tin-based antifouling. Check locally to see if you require a permit to use this material. Because of corrosion problems, never use copper based paints on an aluminum boat.

PREPARING AND PAINTING COPPER-NICKEL

The preparation should include good quality grit or sand blasting followed by high build epoxy filler/primer or epoxy mastic. For final coatings, polyurethane-based coatings are recommended. As with painting of all metal boats, advice and assistance should be sought from a 'local' paint manufacturer or at least one who has a readily accessible and knowledgeable technical department.

FINISH PAINTING ALL METALS

Most paint manufacturers have a separate specification for painting the various metals. Many of the procedures are similar and consist of roughing the hull surface, and/or using chemical preparations to thoroughly clean off any impurities. Next comes the installation of prime coats, more than one barrier coat. The process is completed with several finish coats to the hull topsides as well as the decks and superstructure.

The bottom paint requires more thickness than in other areas of the hull. Paint located on and below the waterline has not only to protect against corrosion, but also must prevent the excessive marine growth that occurs with varying ferocity, depending on your cruising grounds. Nature helps out; the area under the water has less exposure to oxygen, which is one of the agents needed to promote rust and other corrosive elements. Your metal boat should be hauled at least once per annum and the bottom should be given a thorough scrub.

The bottom paint must be checked for flaws and a new coat of antifouling applied. Make sure it is installed according to the paint manufacturer specifications. Even if your boat is continuously moored in fresh water, you will still need to undertake the regular haul-out, scrub and renewal of antifouling. Details on the installation and replacement of anodes together with other actions you should take to protect the underwater areas of your hull, are covered elsewhere.

PAINTING DECKS AND SUPERSTRUCTURE

In general terms you will use the same paint on the decks and superstructure as you have used on the hull topsides. The cabin sides and ends will almost certainly be painted using the same methods and materials as the hull. With a few exceptions, the preparation methods for the decks, cockpit and cabin tops will follow a similar routine. Do not have too many coloured 'stripes' and do not 'chop up' the area into too small a sections, or you may end up with a pattern that looks 'fussy'. It takes careful thought and some experience to lay out a successful two-colour paint scheme for the decks and cabin tops. The designer of your boat may give you some advice and assistance in this area.

If you are planning to install one of the composite patterned deck covering materials such as 'Treadmaster', then obtain this material in advance and carefully study the installation instructions. You must ensure that the adhesive used to install the decking will be compatible with paint used on the deck. Having the decking material on hand will also allow you to make a better informed colour choice for the painted areas of the deck, that is those areas that will remain exposed, after the patterned material is in place.

If a timber 'laid deck' is planned then again you will need to make sure that the preparation is in keeping with the materials you will be using to install the timber decking.

No matter what arrangement your decide to feature for your decks and superstructure, make sure you give the area adequate coats of paint. Our steel power cruiser has five hand applied finish coats; a perfect finish after almost seven years of constant exposure to the elements, proves the worth of a good paint job!

ANTIFOULING

The technology that governs which antifouling we should use is constantly changing. On boats with copper-nickel hulls you will not have to worry; these hulls do not need antifouling. The natural action of the metal keeps the marine growth at bay. Steel and aluminum boats need a preventive coating to the areas below the waterline.

Just when we believe that we have found the answer to antifouling problem, along comes an environmentalist to point out the toxic problems caused by the use of certain protective bottom paints. For this reason it is impossible to make specific recommendations; at least ones that would be worthwhile in the future. As is the case with the entire paint job, my advice is to select one manufacturer and use their system from the first etch primer through to the final coat of anti fouling. When applying antifouling, you will need to estimate the load waterline and make sure your antifouling is carried to 2 1/2 in / 60 mm above this line. The reason for painting the antifouling above the true waterline is that the water is never static and if you finish the antifouling right at the waterline, you will soon have an ugly growth of weed at and just above the true LWL.

BOOT TOP

Boot tops look smart but should not be installed until after the boat has been launched and trimmed. After you have conducted trials loaded stores and water and determined the exact load waterline, only then should you consider installing the boot top. Boot tops are not just a straight parallel line; they need to be applied so the line when viewed from the side appears parallel or appears to have slightly more width at the ends. These lines are difficult to get right, especially on sailboats where the aft sections sweep underneath the hull and require quite a wide line to give the correct appearance. Avoid excessive upward sweeps of boot top at the bow.

If you start with a level line parallel to the LWL then this can be the bottom of you boot top; next using a water level, strike a second line above and parallel to the first, you will see how this line widens out at the stern. Study other boats that are out of the water for the winter, and you will get the idea. Do not copy the ones that do not 'look right'. Powerboats will not present the same problems because the hull sides are more or less parallel. A boot top made of tape that is of constant width can work with a powerboat where it would look totally wrong on a sailboat hull.

This Roberts 342 was built in Australia

This steel Waverunner 34 was built in the UK. Note that a hull stripe is almost mandatory on a contemporary boat.

Chapter 11
ENGINEERING FOR METAL BOATS

Engine compartments - Accessibility. Engine room insulation. Engine bearers and beds. Engine mountings, Stuffing boxes and bearings. Exhaust Systems. The sailboat auxiliary engine and horse-power requirements. Understanding horsepower. Powering your motor cruiser. Powering displacement hulls. Powering semi-displacement hulls. Powering planing hulls. Propeller types. Ventilation. Steering arrangements. Fuel tanks and capacities. Water tanks. Cooling systems. Bilge pumps. Spare parts and materials. Ballast.

The first item to consider is the engine and by engine, I mean diesel engine. In my opinion petrol or gasoline powered engines have no place in any metal boat; or any other cruising boat for that matter. Those who build or buy metal boats are usually 'thinking' individuals and safety is one of the reasons they choose metal. Petrol or gasoline engines do not fit this profile!

ENGINE COMPARTMENT - ACCESSIBILITY

When choosing your engine you must make sure that there is sufficient room to install or retro fit your choice. It is not just a matter of shoehorning the engine into a given space; you will need room for insulation and servicing. If access is difficult then there is always the chance you will neglect essential maintenance work.

Out of the several boats we have owned, I have never been totally satisfied with the accessibility of all of the items that need servicing on a regular basis. Unfortunately total accessibility is something to aim for and hopefully achieve. For example, batteries need regular inspection, testing with a multi meter and/or hydrometer and topping up with distilled water. These inspections are likely to be far less frequent if the batteries are in some difficult to reach location. The oil dip stick and the water filters should be inspected every day that the boat is in service. Primary fuel filters fitted with water traps need to be drained on a regular basis. Water impellers need to be changed occasionally, sometimes in a hurry. Main fuel taps should be easily accessible, and the list goes on. Can you easily obtain access to the injectors,

stuffing box, and fuel tank drain? Is there a drain in the bottom of your fuel tank?

Some single engined semi-displacement powerboats and others have insulated engine boxes in addition to an all insulated engine room. This makes for very quiet running but it does restrict accessibility to some items on and around the engine. In sailboats the engine is often installed so that it intrudes into the accommodation and consequently it is inaccessible and almost impossible to service. If you are building a new custom boat or rehabilitating an older one, here is your chance to do yourself a huge favour; consider accessibility as a number one priority.

ENGINE-ROOM INSULATION:

Engine-room insulation in one form or another is essential if you want to avoid the annoyance of the noise emitted by the engine(s). In a sailboat the engine box is usually a fairly close fitting affair and the problem is also one of accessibility as well as keeping the noise to a minimum.

There are several combinations of materials that you can use to insulate your engine and/or engine compartment and keep the engine noise from intruding into the accommodation or other areas. Whichever material you choose, make sure, that in the event of fire, no toxic gases will be given off by the insulation.

Here are some suggestions: Aluminum covered Styrofoam. Fiberglass insulation with lead insert, fiberglass and foam, layers of lead, foam and aluminum or vinyl foam sheeting. Most boat owners have found that a material that incorporates a layer of lead is usually most effective in reducing the amount of noise that escapes from the engine space. The classified pages of your local boating magazine or the yellow pages of the local telephone directory will reveal many sources for these products.

Insulating the engine-room in powerboats is relatively easy to achieve, as there is usually more room to lay out the insulation without interfering with access to the vital organs. In some powerboats with large relatively cavernous engine compartments, it is necessary to insulate the engine separately by having a separate insulated box around the motor. In a single engined powerboat, while an insulated sound box reduces the noise to almost a whisper, it does make access to the engine more difficult and it certainly earns its share of rude comments especially during service checks.

ENGINE BEARERS AND BEDS
The engine bearers or beds should be made as long as possible to adequately spread the various loads imposed by the engine. Beds that are two or more times the length of the engine are recommended.

Space restrictions may hamper this ideal, just make them as long as possible. In our powerboat designs we always try to mate up the engine bearers with fore and aft webs that run almost the full length of the boat. These fore and aft webs also add strength

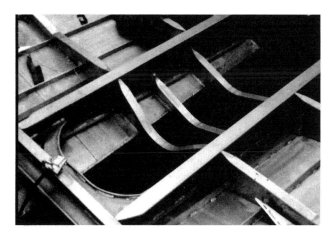

These engine beds embody all of the features described in the text.

throughout the hull and have the secondary use of helping to support the sole.

The engine bearers should be made of plate that is two to two-and-one-half-times the thickness of the hull plating. Naturally the exact thickness should be specified in your plans. The size and horsepower of the engine and its size relationship to the hull will all have to be considered when designing the beds and their supports.

The transverse web supports in our designs are part of the regular frame web construction sequence with additional webs added as required by the spacing of the frames. For example, if the frames of the hull are spaced say 10 to the waterline length, then additional webs will be required between the stations.

It is a difficult job to match the height of the beds with the line of the shaft and stern bearing. If you do not already have the engine one site, then using a three-dimensional plywood mock-up of the engine can help.

MOUNTINGS, COUPLINGS, STUFFING BOXES, WATER SEALS AND SHAFT BEARINGS
The long subheading illustrates how these items are linked. You must consider the 'drive train' of your engine as a single integrated unit. Most engines are mounted on flexible mountings and feature a suitable coupling such as an 'Aqua Drive' unit to complete the vibration free installation. The Aqua Drive and similar units allow for slight misalignment between the shaft and the engine transmission. This is a

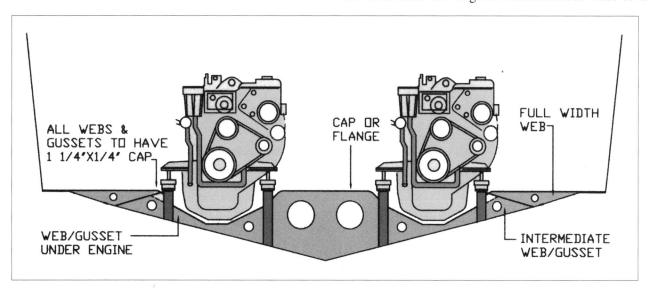

The twin engine bed arrangement shown here will fit in most powerboats over 35 ft / 10.67 M and will leave room for fuel tanks to be installed outboard of each engine.

Engine bearers in ROBERTS SPRAY hull. A longitudinal steel web with lightening holes would improve this installation.

necessary feature because when the engine is mounted on flexible mountings, there will be some movement between the engine coupling and the propeller shaft.

STUFFING BOX

You will need some form of gland to prevent the water entering your boat where the propeller shaft leaves the propeller tube at the inboard end. Your main choices will be between a traditional stuffing box and one of the newer devices, such as a 'Deep Sea Seal'. If you choose a stuffing box it may have an external grease lubrication system or depend on the natural oils of the 'stuffing' and the water for lubrication.

Grease fed stuffing boxes usually employ a remote cylinder that one packs with waterproof grease. One or two turns on the plunger each day forces enough grease through the line to the bearing; this assists in keeping the water at bay. All stuffing boxes, also known as packing glands, will drip twice or so per minute and produce about a cup full of water per day. If they are over tightened and do not produce this drip, then the bearing and the shaft will probably suffer from excessive wear.

PATENTED STERN BEARINGS

Stern bearings, such as the unit marketed as the 'Deep Sea Seal', have long been used on large ships, but only in the past few years have they been installed in pleasure and work boats of all types. The 'Deep Sea Seal' has an excellent reputation and have been fitted to many thousands boats around the world.

The basic DSS has been improved with the addition of an additional 'red' clamp that allows the unit to be serviced while the boat is still afloat. There are other manufacturers of these devices and you should

investigate the various types, before making your choice. See supplier's addresses in appendix 4.

If your boat has twin engines, it is a sure thing that on many occasions you will want to run on one engine. If your engines are equipped with Deep-Sea Seals, or similar water lubricated stern bearings, you should consider the necessity of supplying water to the bearing of the shut down engine.

The Pedro 41 'Van Hoff', a custom built, steel hull with aluminum decks and superstructure, trawler yacht owned by our friends Mike and Caroline Hofman, is fitted with a crossover water supply to both Deep Sea Seals. I confess I showed only moderate interest when Mike explained this system. The twin water supply was necessary, because, as with most twin engined vessels, for the sake of fuel economy, 'Van Hoff' is often operated on one engine. In light of subsequent events not fully detailed here, I should have taken more notice! There follows a clue!

Even if you have only one engine, consider the possibility of engine failure and then when your vessel is towed, do you let the shaft rotate and if so, how do you provide water to the bearing! If the situation persists for more than a short time, freewheeling un-lubricated stern bearings can be damaged. In all single or multi-engined craft, it may be wise to consider installing shaft-locking devices that are available to suit most size engine/shaft combinations.

AFT SHAFT BEARINGS

Your boat will require a bearing where the propeller shaft leaves the outer end of the tube. The choice is between a fibre bearing, a tufnel bearing or a cutless rubber bearing. Cutless bearings are well proven and when properly set up with two small water scoops at the aft end of the tube to introduce water to lubricate the bearing, they will give long and trouble free service.

If the distance between the inboard stuffing box or seal and the outboard end of the tube is over say 6ft 6 in / 2.00 M, you may require an intermediate bearing generally known as a 'plummer block'. This may be a cutlass bearing that has been slid down the tube to the mid point location.

If your shaft protrudes from the tube by more than a few inches, you may need a Y bracket bearing to support the outer end immediately ahead of the propeller. Decisions as to whether you need an intermediate bearing and similar questions are best

Either a 'Y' or a 'P' bracket will be required to support the shaft between the hull and the propeller.

addressed to the designer of your boat or a qualified marine engineer.

EXHAUST SYSTEMS

Most diesel engines do not come completely equipped with a suitable exhaust system. In the past, one exception was the range of diesel auxiliaries supplied by Vetus den Ouden. Unfortunately the engines and equipment are now sold separately. Vetus do have a good range of exhaust systems that are available all over the world, see appendix 4.

Diesel engines fitted to sail or powerboats will need a properly engineered exhaust system. Engines mounted below the waterline, and most are, will need special attention to ensure that anti-siphon devices are fitted to the system. There are two basic ways of cooling an engine and both have a bearing on the type of exhaust system required.

Most air-cooled engines (noisy) have a 'dry exhaust' system and this means that no water is added to the necessarily heavily insulated (lagged) exhaust. In the confines of a sailboat, dry exhausts are hot and noisy. This type of exhaust can be used to good effect in some types of traditional powerboats. Dry exhausts combined with a vertical stack are often seen on fishing and work boats.

A wet exhaust system is used to cool the exhaust gases soon after they leave the engine. The water and gases are expelled together with the cooling water. This system is necessarily inter-related with the cooling system of your engine. A stainless steel 'water lift' muffler is a nice addition to any exhaust system and will help to quieten the noise emissions.

Stern-drive equipped engines and outboards have the exhaust systems built in. Outboards are outside the scope of this book but you may be considering a diesel powered stern-drive for your metal powerboat. Stern-drive exhausts usually exit via the centre of the propeller, no doubt adding a minuscule amount of thrust in the process.

HEAT EXCHANGER COOLING

Most modern diesel engines feature fresh water, heat exchanger cooling. This method uses a special tank of fresh water, which runs through the engine's cooling system. The fresh water tank contains internal piping and is, in turn cooled by seawater being pumped through the pipes. This method prevents the internal cooling system of the engine coming into contact with salt water.

Most modern diesel engines are cooled in this manner. One problem with this method is that in the event that the outside intake for the cooling water becomes clogged, then the whole system overheats. A sensor in the system can warn you about this condition, before your engine overheats. Make sure your engine(s) are equipped with this warning device.

Raw water-cooling is usually found on older model slower revving diesels. The method is to pump outside (sea or fresh water depending on the boats operating environment) water through the engine casing and then out through the exhaust and thus cooling the engine in the process.

KEEL COOLING AND SIMILAR METHODS

There is a third method where no external water is required. The most common of the self contained cooling systems involves adding outside keel cooling pipes which are usually tucked in at the keel/hull intersection and allows the engine cooling water to recirculate and be cooled by the surrounding sea water.

The most interesting version of this method is only possible with boats that have a hollow metal keel. It involves selecting a section of the keel and boxing this off to store the required quantity of a 50/50 mixture of anti freeze coolant and fresh water. This mixture is run through the engines' cooling system and providing that the surface area of the selected portion of the keel is adequate to allow for the ambient outside water temperature, then the system works extremely well. This latter arrangement employs two header tanks and works in a similar manner to the engine cooling system in your automobile.

An additional benefit of these engine-cooling systems, can be the incorporation of an insulated hot water tank, known in the UK as a calorifier. This tank has an internal pipe coil through which the hot water from the engine cooling system is circulated; this hot pipe in turn heats the domestic hot water. In our previously owned sailboat K*I*S*S, we found that running the engine for about 20 minutes every other day was sufficient to provide hot water for two days of showers, plus other daily hot water requirements.

Any internal cooling system where there is no outside cooling water requires a lagged dry exhaust.

Considerable care is required in routing any exhaust line, especially the dry variety, which, despite the lagging, can get hot. If you have a dry exhaust, then make sure that you pay particular attention to the ventilation of your engine space and the surrounding area. The main negative feature of this arrangement is that dry exhausts are usually noisier than the water-cooled systems.

MUFFLER

Many exhaust systems involve the use of a water lift muffler. The engine cooling water is fed into the exhaust tube just aft of where it leaves the engine and then into the muffler where the pressure of the exhaust gases forces the water out of the boat. This latter system can be one of the quietest available. Quietness in your exhaust system is a very desirable feature.

If you are purchasing a ready built new or used metal boat, then the engine cooling and exhaust system will already be in place and usually it is an expensive proposition to change from one system to another. If you are custom building, then you should choose carefully. Check other boats; weigh up the advantages and disadvantages of each system, before you make your final decision.

Raw water cooling (no heat exchanger) is the least desirable because the innards of your engine are constantly exposed to the ravages of salt or outside water containing all sorts of pollutants. Your choice should be between a system with a regular heat exchanger and where you use outside water to cool the heat exchanger, or a system where you have outside piping to allow keel cooling or you can choose the fully internal system.

No matter which system you choose, remember the advantages of having your hot water tank (calorifier) as part of the engine cooling system.

SAILBOAT AUXILIARY

You will want to know whether your cruising boat has sufficient power to do the job. The auxiliary is often under valued until you need it most. There are many formulas used to ensure it is up to the task; for preliminary calculations, we use a power-v-weight ratio. This calculation will reveal if your sailboat has enough power to propel it in the direction you want to go when for one reason or another, the sails can not do the job.

We can start with a 'ball park' calculation and estimate that for any sail boat, two horsepower per 1,000 lbs /

454 kg displacement is a reasonable requirement. The addition or reduction of horsepower from the above calculation will depend on your philosophy. In general, USA sailors prefer more power than their European counterparts.

All inboard engines fitted to sailboats require gearing down by way of a transmission gear box, to produce the power required to drive the vessel in anything but a flat calm. We usually recommend a 2:1 reduction; thus halving the rotation rate of the propeller verses the engine revolutions. You will find that most manufacturers have a range of reduction options between 1.9:1 to 2.15:1, any one of these can be considered to fall within the 2:1 recommendation.

Generally speaking, the larger the reduction the larger the propeller diameter required to obtain the correct revolutions. For this reason it is not practical to install a very small engine that is geared down to say 3 or 4 to 1. The problem is that the large propeller required, would destroy the sailing performance.

Single or twin engines; in a sailboat I feel that unless your boat is over 55 ft / 16.76 M, this is hardly worth discussing. By over 55 ft I mean considerably over!

ALTERNATIVE POWER

Hydraulic drives electric drives, jet drives and the like has no place in a sailboat. Over the past 30 odd years

LWL	Tons Displ.	5 Knots	6 Knots	7 Knots	8 Knots	9 Knots
25 ft/7.62 M	2.0	5	5.0			
25 ft/7.62 M	3.0	6.5	6.5			
25 ft/7.62 M	4.0	8.7	8.7			
25 ft/7.62 M	5.0	12.0	12.0			
30 ft/9.14 M	2.0	1.9	3.6	6.4		
30 ft/9.14 M	3.0	2.5	5	9.7		
30 ft/9.14 M	4.0	1.9	6.4	13.0		
30 ft/9.14 M	5.0	3.3	7.7	16.0		
30 ft/9.14 M	6.0	3.5	8.8	19.0		
30 ft/9.14 M	8.0	4.0	11.0	26.0		
40 ft/9.14 M	4.0	2.8	5.2	8.5	13.0	
40 ft/9.14 M	6.0	3.5	7.0	12.0	25.0	
40 ft/9.14 M	8.0	4.0	8.4	15.0	26.0	
40 ft/9.14 M	10.0	4.4	9.9	18.0	33.0	
40 ft/9.14 M	12.0	4.6	11.0	21.0	40.0	
40 ft/9.14 M	14.0	5.0	12.0	24.0	46.0	
40 ft/9.14 M	16.0	5.2	13.0	27.0	53.0	
40 ft/9.14 M	18.0	5.6	14.0	30.0	59.0	
40 ft/9.14 M	20.0	5.9	15.0	33.0	66.0	
50 ft/9.14 M	8.0	4.1	7.2	13.0	19.0	28.0
50 ft/9.14 M	10.0	4.6	7.9	15.0	23.0	35.0
50 ft/9.14 M	12.0	5.0	8.8	17.0	27.0	42.0
50 ft/9.14 M	14.0	5.3	9.6	20.0	30.0	49.0
50 ft/9.14 M	16.0	5.6	10.0	11.0	34.0	56.0
50 ft/9.14 M	18.0	5,8	11.0	23.0	38.0	63.0
50 ft/9.14 M	20.0	6.0	12.0	25.0	41.0	70.0
50 ft/9.14 M	25.0	6.5	13.0	30.0	50.0	87.0
50 ft/9.14 M	30.0	7.0	14.0	34.0	57.0	105.0

we have been asked to design every imaginable type of 'alternative' power arrangement. After completing many, sometimes longwinded investigations, we have reached the conclusion, diesel power is the way to go.

If you have a particular hobby such as steam and you wish to combine this with your boating activity then, there may be an argument for installing an engine that allows you to indulge in your pet interest. It is worth noting that you will probably need to remove this unique installation, before you sell the boat.

UNDERSTANDING HORSEPOWER

When considering 'horsepower,' there are several terms used to convey the 'power' generated by the engine at certain revolutions. Terms you will encounter include brake horsepower (BHP). This is the power put out by the engine but does not include the power loss caused by the transmission gearbox or other losses due to such items as alternator, water pump and general friction of the transmission system. Shaft horsepower (SHP) represents the available power at the propeller.

Usually more than one rating is shown. For instance maximum, this is the power you could get for a very short time before you burn up the engine; intermittent, this is the power that the engine can deliver for the limited period usually 30 to 60 minutes; continuous, this is the rating that the engine can operate at for long periods without damage.

Continuous is the rating that will be of primary interest when you decide what horsepower is required to move your boat at the desired speed. Increasingly you will find that the power ratings are given in Kw and the conversion is as follows: 1 Kw = 1.359 HP

POWERING YOUR METAL MOTOR BOAT, POWERBOAT or SHIP!

Depending on which side of the Atlantic or Pacific you reside, you will refer to your motor driven vessel as a Powerboat or Motorboat. If it is large enough you may even refer to it as a 'Yacht'. When you meet a person from the Netherlands, they will refer to your modest power cruiser as a 'Ship'.

Because of the variables involved, this is a much more complex subject than powering a sailboat. Due to space restrictions, we can only give a brief overview of this subject. If you are interested in learning more, you should check out the recommended reading in appendix one.

BRAKE HORSEPOWER FOR SAILBOAT AUXILIARY ENGINES

The chart opposite shows reflects data collected by John Thornycroft of UK. The figures represent the various BHP (brake horsepower) requirements for auxiliary engines installed in sailboats. The calculations assume a 3 bladed propeller. The BHP quoted is at the engine and allows 15 percent for engine and shafting losses.

POWERING A DISPLACEMENT HULL

Powering any displacement hulled motor vessel follows much the same rules as those used to calculate the requirements for sailboats. The exception is that while the sailboat has its sails to use in an emergency, the displacement motor boat totally relies on its engine. Most displacement powerboats are fitted with only one main power plant, so you should select yours with care. To estimate the horsepower requirements, start with an estimate of two horsepower per 1,000 lbs (454 kg) displacement. This should be taken as the minimum requirement.

You can gear down your engine to give maximum performance at lower speeds and reduce the number of horsepower required to drive your vessel. This option results in a larger diameter propeller and there may not be room for it. There are other disadvantages to taking this minimum power route; one day you may need extra power to get out of a sticky situation, or tow another vessel.

Conversely a diesel engine likes to be worked moderately hard, so it is not advisable to have and installation where only 50 percent or less of the power can be used without driving the stern down to an unacceptable level. If you want more power, then you may wish to consider a semi-displacement hull that can make better use of additional horsepower.

POWERING A SEMI-DISPLACEMENT HULL

A fact you must consider is that it takes excessive power to drive a semi-displacement hull faster than 1.5 times the square root of the waterline length. For example, this type of hull measuring 36 ft / 10.97 M on the waterline would have a square root of 6. So 6 times 1.5 equals 9 knots. A broad definition of planing is when a boat reaches a speed of 2 times the square root of the waterline length.

Taking the 36 ft / 10.97 M example shown above, square root of 6 x 2 gives us a 12 knot planing speed, at this speed the necessary horsepower and fuel requirements will turn a comfortable economical cruising boat into an expensive proposition. Please note that 2 times S/R/WL is only the start of planing and to make a semi-displacement hull reach a full or near level planing attitude, will take considerably more power and use more fuel than consumed by a similar sized planing hull. The point is that it makes no sense to grossly overpower any semi-displacement hull. 'You will be just spinning your wheels', in this case your propellers. This whole subject will be fully covered in my forthcoming book Choosing a Cruising Powerboat / Motorboat. See appendix one for details.

Next we have to consider the weight of our vessel. Weight in this instance means loaded displacement. This includes not only the weight of the finished boat but includes fuel, water, stores and the crew. In addition, there are all of those items that are brought aboard for a particular use or occasion, and then never leave the boat.

Now there are many degrees of 'semi-displacement hulls ranging from a near displacement vessel through to almost a full planing hull. The degree of rise in the chine or buttock lines aft will determine how fast the hull may be driven. Simply put, the more stern there is in the water at rest, then the faster the hull may be driven. Overpowering a hull will cause the stern to drop and create a large stern wave. In certain instances this wave can overwhelm the vessel.

POWERING A PLANING HULL

It was only a few years ago that it was thought impossible to build a successful small to medium sized steel planing hull. Fortunately modern building techniques and technical advances in design have not only made this possible, but practical as well. As mentioned above, planing occurs when the boat reaches a speed equal to two times the square root of the waterline length. A planing hull will then make the transition from 'just planing' to 'full planing attitude' with less fuss, less extra horsepower and less extra fuel than as similarly sized and equipped semi-displacement hull or semi-planing hull.

Aluminum has been used to build hundreds of thousands of small, medium and large planing hulls. Although at first glance this material may appear to be the ideal metal for a fast hull, I have reservations about this material when used in any type of hull, preferring to recommend it for decks and superstructures. You will find my thoughts on this material scattered through this text so it is not necessary to repeat them here.

Now for those who prefer aluminium; you will find that the performance of planing hulls is related to WEIGHT - VERSES - POWER. Unlike displacement hulls, and to a lesser extent in semi-displacement boats, waterline length plays a smaller part in the performance characteristics of a planing hull.

So in simple terms, the more power and the less weight you have in your planing hull, the faster it will go. Fortunately for designers like myself, it is not that simple. A well-designed planing hull equipped with modest power will outperform an overpowered, poorly designed vessel.

POWERBOATS - 'TAKE-HOME' ENGINES

Before we consider the subject of single or twin engines, we should touch on the possibility of installing a 'wing' engine, or using the diesel that powers the 'gen-set' as a take-home arrangement. Some owners have installed an electric drive that is powered by the 'gen-set' and have used this as emergency propulsion.

Circumstances have caused me to give this matter considerable thought. In the near future we will be designing a range of long distance power cruisers. These vessels are generally referred to as 'Passage-makers' and to be successful, need a minimum range of 3,000 miles / 4,828 km.

Some vessels in the 50 foot plus / over 15.25 M can be built to cover up to 6,000 miles / 9,656 km without refuelling. For various reasons, most of these long distance vessels are fitted with a single engine, hence the interest in alternative propulsion methods. As a safety factor both for medium distance and local cruising, my choice would be for a wing engine.

POWERBOATS - ONE OR TWO ENGINES

As mentioned earlier most displacement-hulled vessels are traditionally fitted with a single engine. Many owners have twin installations and the bulk of them quote safety as the prime reason for taking this route.

We have always quoted that when you install twin engines as opposed to a single engine of the same total horsepower, you will lose 20 percent in total output. More recently we have decided that the effective loss of power may be even higher. Other examples show that the additional fuel consumption of the second engine is not justified, by the small increase in performance when the two engines are used.

If you are considering a new boat, and then you should in the interests of safety, consider twin engines, however you should be aware that in the interests of economy, you might be operating only one engine for much of the time. You would be well advised to lay out your engines and systems with the above facts in mind. Owners, who regularly take this course, rotate the use of each engine on a four hourly or daily basis.

PROPELLERS

It would be nice if we could buy a propeller to match our hull material! Builders using copper-nickel are well served as the bronze propellers that are readily available are a close relative to the hull material, so the interaction between different metals that causes corrosion is at least reduced. Steel or cast steel propellers are very difficult to obtain so steel boat owners are forced to use the bronze versions or join their aluminum boat owning friends and opt for an expensive stainless steel 'wheel'. So there you have it, Steel boat; bronze propeller, Copper-nickel boat; Nickel aluminum bronze propeller (must be more noble that the copper-nickel hull), Aluminum boat; stainless steel propeller.

Propeller nomenclature is simple, but unfortunately choosing the correct size and pitch of the 'wheel', is somewhat more difficult. First the simple part. The DIAMETER refers to the size of the circle scribed by the tips of the propeller blade. The RPM, refers to the revolutions that the shaft achieves in one minute, this figure is usually a factor of the engine RPM but due to the transmission reduction 1.5:1, 2:1 and so forth the shaft RPM will be different to the engine RPM. When calculating propeller sizes, it is the shaft RPM that is important.

The SLIP refers to the loss of motion due to the fact that the propeller is rotating in a liquid and not a solid. Slip is the theoretical difference a propeller of a given pitch would travel and what it actually is expected to achieve, usually expressed as a percentage.

The PITCH is the distance the propeller would travel in one revolution if it were rotating in a solid. The PITCH RATIO is figured by dividing the pitch by the diameter. Fast powerboats sometimes have a diameter and pitch of the same number; this is referred to as a 'square wheel'.

PROPELLERS FOR POWERBOATS

In powerboats you will want to install the most efficient propellers that will allow the engine to reach its operating and top RPM when required. In some designs, the aperture is not sufficiently large enough to allow the correct propeller to be installed and in this case, a change from a 3 bladed to a 4 bladed 'wheel' may prove successful. If you are experiencing cavitation because the tip clearance is too small or because of the shape of your particular hull, then a change to 4 blades may remedy the situation.

The design and matching of a propeller to the hull, engine and reduction ratio is something of an occult art. As designers we do our best, but even the most detailed calculations can result in a propeller match that can be improved with trials conducted over a variety of conditions. You can also contact one of the many well-known propeller manufacturers in USA, Australia, UK and elsewhere, these manufacturers will usually be most helpful. If you have a propeller problem do not disregard it, seek assistance as required.

PROPELLERS FOR SAILBOATS

The most efficient propeller from a sailing point of view (excluding none at all) is the two blade folding variety. Two blades mean a larger diameter and this can cause problems where space is restricted. Some of these two bladed folding propellers are inefficient and others have a reputation for not always opening on demand, which could be disastrous. If you do decide to choose a two bladed type, make sure you are able to get a first hand recommendation from another person who has already had experience with the brand you favour.

The elimination of drag is the aim of every sailboat owner. One way around the problem is to use a feathering propeller. These units are complex and expensive. Finely engineered feathering propellers may be suitable for larger yachts where the owners have the resources to cover the initial expense and possible high maintenance costs. Unless you have a very deep pocket, you are best advised to accept a small loss of speed under sail and select a fixed three bladed wheel.

ROPE CUTTERS

These devices are mentioned here because they may require a slightly longer shaft to be fitted. Suitable for both sail and powerboats, rope cutters are designed to be clamped on your shaft just ahead of the propeller. These units can be very effective in cutting rope or a similar obstruction that would otherwise foul your propeller.

FUEL FILTERS

Does your engine have a separate primary fuel filter? Not all boat manufacturers fit these essential items as standard. The fuel filter that comes with the engine is basically a secondary filter, so a good primary fuel filter that incorporates a water trap is needed between the fuel tank and the engine. The filter should have the capacity to handle a considerable amount of dirt and water. Twin primary filters can be arranged so one can continue while the other is unclogged or changed. The installation of duel primary fuel filters, should be a serious consideration in single engined craft.

I prefer the primary filter to have a glass bowl, so one can quickly observe if water is present. The sealed filter units have expensive cartridges that need to be replaced in total rather than simply replacing the internal filter. Unfortunately these glass bowl versions are now outlawed in Europe; the argument being, that in case of fire, they present an additional danger.

The foregoing was written last week. Today I met a fellow boat owner who had his boat towed into port. His story gave me food for thought. The boat is a steel, Dutch built 34 ft / 10.36 M motor cruiser. The experienced owner was alone off the Spanish coast near Barcelona, motoring along in heavy seas when the single engine stopped. On investigation, it was found that the glass bowl on the primary fuel filter had shattered. This had allowed diesel fuel to spray in all directions and of course the engine stopped due to lack of fuel. Fortunately there was no fire. No replacement bowl was available and the engine was too hot, and the motion too violent, to allow the owner to deal with the situation. He was forced to swallow his pride and call out the Spanish Coast Guard who responded promptly. Within half an hour the disabled vessel was under tow; another hour and she was safely in port. The owner believes he over-tightened the glass bowl on the filter and when it expanded due to the heat from the engine, it shattered. There are two lessons there; reconsider the use of glass bowled filters, or at least, do not over tighten them.

You will need to change the filters at regular servicing intervals. In the case of a fuel blockage, you will need to change them as required. This is a very messy job and is one area of boat maintenance that you must understand. You should practice preventative maintenance wherever possible. When reassembling filter units make sure you have the 'O' sealing rings in the correct order and position, sometimes the top and bottom rings look similar but are different enough to allow fuel or oil to leak out when the engine is fired up. Start the engine with caution after servicing these items.

VENTILATION

In both power and sailboats, ventilation of the engine space is an important feature. Your engine needs a considerable amount of fresh air. Install two vents of adequate size, one ducted below the engine to bring the fresh air in and the other ducted high up in the engine space to take the hot air out. Generally a blower is not required in the northern latitudes however, in hot climates you may need one to turn the air over at the correct rate. An engine space blower is simply a ducted fan that is designed to either import or export larger quantities of air than would circulate naturally.

INSTRUMENT PANELS

Your engine will usually be equipped with an instrument panel, but you may want to add to the instruments supplied in the standard package. The minimum engine instrumentation should include a tachometer/revolution counter, engine hour meter, fuel gauge (notoriously inaccurate in boat installations; have a dipstick handy) and a volt/ampere meter. You will require an instrument light switch including a dimmer control for night use, an audible alarm to indicate if you fail to switch off the ignition after the engine has been stopped, an engine stop button and a water temperature gauge.

Warning lights and/or buzzers may represent some potential problems; in my opinion, warning lights are not as effective as proper gauges. Audible alarms are recommended for water temperature, alternator output and the other 'vital life signs.' Your electrical panel complete with fuses is usually located in a separate box, however in some boats with inside steering it may be incorporated in to the main panel.

ENGINE WATER PUMP

Your cooling system will include a water pump that is necessary to draw water from outside the hull and force it through the cooling system. The pump will include an impeller that will need replacing from time to time. Most water pumps are located in most inaccessible places. Make sure you know where yours is located and check that you have a spare impeller. Also check for difficulty of removing the impeller and covering plate. 'Speedseal' is a product made in the UK and consists of a water pump cover that is attached with only two knurled screws. This unit can be installed and removed with one hand, replacing your regular water pump cover with one of these units may be worthwhile.

ENGINE WATER FILTER

If your engine uses water drawn from outside, either directly as raw water-cooling or by way of a heat exchanger, then you will require a water filter. This filter is used to remove any foreign matter that could damage the water pump impeller or otherwise clog the cooling system and in turn cause the engine to overheat. The usual arrangement is to have the water filter located immediately after the seacock where the outside water enters the system.

The filter should be easily accessible, as it should be checked daily and more often especially if you are motoring in weed infested waters. This unit is often made of clear plastic, presumably so you can see what is going inside, do not let this discourage you

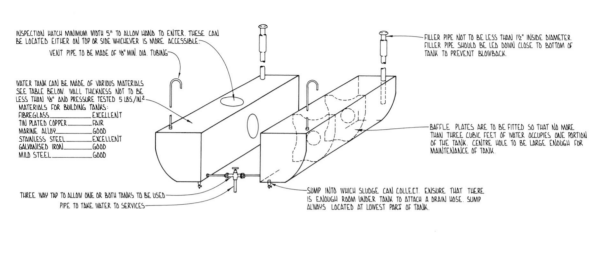

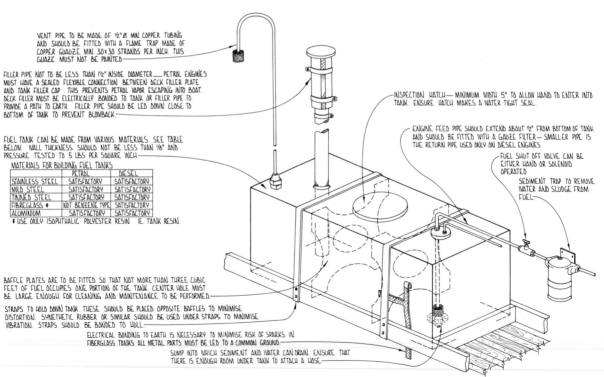

Your tanks will need to embody all of the features as shown in these sketches. See also text.

from removing the top for regular inspections. Plastic bags are one of the most common foreign bodies lurking in our waterways and these are not always visible without removing the top of the filter. Most filters have a rubber-sealing ring and you may find that a light coating of Vaseline will prevent the unit from sucking air. In any case, the rings will need replacement every two years or so. If you have a diesel powered generating set then you should have a separate water filter for this unit. If possible locate the two filters so you can check both at the same time.

BILGE PUMPS

Take some time planning and laying out your bilge pumping systems. Bilge pumps can be electrically, mechanically or hand driven. Usually the first line of defence is the automatic electrically powered unit situated in the lowest point of the bilge. At least one of your bilge pumps should be situated in a ёstrumí box. This is a special 'well' situated low in your bilge, created to hold a gauze covered end to the pipe that is in turn connected to the bilge pump. If you have an automatic shower pump-out system, this can double as another bilge pump. The shower pump will often be located in a different compartment to the main unit.

You will need at least one, preferably two hand operated bilge pumps and one of these should be a large capacity portable unit that is mounted on a board thus allowing it to be operated in any part of the vessel. The Edson 18 and the Whale Titan are both excellent hand operated pumps.

FUEL TANKS

If you are building or refitting an aluminum boat then you may find that the same material has been used for the tanks. There have been many problems with aluminum tanks. They tend to be susceptible to vibration and can fracture along the weld lines where baffles are attached inside the tanks. If you do use aluminum for tanks, make sure they are made from a high magnesium alloy such as 5083 or 5086 specification. It may be better to consider poly-propylene fabricated or moulded tanks.

Aluminum and steel tanks are sometimes built with the hull acting as one side of the tank. It is preferable to have the tanks built as a separate unit and tested before installation in the boat and this will ensure that there are no leaks. Air pressure of about 3 psi can be used to test the tanks.

On no account simply connect the tanks to a high-pressure air hose, or you may cause the tank to explode. Because of the risk of explosion, some experts recommend hydrostatic testing rather than the air test mentioned above.

Diesel fuel tanks can be built from a variety of materials including high-density polyethylene, stainless steel, aluminum or mild steel. Most builders choose regular mild steel. This material has the advantage of low cost, ease of fabrication and low maintenance requirements. The diesel fuel inside the tank takes care of the interior and providing you keep the outside wall painted, your steel fuel tanks should give you long service.

These tanks were fabricated and tested outside the hull and then installed as shown. As it is usually impossible to remove tanks without destroying the interior joinery, you had best make sure your tanks are thoroughly tested before installation

Tank capacity is a subject where there is often a difference of opinion between the designer, builder and the owner. Most designers would like to specify small easy to remove tanks, the builder wants tanks large enough so that he can offer a cruising range greater than the competition and the owner often requests an enormous cruising range under power.

All tanks should be fitted with inspection hatches and be capable of being cleaned through these openings. Fuel is drawn off by way of a pipe that enters the tank from the top and extends to within 1 in / 25 mm of the bottom. Arrange the tank and fuel line so that any sludge will collect below the drawing off line. A drain cock from the bottom of the tanks will allow you to flush out the tank. In some areas these drains are not legal, check locally but if possible; fit the bottom drain. All tanks will need breather pipes, see drawing for these and other details. If you are purchasing a used or new production boat, your tanks may not meet all the criteria outlined in this chapter and they may need attention in one or more areas that we have already mentioned.

If you are building or retrofitting your boat, then choose tanks that give you a sensible cruising range. If you plan to install a diesel powered generating set, diesel cooking stove and/or a diesel powered heating system, then take the usage of these items into your calculations. Remember that to avoid condensation and to minimise the chance of bugs infecting your fuel, you should keep your diesel tanks topped up whenever possible. It does not make sense, to be carrying excessive weight in the form of over large amounts of diesel fuel.

Sailboat owners should make careful calculations of their requirements. Armed with the knowledge that you will need to use the engine for a percentage of the time, allow for this and then add the other uses such as diesel heating. Now decide on the size of your fuel tanks.

No matter what type of material you choose for the fuel tanks or any other liquids, make sure they are firmly anchored in place. The thought of a loose tank, either full or otherwise; charging about the boat in a rough seaway, should be enough to ensure you carefully check all tank supports and containment arrangements.

MICRO-ORGANISMS AND BIOCIDE ADDITIVES

All diesel fuel systems have the potential for microorganism contamination. Neglected or unprepared fuel systems will continue to provide life support to these pests once they are introduced into the system. Problems show up in shortened fuel life, clogged fuel lines and increasingly corroded fuel system components including the tanks.

The degree to which microorganisms grow and prosper in the fuel system is relative to how fast the fuel is turned over. Boats with small fuel tanks or with high horsepower engines are less likely to have this problem. For several reasons already covered, cruising sailboats tend to have larger tanks and turn the fuel over less often.

If you leave your boat for extended periods without making sure that the fuel tanks are totally full, then you run the risk of introducing these foreign bodies into your fuel system. Partially empty tanks allow water condensation to form and the least effect of this is that your water trap/fuel filter will be working overtime. A more serious result of partially filled fuel tanks, is that you will create a situation where the microorganism commonly referred to, as 'the fuel bug' will thrive. These 'bugs' occur in the form of algae,

bacteria, yeast, mould and fungi. This is a problem faced by all owners and operators of diesel engines, no matter where the engines are located or in what type of transport, the engines are installed. Boats used and laid up in warmer climates are more susceptible to the 'bug' however, many cases have occurred in the UK and colder parts of the US, so this problem is not confined to tropical areas.

To avoid and/or eliminate 'bugs' from your fuel it is necessary to understand how these pests thrive in your tank. The various microorganisms need water to survive, since they live at the interface between water and diesel fuel, using the fuel as a food source. Diesel contains carbon, hydrogen and dissolved oxygen, and is a good nutrient source for the bugs.

Once you have removed water from the system, preventative measures must still be taken against microbial growth. In a marine environment, moisture is always present, and diesel bugs can grow quite rapidly. They can be present in the air, or in fuel taken aboard after you thought you had cured the problem. Some bacteria can grow into a mass many times their original size in just 24 hours. Other types can corrode fuel systems without being so obvious; these may show up as black grit resembling coffee grounds, either in the filter or if you still have one, in the water separator sight bowl.

If you purchase a boat that has been unused for some time, then you would be wise to remove all of the existing fuel from the tanks and have them flushed out and filled with fresh fuel, before you use the boat. If in doubt about the cleanliness of existing fuel or if refilling after flushing out the tanks, you should add a biocide chemical to your fuel. This will ensure any remaining bugs are destroyed, before they multiply and clog your fuel system at some inappropriate moment.

There are many brands of biocides available and they have one major factor in common; they are all expensive, usually costing around £12 / US $20 for sufficient to treat a 150 gallon / 680 litres fuel tank. Another shared feature is that they are all composed of highly toxic chemicals, so highly concentrated, that they need to be handled with utmost care. It is well to keep in mind that over time, biocides lose their effectiveness and have to be replenished.

If you have a bad case of the bug, do not be afraid to give your fuel tank a double dose of biocides. These chemicals are extremely toxic, that is why they work! Select a safe storage method and wear disposable rubber gloves when handling biocides. Needless to say keep these chemicals well away from the reach of children.

WATER DISPERSANTS

These additives are only successful when used as a preventive rather than a cure. The biocides should be used if your tank is already infected with the bug. Water dispersants are designed to absorb water into the fuel and in this way remove the water before the fuel reaches the filters. Before using these additives, you must first drain off as much water as possible. There are other benefits claimed for these products, including the fact that they inhibit separation of the waxes and gums that are present in diesel fuels. Only use these products if you have minor water problems or as a preventive method.

MICRO-ORGANISM FUEL FILTERS

For those of us who plan to operate our boats in areas and under conditions where the fuel bug is likely to be an ongoing problem, then we may want to consider a more positive solution to micro-organism growth. Developed over 10 years ago in New Zealand, this new technology called De Bug ™ Fuel Decontamination unit uses patented and unique 'multi magnet' technology to kill micro-organisms. When correctly sized to the fuel flow of the particular engine installation this unit kills 97% of the 'bugs' in a single pass.

The De Bug filter contains calculated magnetic fields produced by ceramic coated magnets located within the unit and this destroys the microorganisms as they flow through the filter. This unit is a one-time installation, it has no moving parts and no electrical power is required. No replacement filters are necessary and the only maintenance required is an occasional cleaning. Unlike the chemical biocides, the dead bacteria cells are destroyed in a way that does not result in a messy residue that can still clog filters.

The De Bug ™ 'fuel bug' filter comes is various sizes and has been used in all types of diesel powered applications both ashore and afloat. The smaller unit is capable of handling up to 35 gallons / 160 lit. per hour. Larger sizes of this unit can handle amounts ranging from 265 gph through to 5,000 gph, and remembering that a near 100 percent (97%) bug kill is claimed, then this is one of the most efficient pieces of equipment you could add to your boat. Do you need it? I do; after the experience of losing engine power in a rather embarrassing situation and all due to 'the bug'; my boat is now fitted with this device.

SPARE PARTS, TOOLS AND CONSTRUCTION MATERIALS

The field of spare parts alone covers a multitude of possible items that can be acquired and carried aboard your metal boat. Add some construction materials and

This builder, Ian Goodson of Brisbane, made a pattern of the inside of his keel and then made a plywood mold in which he cast lead for the section of keel on his ROBERTS 36 hull.

Lead ingots make good ballast if your pocket allows.

you can see that a large number of items could be assembled under this heading. Perhaps this is a good time to review those items that you have already decided to install and decide if you really need them. Now consider how likely they are to need spare parts, in order to remain in service.

One area where you will need to carry an adequate number of items is in your engine spare parts package. Filters; you must have at least two replacement sets for each filter installed on your boat. If you have more than one of a particular type of filter, then you need two spare filters for each one. Filters clog up at the most inopportune moment usually one set of spares is just not enough. Don't forget the spare oil filters, while not so often needed as fuel filters, they are required at regular intervals.

Hoses, cooling fan belts, alternator belts, impellers, the list goes on. Ask your engine supplier to suggest a complete list covering your expected requirements. Most manufacturers have recommended lists for 'local', 'coastal' and 'offshore' cruising. Look over these lists and choose the one most appropriate for your needs.

On the subject of marine engine 'manufacturers', the word manufacturer is misleading. Most marine engines are 'assembled' or 'marinised' from another manufacturers basic engine. Many of the filters, fan belts and other consumable spare parts are available at less cost when some other manufacturer supplies them. The engine manufacturers naturally discourage your from obtaining these outside sourced spares. You will need to decide if the purchase and use of these less expensive, 'unofficial' spare parts are in your interest.

WEIGHT EDITING

It is impossible for the designer to know how the builder keeps track of the materials used to build the boat. Only the builder knows what has been added to the basic construction, in addition to those materials and gear specified in the plans.

If you want your ballasting to be correct and as efficient as possible, keep accurate records and generally follow the designer's recommendations as closely as possible. It may be worth having the hull weighed before installing the ballast.

The crane that is used during the moving of the boat from the building location to the launching site can often undertake this weighing operation. Perhaps a small side trip to a weighbridge could achieve the desired result. With the minimum of planning, it should be possible to add the ballast just prior to launching the boat.

When you do install the ballast make sure that you install it by weight not by volume. Weigh each portion of the ballast as it is installed in the keel. This is a time consuming and thankless task, but you may be rewarded if you need to trim the boat, add tankage or otherwise change the ballast arrangements.

BALLAST

In a metal, sailboat or trawler yacht, the keel sides, bottom of keel and web floors all form part of the ballast. In some cases such as in ultra-shallow draft boats, the bottom plating may also be considered to contribute to the ballast. Back in the early seventies, we did not make this sufficiently clear and this caused some builders of our designs, to install more ballast that was intended. Fortunately in most, if not all cases, this did not materially harm the handling of the boat. Carrying too much ballast can detract from the performance.

No matter who designed your metal boat, make sure you are aware of the amount of ballast that has to be added in addition to that already created by the keel and supporting structure. Of course the above mainly applies to steel and copper-nickel hulls; aluminum hulls require the full amount of ballast quoted by the designer. In any case, during the construction stage, it is wise to only install between 70 and 80 percent of the total ballast required. The remainder can be added for trim ballast as and when required.

Home made lead melting device. Lead must be installed in bars and only consolidating amounts of lead melted into the keel in this manner.

Another point to remember is that some confusion may occur by the quoted displacement / ballast ratio. Total the amount of the 'naturally acquired' ballast and the added ballast before making any judgmental comparisons in this area.

Over the years many different materials have been used as ballast, but today the choice lies between lead, cast iron or scrap steel. Cast iron is now about the same price as lead and it is mostly used, as bolt on ballast consequently; it is less suitable for metal boats. The designer may have already made your choice of ballast, after taking the relative centre of gravity of the ballast into account, when figuring the stability of the vessel. Always consult the designer before making any changes to the amount, type and location of the ballast.

Some builders have found it convenient to install the ballast at an early stage. If you are building upright, then it may be a good idea to install the bulk of the ballast before the final bottom plate is installed. This means that you do not have to carry the ballast material up and over the sides of the hull. Some builders have constructed the keel separately and after setting this in position, have installed most of the ballast before even setting up the frames. All these factors should be taken into consideration, before you decide to build your hull upright or upside down.

LEAD BALLAST

Lead weighs 710 lb per cubic ft / 3,466 kg per cu M, and this combined with the low melting point of 621 Degrees F / 327 degrees C, makes lead the superior ballast material. If you are building on a tight budget then all of the advantages may be purely academic. The price for lead will vary from one dealer to another so it is worth shopping around. You may collect scrap lead from a variety of places including garages and tyre outlets where those small lead weights are used to balance the wheels on your car. It takes a great number of these small weights to make up a ton of lead, but this is only one possible source.

The lead may be installed in standard 'pigs' or melted and recast into shapes of a suitable size and weight and then installed into the keel. Melting lead can be a hazardous operation and utmost care should be taken when handling this material. Wear gloves and other protective clothing when handling lead.

When melting lead, always wear a protective-breathing mask. The ones used for avoiding paint fumes are not suitable and special respirators are available that will filter out the lead particles and

gasses given off during the melting process. Totally avoid the fumes given off by this material.

To melt lead you will need some form of vessel to hold the chunks of lead while heat is applied to turn it into molten form. The type, size and complexity of the 'melting pot' will depend on the amount of lead you plan to melt. When melting lead, less is better, so try and choose one of the installation methods that requires the least melting before the lead is installed in the keel. For example, install large chunks or 'pigs' laid into the keel and then use small amounts of molten lead poured over and around these larger pieces to solidify the whole mass. For large melting jobs, an old cast iron bath is ideal and used to be available from the wreckers, however these days many of these older items are prized as artefacts and are no longer available for other uses.

If you have to construct a purpose built melting pot, then it should be about 2 ft- 6 in / 762 mm in diameter or 2 ft / 610 mm square about 3 ft / 914 mm high and raised about 2ft-6 ins / 762 mm from the ground. Either use strong pipe legs or a similar very strong structure to support your melting pot. The melting pot will need to have at least 1/4" / 6 mm plate walls. Do not use oil drums or similar containers, they will be far too light for this purpose. At the bottom of your melting pot, you will need to install a tap or valve to allow the molten lead to be drawn off as required. A pouring bucket or ladle will be needed to transfer the lead to your mould or directly to the keel for pouring over the large solid pieces that you have already installed.

If you only require a relatively small amount of molten lead, then the melt and pour in place arrangement as shown in the photograph below may suit you better than a melting pot situated some way from the keel. As lead solidifies rather quickly and as you want to eliminate voids between your large pieces and the molten filler lead, make sure you install the lead in small enough amounts and in a sequence that will achieve the desired result. There should be no voids and using this method, the lead can be 'welded' together.

Many builders have made patterns of each keel area between the webs where ballast is to be installed. Heavy pine planking say 1 1/4 in / 35 mm thick can be used to build a mould for these blocks of ballast. Using a well-constructed melting pot and adequate ladling or pouring bucket, then pour and mould each section. A lifting eye or wire loop can be installed in the top of each lead block and the completed ballast

This ballast is tractor track pins set in resin putty and cost builder only the transport of the scrap. Many BRUCE ROBERTS designs call for scrap steel ballast.

section is then installed in the keel. The keel will still need to be lined to avoid the lead interacting with the steel, aluminum or copper-nickel.

Never melt the bulk of the lead directly into any keel; not even a steel one. The heat generated, as the lead cools will surely buckle the sides of the keel. The heat could ruin the shape as well as doing other damage to the structure of the keel. Lead can be cut with some difficulty; it tends to clog up the teeth of any saw. Some boat yards have been known to use chain saws to cut the lead; this seems to add one hazardous operation to another. An oxyacetylene torch can be used to burn off chunks of the material. You can weld angle or plate over the ballast so that in the event of a 'knock-down' you can be sure that it stays in place. Another method of securing the ballast is to cut holes in the web floors and allow the ballast to extend from one keel compartment to the next. There are many simple and ingenious ways to ensure that the ballast is effectively one unit and will stay in place under all conditions.

It is desirable to make some provision to separate the lead ballast from the interior of the keel plating. This applies to all metals. One method is to coat the inside of the keel with tar epoxy, but watch out for the fumes as you install any molten lead ballast. Another method is to line the inside of the keel with sheet zinc before installing the ballast. The zinc will melt as any

molten lead touches it and will float up the insides of the keel, giving the inner surfaces a coating and protecting it from any interaction with the lead. Bitumastic is another material that has been successfully used to line the steel keel before the lead ballast is installed.

BALLAST MIXES

It is possible to purchase ready mixed ballast, which is usually supplied in granule form. This ballast is very easy to install but because it has been 'processed' for your convenience, it is relatively expensive. A check of the classified advertisements in your local boating magazines should reveal the suppliers of this type of ballast.

SCRAP STEEL BALLAST

If you are installing scrap steel ballast, you should obtain the largest possible pieces of material that you can conveniently place between the webs in the keel of your boat. One material that is particularly suitable for installing in keels, are the pins that are used in the tracks of crawler tractors and other earth moving equipment. These track pins are usually about 12 in / 305 mm long by 2 to 3 in / 50 to 75 mm in diameter and have proven in the past to be ideal as ballast material. The pins may be set either on end or installed on their sides. You will need to insert small steel rods in between the round pins to achieve as solid a mass as is possible.

When using scrap steel ballast, it is most desirable that you obtain a ballast density of 350 pounds per cu ft / 1708 kg per cu M. This is a minimum figure and it may be useful to make a test 'brick' utilising the materials you have available and then weigh the brick to make certain it reaches the proper level of density. If you use scrap steel punchings, you may have a problem in reaching the desired density, so larger pieces of metal are preferred. Railway line combined with other steel materials may be suitable.

After the scrap steel ballast has been installed, and any small pieces of steel have been added to insure that the minimum voids occur, then it will be necessary to add some mixture so that the whole mass can be bonded together. You must ensure that air is excluded from the ballast mix so as to avoid corrosion problems with the ballast. If you have voids in the ballast, bilge water will find its way to the lowest point. This water can set up a corrosion process that may remain undetected, until serious damage is done to the ballast, or more importantly to the keel. It is important to eliminate all voids from the scrap steel ballast. Hot pitch or similar material can be poured over and into the ballast and it will effectively find its way into the same voids that would harbour bilge water. The pitch will seal off the fill and seal off the voids and prevent corrosion problems in the future. Tar epoxies or other suitable epoxy materials that have been thickened with suitable fillers, can be used in place of the hot pitch. This would give a superior, but more costly result.

WARNING

In the past, some builders have used cement (concrete) for bonding the lead or steel ballast into position. We have often warned against this practice and recently have been made aware of two examples where the cement caused the steel to rust out from the inside. In one case this caused the loss of the boat and in the other, the whole bottom plating had to be replaced. Under no circumstances use cement or concrete in your ballast mix.

After the ballast is installed (except the trim ballast) you may consider welding 'L' angle or other reinforcing across the top of the ballast mass. Some builders have plated over the ballast; the timing for this operation is difficult, as you need to have the trim ballast installed and by this stage you have all of the exterior paint work completed. The welding of the plate over the ballast will disturb you paint job. Careful planning is necessary, to overcome this and other scheduling problems.

When you have finally completed the installation of the primary and trim ballast, then you can seal off the top of the ballast using epoxy filler trowelled to a smooth finish. A thin plywood liner could be used to complete the finish of this area above the ballast, making an ideal storage compartment.

You will need to make provision for the flow of bilge water. In modern, well-maintained metal boats, the

This Centennial Spray 38 was built in Sweden in round bilge steel. Most Spray designs will accept scrap steel ballast thus considerably reducing the cost of the hull.

amount of bilge water will be small and mostly caused by preventable condensation.

SUMMARY - BALLAST

When considering the ballast material, your plans may give you a choice; shoal draft using lead ballast or deeper draft using the scrap steel option. You might want to consider that no matter which draft option you choose, lead would offer the best alternative. Although lead ballast is more expensive than steel, it can be installed in a smaller space, which in turn will leave more room for the stowage of stores and perhaps the installation of additional fuel and water tanks. As mentioned elsewhere, the storage of canned goods and other relatively heavy stores under the sole, is a very practical idea. The weight is located where it will provide some benefit as ballast. The stores are much less likely to be thrown about in rough weather, than similar stores located above the waterline.

Another reason to choose lead ballast is that it will definitely add to the resale value of your boat. It should be remembered that almost every boat is sold sooner or later. By installing lead ballast you are helping to protect your investment. It is a general rule, that every Pound/ Dollar you spend on materials and equipment is multiplied by a factor of 2, 3, or even 4 (depending on the item), when it comes time to sell the boat.

THE SUMP

You will need to arrange a sump or suitable collection point for any bilge water. This sump is usually under or nearly under the engine so that any spilt diesel fuel and other unwanted liquids can be pumped or sponged out. A hand operated bilge pump with a hose attached is useful in this area so that you can pump any contaminated water into a separate container for proper disposal ashore.

Pumping oily bilge fluids directly into the surrounding water, can in environmentally aware areas, cause you major problems. For instance in Florida a heavy fine can be the result of pumping even the smallest amounts of polluted water into the local canals. Any bilge pumps located in the sump or elsewhere should be fitted with a strainer. In the event of any large particles being present you need to ensure that they will not find their way into ,and totally block, the pump.

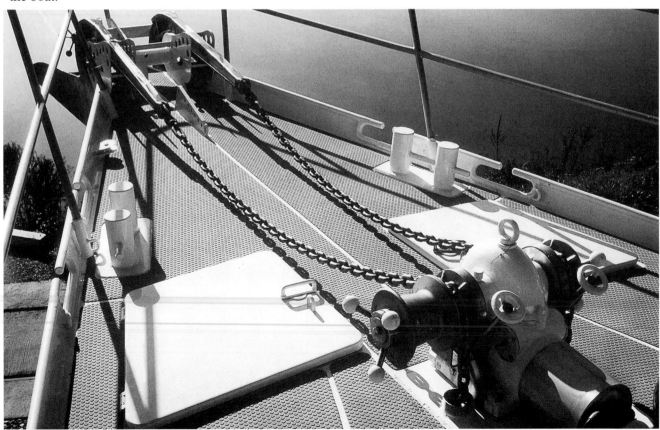

Need a break from the main project-make a few deck fittings like these made by Herbert Fritz.

Chapter 12
CORROSION PREVENTION

Galvanic behaviour of metals. Selective corrosion. Galvanic Corrosion. Crevice corrosion. Cathodic protection. Sacrificial anodes

You will find various references to this subject elsewhere throughout this text; however I feel that it is important to give the subject a through coverage under its own heading. In seawater, corrosion is electrochemical in nature and it is important that every boatbuilder, who works with metal, is familiar with the cause and effects of the more common types of corrosion. You should know how to avoid any problems in this area.

Corrosion is not a problem confined to metal boats or a recent phenomenon; it has been around for centuries. Corrosion can cause damage and even the loss of every type of vessel including those built of timber, fiberglass and Ferro-cement. The result of corrosion is why keels and rudders fall off, why stainless tangs break and why rigging fails. It is often the cause of fastening disease, an age-old problem with wooden boats. The result of corrosion can be severe to the point of failure for rudderstocks, through hull fittings, propellers and seacocks. There have been instances where the seacocks have been caught in the final stages of disintegration just before they crumbled away and let in the outside water. This is a serious subject and worthy of your attention.

When a metal is immersed in seawater it will achieve a certain electrochemical potential. This potential will differ from metal to metal. Different potentials can also occur locally from area to area in a single metal surface for example, at or near a weld area, different types of phases within a metal structure or areas exposed to different levels of oxygen. It is the potential difference between metals when in contact with each other, or areas on the same metal surface, which under particular circumstances can act as a driving force for the corrosion to occur.

GALVANIC CORROSION
When two different metals are immersed in such a good electrolyte as seawater and connected through a metal path, current will flow causing corrosion of the metal with the lower potential. The metal that corrodes is called the anode and the metal, which has the higher potential, is nobler and is, called the cathode. When this type of corrosion occurs it is termed galvanic or bimetallic corrosion.

Although the less noble metal in the galvanic couple will corrode at a higher rate than it might otherwise have done, the more noble metal will corrode at a lower rate. This can be used to advantage and is the basis for cathodic protection.

THE GALVANIC SERIES OF METALS IN SEAWATER

The position of the metals on the scale may vary slightly depending on the exact composition of the particular metal.

Cathodic or noble
Platinum
Gold
Graphite
Silver
Titanium
Hastelloy C
Stainless steel (304 and 316 passive)
Nickel
MONEL (400, K-500)
Silicon bronze
Copper
Red brass
Aluminum bronze
Admiralty brass
Yellow brass
Nickel (active)
Naval brass
Manganese bronze
Muntz metal
Tin
Lead
Stainless steel (types 304 and 316 active)
50/50 lead tin solder
Cast iron
Wrought iron
Mild steel Cadmium
Aluminum alloys
Galvanised steel
Zinc
Magnesium
Anodic

THE GALVANIC SERIES IN SEA WATER HELPS PREDICT WHICH ALLOY IN A METALLIC COUPLE IS MORE LIKELY TO CORRODE.

The metals and alloys lower in the series have lower potentials and will be corroded by those higher in the list. The degree of corrosion which occurs depend not only on how far apart they are in the galvanic series and thus the size of the potential difference, but also on the relative surface areas of the cathode and anode.

Alloys close together in the series, e.g. copper and bronze, will be less prone to galvanic corrosion than those farther apart, e.g. copper and steel. Corrosion can be expected to be greater if the exposed surface area of the more noble metal is large compared to that of the less noble alloy. An example of this is that steel bolts in a MONEL structure will corrode very quickly and for MONEL bolts in a steel structure, the corrosion per unit area could be so small as to be insignificant.

There are various ways of controlling galvanic corrosion. Choosing metals close together within the galvanic series can be a good way of reducing galvanic problems. If and where possible you should use only similar metals throughout the vessel e.g. steel in your steel hull as well as the other fittings being made of steel. In this way no galvanic current will flow.

It is not always possible or desirable to use one metal throughout the hull, deck and superstructure. Galvanic current can be prevented from flowing by electrically insulating the two metals from each other. Insulating washers and sleeves can be used on bolts; non-conductive gaskets can be used on flanges.

Paint coatings can also be used as protection against galvanic corrosion. In this case, the temptation is just to coat the alloy in the metal couple, which is likely to corrode. As coatings may have imperfections or 'holidays' in them or can be damaged, the current can pass through in very localised areas. The large area of the un-coated cathode produces high rates of corrosion in the small areas exposed through the coating. Always apply coatings to the more noble metal or to both metals rather than to the anode alone.

Non metal fittings are another possibility, however some classification authorities are reluctant to accept this solution; they suggest that fire and degradation from sunlight could be a problem. I have seen examples of the latter, where plastic (presumably nylon) skin fittings were wiped off when the vessel rubbed against a piling. This vessel had spent a considerable time in a sunny clime and the sun had effected the fitting to such and extent, that is had very little strength. There are some plastic seacocks and skin fittings and the like, which are claimed to be unaffected by the sun and ultraviolet rays. You should check these out for yourself, before purchasing these items and fitting them to your boat.

The best overall protection is to stay with one metal, especially in the hull where you have a good chance of maintaining all steel, all aluminium or all copper nickel structure. In practice, the solution is to use a combination of the above methods to minimise chances of galvanic corrosion.

In the interior of your metal boat, you can choose the closest compatible metal to attach the interior joinery to the metal hull. There is no point in using regular steel screw, as they would soon rust in the marine environment. You can use stainless steel screws or MONEL screws and bolts (expensive) or you can plan your interior to avoid, as much contact of dissimilar metals as is possible.

Galvanic corrosion can occur on the same metal. For example type 303 free machining grades of stainless steel suffer extraordinarily severe corrosion in salt water. These metals contain high densities of manganese sulphide or selenium inclusions, which create many, built in metal to inclusion galvanic cells. These grades should never be used in salt water.

SELECTIVE CORROSION

Selective corrosion can occur in certain alloys when one component of the alloy make-up corrodes away more quickly than another. I have seen this with brass seacocks, which contain copper and zinc. The zinc dissolves in seawater and leaves behind a weak and spongy mass of copper. This is called dezincification.

Cast iron also can exhibit a form of selective corrosion called graphitisation. The matrix of cast iron contains flakes or spheroids of graphite. The iron can corrode leaving a weak, brittle network shell of graphite. The external appearance remains unchanged, which can make the condition difficult to detect. A further consequence is that the graphite shell is galvanically very noble and can then cause galvanic corrosion of adjacent parts.

Stainless steels can undergo selective attack in heat affected weld zones. This is completely avoided if welding is carried out by using carbon L grades or titanium or niobium stabilised grades of stainless steel.

CREVICE CORROSION

In seawater stainless steels have very low general corrosion rates. If they corrode, it is normally in localised areas under hard fouling or tight man made crevices such as gaskets. Oxygen in the crevice is used up forming an oxygen concentration cell with the oxygenated conditions outside the crevice. This can lead to corrosion reactions within the crevice. The 316 alloy has better resistance to this than the 302 or 304 alloys. Cathodic protection by anodes or galvanic contact with other less noble alloys can also help.

STRAY CURRENT CORROSION

This is another type of corrosion that can be prevented. Unlike galvanic corrosion, which is caused by two different metals in water, stray current corrosion results from an outside electrical source, such as direct current from the ship itself or alternating current from a shore electrical hook-up. You will find additional information on the cause and remedy for this situation elsewhere including Del Kahan's essay in appendix 3.

In most cases the villain comes from one of these sources; a current leak in the wiring from frayed or broken wires; improper or crossed grounds, electrical leaks from loose, broken or poorly insulated terminal connections, or bad marina shore-power equipment.

When connected to shore-power, you should always use heavy-duty extension cords. The length should be only sufficient to transfer the current from the power source to your boat. Power tools often generate stray currents and on board radios can also cause problems in this area.

Unfortunately, while galvanic corrosion occurs relatively slowly and over a period of time, electrolytic corrosion can occur rapidly, depending on the strength of the stray current. The stray current can be a mere trickle of DC volts from an area that is damp, to a blue sparking short circuit on board from a marina's 220/110-volt system. Stray current can also give shocks to the crew and can cause fire or explosion.

Warning signs can range from blue sparks and a crackling noise from a shorted out power cable, to heavy static on radio speakers because of voltage drop. Electrical equipment that does not function up to expectations, can be suspect to the effects of stray current flow which ends up somewhere other than where you want it. Voltage can be traced by use of a multi-meter. Metal damage resulting in the grounded area from electrical leakage shows up as massive rusting and scaling on steel parts, abnormal brightness on bronze and the total disintegration of aluminum parts.

Stray currents, like galvanic corrosion, can be eliminated when electronic devices are installed on the vessel. A custom builder should take the approach that both types of corrosion are predictable problems which not only can be 'built in', but can equally be built out of the boat and totally eliminated.

Using high quality wiring, fittings and switches designed for the marine environment by a reputable marine manufacturer, should form part of your self insurance against most of the potential problems described in this chapter and elsewhere. Shore power needs particular attention since this has the greatest potential for danger. You will want to use heavy-duty cord, which is moisture resistant and specifically made for marine use. Use watertight marine connectors at both ends and if possible, use a 'moulded cord set' which is the last word in connecting shore power to your vessel.

A ground fault circuit interrupter should be installed in the vessel's panel or fuse box. This will help prevent electrical accidents, especially those that result from current flowing from a hot wire to a ground. It will also reduce the chance of bodily harm from electric shock in the marine or damp environment.

CATHODIC PROTECTION

Many people are under the false impression, that boats that cruise exclusively in freshwater do not require any special form of cathodic protection. On boats, the most commonly used method is to install anodes to various underwater locations on the outside of the hull.

M.G. Duff the UK experts on this subject have produced two excellent pamphlets. One for boats operating mostly in salt water and the other covering the fresh water environment. These publications explain the special requirements needed to protect your stern gear, rudder and associated underwater equipment from the ravages of mysterious gremlins that can damage your propeller, prop shaft, rudder gear and even the hull itself.

Most metals are extracted from ores by various processes and as such they are prone to return to their natural state under the action of oxygen and water. We have all seen unprotected metals such as steel and aluminum and steel react in this way.

Cathodic protection is a means of transferring the corrosion electrochemically to another less noble metal. The concept is not new. For instance Samuel Pepys back in 1681 noted in one of his dairies, that the removal of lead sheathing on ships of the line, reduced the corrosion on the iron rudderposts. Over 100 years ago, experiments were conducted in this field and proved that when two metals were electrically connected and immersed in water, the resulting corrosion of one of the metals is speeded up, while the other receives some level of protection. Once we understand this concept, then the remedy to controlling hull corrosion and protecting immersed fittings becomes relatively simple. Sacrificial anodes of reactive metals can be applied to a metal and protect it.

A word of caution, cathodic protection of a copper nickel hull is unnecessary as the alloy already has good corrosion resistance to seawater. The use of cathodic protection will also reduce the effectiveness of the antifouling of the material. Hull attachments below the water line should if possible be copper nickel, or if not, the fillings should be made of a slightly more noble metal.

SACRIFICIAL ANODES

Sacrificial anodes are usually made of magnesium, aluminium or zinc. For metal boats, anodes are either zinc or magnesium and come in various shapes and sizes. These protective devices are relatively inexpensive and a complete spare set should be carried at all times. An unexpected haul-out could reveal the necessity to replace the anodes, so a set should always on hand. For freshwater, use magnesium anodes and for saltwater or heavily polluted water, use zinc anodes.

If you are building a new boat, the designer will be able to recommend the type, number and placement for the anodes and they can be either welded or bolted to the hull. We recommend the bolt-on method, as the replacement of this type will not cause the paintwork to be damaged by additional welding. Bolting on replacement anodes, is a much simpler process than removing and replacing old spent ones, that have been welded in place.

When you are setting up your anodes for the first time, simply use the anode attachment straps and bolt holes, to mark the position of the threaded studs to be welded to the hull skin. The fact that you are going to reuse the same locations and bolting arrangements, is another good reason to have more than one spare set to hand. On one occasion I was required to redrill several anode straps to match existing studs when unable to purchase the same brand with matching holes. The studs and surrounding area should be painted after the studs are installed; under no circumstances paint the anodes as this stops them from working.

The position and placement of the anodes depends on the size and displacement of your boat. The anode manufacturers have special charts showing the relationship between the size of boat and the number of anodes required and where they should be located. It is common practice to have one anode on each side of metal boats up to 25 ft / 7.62 M, these are placed below the waterline at about 25 percent forward of the stern. Boats up to 35 ft / 10.67 M require 4 anodes, 2 per side, one at 25 percent and one at 50 percent forward of the transom. Boats up to 44 ft / 13.41 M can use the same amount and placement but larger anodes can be used. For larger boats, it is normal to have three anodes per side.

In addition to the above placement of anodes, each boat should have a small anode placed around the shaft, another on the rudder and a third in the area of the bow thruster if fitted. When placing the anodes, either makes sure that they are adjacent to the seacocks if these are made of dissimilar metal or fit additional anodes as required. For a foil shape rudder, the anode can be fitted using the threaded stud method at about 25 percent below the waterline. On a powerboat single plate rudder, the anode can be through bolted in position, using a bolt of the same metal as is used to construct the rudder.

If you fit a bronze seacock on a steel or aluminium hull, then make sure you insert a heavier metal section in the hull skin in the area where the metal stand-pipe is located. It is recommended that the standpipe be carried inboard until the bronze seacock can be fitted clear of the waterline. The seacock will be isolated from the standpipe by liberal bedding compound installed between these two items.

Please note that the installation of the anodes for a metal hull differs from that of a wooden or fiberglass boat, in that the metal hull and metal fittings inside conduct galvanic current to the anodes. You do not have to run wires from the engine, engine shaft or other similar items to the anodes. The reason is because the engine and other fittings are already grounded to the metal hull and carry the galvanic current to the anodes.

If you keep the hull of your steel or aluminium boat well painted, especially the area below the waterline, then this alone will contribute to your maintenance of the boat and reduce the demand on the anodes. Anodes will need replacing before they are totally used up; deterioration of the anodes shows that they are working. As mentioned elsewhere the underwater sections of a copper-nickel hull will not need any painting or anti-fouling protection.

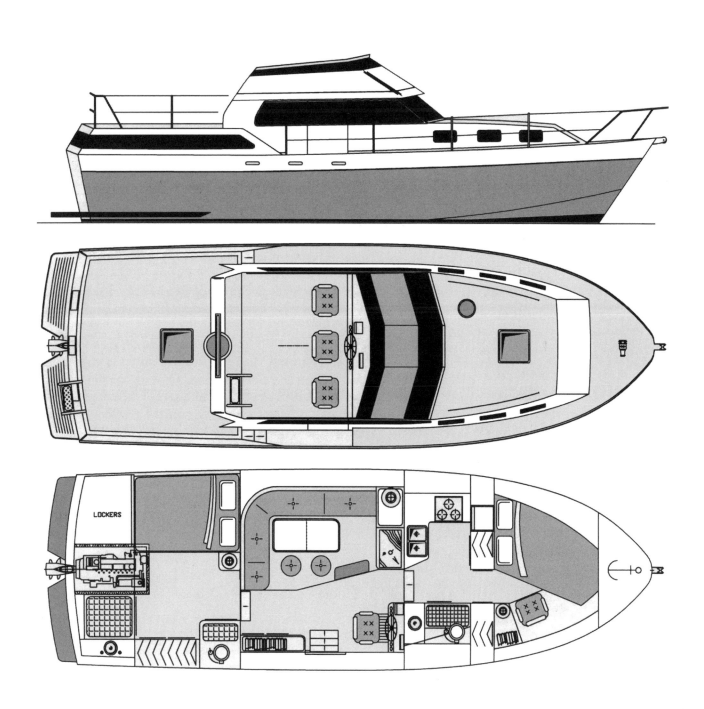

Powerboats like this Waverunner 342 will require special attention when considering anodes. Most boats of this type have a considerable amount of electrical equipment, which can give rise to all types of corrosion problems if not correctly wired and protected.

Chapter 13
METAL BOAT INTERIORS

Insulation. Lining materials. Cabin soles. Building bunks. Head and shower compartments. The galley. The galley stove (gas, diesel, alcohol, paraffin). Heating. Stowage for food and stores. Hot and pressure water. Water tankage. Comfortable seating; measurements and suggestions. Chart table. Sail stowage. Refrigerators and ice boxes. Ventilation.

FOAM INSULATION

Now is the time to consider how you are going to select and install the insulation that is so important in any boat. Even fiberglass boats need insulation as they 'sweat' in the same manner as other boats, including metal ones.

If you are planning spray-in-place foam insulation then this should be installed after the deck and superstructure are in place, but before you start work in the interior joinery. An alternative is to install 'bats' or sheets of foam glued or held in place by the

Sprayed in place foam offers the best insulation and has other benefits in that it can protect the interior the metal. Install in the hull (above the sole line) and in the deck and superstructure areas as well. Make sure you have adequate thickness and that you get what you pay for, see text.

'ceiling'. See below in the section covering lining materials for details on installing the ceiling planking.

My choice for foam insulation is the type of urethane foam that has fire resistant and non-toxic properties and is sprayed in place. In steel boats, the interior of the hull should be first grit blasted and primed, or built of pre-primed materials. The foam will now be sprayed to a depth between 1" / 25 mm and 2" / 50 mm; the thicker the better. It is a good idea to cover the stringers and they will most likely be about 1 1/4" to 2" / 30 to 50 mm deep. The foam will form a skin and should be of a type that is forms a skin on the surface that is impervious to water. Make sure you choose a variety that in the event of fire does not give off toxic fumes. You will also need to make sure that the foam is of the self-extinguishing type.

The supplier of the foam usually has all the equipment needed to install the material and charges by the cubic foot / cubic metre or by the pound / kilo. Make sure you obtain an estimate of the cost for the boat to be sprayed to the desired thickness. Be very careful that you get what you pay for. Measure the depth of the foam and check that it is reasonably constant thickness throughout the boat.

LINING MATERIALS

There are a variety of materials that can be used to line the interior of your metal boat. This is one area where the wrong choice can damn your boat and scream 'AMATEUR'. If you want to achieve a decent resale value, then you had best get it right.

If you are building a 'traditional' style metal boat such as a Spray replica, or if you like the warmth of an all timber interior, then ceiling planking can go a long way to achieving the right effect. Ceiling material should be 1" x 5/8" / 25 x 15 mm light coloured fine grained timber that is rounded or arrased (bevelled) on the outer edges. Install the planks longitudinally and space them at about 1/4" / 6 mm apart. You can plank only those areas that are visible after the joinery is complete, or you can plank the entire accommodation area and use the material as the lining for the various lockers. If you take this latter course then you had better reduce the spacing to say 1/8" / 3 mm so you will not lose small items though the gaps in the planking. If you only use ceiling where there are no lockers then you may have a problem getting a fair curve where there is no frame to attach one end of the planks.

The lockers can be lined with plywood; do not forget to put finger holes in the lining. Leave the bottoms loose with a neat fit but not tight; you will often want to get under and behind the locker to have access to cables and the inner hull.

Lining the entire interior of the accommodation with light plain painted or veneered fancy plywood can produce a pleasing result when combined with solid timber trim. Too much varnish or areas of paintwork that are too large can spoil the interior appearance so you will need a balance between the two finishes. If you are unsure of this balance, then use as much varnish as you like, you can always paint over it at a later stage. The reverse is obviously not so simple.

For deck-heads and the interiors of the cabin top you can use plywood that is painted. Use some timber trim to relieve and break up the area. Timber planks similar to that used for 'ceiling' but say 2 in / 50 mm wide can also be used to line deck heads and cabin tops. There are several alternative vinyl type products that have a light foam backing and are ideally suited to deck-heads and certain bulkheads. Be careful using this material for bulkheads in the main living areas as it can cheapen the look of your interior. The foam-backed vinyl can look acceptable in some parts of sleeping cabins. The use of vinyl is fine for deck head and cabin top linings in any part of the boat. Use timber trim as needed to break up any large expanses of lining material.

In the past some builders both professional and amateur, used carpet and carpet like materials for lining the hull and deck heads. These materials are inexpensive and easy to install but look so cheap! We do not recommend this route, besides the interior would look 'dated'.

CABIN SOLES

The sole framing will need considerable planning. Usually L angle is used for the main framing and some timber can be used where it would be attached to vertical plywood surfaces such as bunk fronts and dinette ends. The size of the angle will vary depending on the span and spacing of the framing. Your plans should give you a guide. As the builder sometimes changes accommodation layouts, you may have to use your judgement. There are few things more annoying than a springy or squeaky sole.

Plywood is universally accepted as the material to use for this area. The thickness will vary between 1/2" / 12 mm and 3/4" / 20 mm, depending on the spacing of the under sole framing. Usually 5/8" / 15 mm is sufficient and the thickness can be less if you plan add teak or other timber surface. This is such an important area that you should try a sample area, before deciding on an overall thickness. A spongy sole is most undesirable, but you will not want to add excessive or unnecessary weight.

While you are still constructing the interior, you should only fit and lay the plywood in position, do not screw it down until the all of the joinery work is completed. It is advisable to arrange the sole so you can remove all parts of it including those areas that form the bottom of lockers and closets. This may mean additional under-sole framing to provide a base at the edge of the particular area of the sole. Under no account 'build in' areas of the sole so they are impossible to remove. The plywood can be screwed down using self-tapping stainless steel screws.

Make sure you have carefully planned hatches to those areas of the sole, which will need frequent or even regular infrequent access. The hatches should be laid out in an orderly manner and have aluminum or similar trim around the edges and be provided with flush 'ring-pulls'. Hatches in unseen areas such as inside lockers may have finger holes in lieu of more expensive hardware. Where carpet is installed, aluminum edge trim is an important feature around the sole hatches.

Carpet covered soles are fine in most powerboats and also in well-maintained and dry sailboats. If your cruising habits mean that you will be bringing a considerable amount of water into the cabin, then carpet is not a sensible option. I personally like carpet, it offers a good footing under most conditions, is warm and attractive and considering the small area of a boat interior, it can be replaced at very little cost.

If you must have a 'teak and holly' sole then do not finish it to a high gloss, rather use a mat finish that will give you some chance of remaining upright in adverse conditions. A slippery surface can be deadly in anything of a seaway.

BUILDING BUNKS

Your first consideration will be how many permanent berths to build into your interior. Less is better! My idea of the perfect number of berths is a spacious double for use in port and in suitable weather. Two single berths suitable for watch keeping and for use in adverse weather conditions plus additional single berths for the permanent crew. The number of berths should not exceed four plus those required for the permanent crew. Boats under say 38 ft / 11.60 M should not have more than one double and two single berths otherwise too much of the interior space is used up in this manner.

All boats are a compromise; you may have to be creative to provide the necessary sleeping accommodation, without turning the boat into one large dormitory. Avoid berths that are too narrow, singles should be a minimum of 2 ft / 610 mm wide and preferably just a few inches / centimetres wider. Doubles should not bear that title unless they have a minimum width of 4 ft / 1.22 M and preferably wider. You will find 4 ft 6 in / 1.37 M is ideal and up to 5 ft / 1.52 M width is fine in a larger boat. For designers and builders, achieving adequate berth length, is always a problem. It is a fact that as each generation becomes taller, they require longer berths to get a good nights sleep. In new designs we use 6 ft 6 in / 1.98 M, as a reasonable length. It is hard to include longer berths than this, without encroaching into other areas of the accommodation.

Berths can be framed up in 2" x 1 1/2" / 50 x 30 mm timber or 2" x 1" x 1/4" L angle. Depending on which metal you use to build your hull, framing in the same material may give satisfactory results. In steel boats and in the interests of saving weight, you may prefer to use timber framing throughout the interior. Plywood of 5/8" / 15 mm thickness will be adequate for all berths and if you have adequate framing then 1/2" / 12 mm may be sufficient. Berths should have hatches in the top to allow access for stowage and inspection of the boxed in areas of the hull. The plywood tops of the berth should also have a few 1 in / 25 mm diameter holes bored at random to allow the air to circulate in the area under the mattress.

Face the berths with a timber board of around 6 in x 1 in / 150 x 25 mm and round off the top and bottom of this face plank to remove any sharp corners. This facing will hold the mattress in position and give a finished look to the berth.

The mattresses should be of good quality foam, between 4 in and 6 in / 100 to 150 mm in thickness and covered with a light cotton or other suitable fabric. Hooray for the Duvet! Duvets make the best bedding arrangement; they are easy to make up, especially where a berth does not have access from all sides. A fitted under-sheet combined with a duvet that is equipped with a slip-on cover makes for perfect

sleeping. This arrangement also provides easy making up in the morning. Duvets, when they are used on settee berths, have the additional advantage of being easy to stow.

HEAD AND SHOWER COMPARTMENTS

If space permits, a separate shower compartment is very desirable, especially on any boat intended to be used as a live-aboard. The shower can be totally separate with its own entrance, or simply a shower stall entered through the main head. On boats where the regular crew is four, I would prefer two medium sized heads and one separate shower compartment. Choices in this area are a personal matter so you should discuss the options with your partner and those family members, who will be crewing regularly on the boat.

The floor of the shower/head can be formed from fiberglass and laminated as a one-piece unit. Do not forget to include a non-skid surface. The actual shower pan can be slightly lowered and fitted with teak slats. This arrangement may allow a wider sole, even if some areas include a slight slope. Separate shower stalls can have a tiled sole, a nice touch if your boat can accommodate the additional weight. The walls or bulkheads in the shower/head area should all be lined with a plastic finish such as Laminex (tm) or Formica (tm). The entire floor area as well as the bulkheads and cabinets, should be designed for easy cleaning.

If you are building or own a small or minimalastic boat, then you may be happy with a 'shower bag'. These plastic bag devices are wonderfully efficient. Provided you have a reasonable amount of sunshine each day, one bag can provide hot showers for two. Shower bags are great water savers and recommended on vessels where replenishment of water tanks is infrequent. Shower bags can be a great back up device and even if used only infrequently, they will pay handsomely for the small amount of stowage space they require.

Drainage for the shower can take many forms. In our sailboat the 28 ft / 8.53 M steel Spray K*I*S*S, the builder had fitted a fiberglass shower tray in the head and drained this into the main sump in the keel. The sump was emptied by way of a manual bilge pump located in the cockpit. This pump also served as the emergency bilge pump. This arrangement was fine except that you had to pump out the water soon after your shower, otherwise the sump would generate sufficient gas to set off the alarm intended to service the gas stove rather than the shower sump. A better arrangement would have been to have a separate 'grey water' tank to temporally store the shower water. In our present boat we have a plastic sump about 1ft / 305 mm square, fitted with a lid and an automatic Rule shower/bilge pump. The 800 gallon / 3,028 Litre per hour unit, is the same size as those of smaller capacity and this unit provides a backup to the regular bilge pumping arrangements. Shower pumps need regular cleaning, usually about once every week; more often if the shower is used by more than two persons.

Manual or vacuum toilets are a must. The electric varieties, while they do reduce the solids to a fine mist, are incredibly noisy. Unless you can find a quiet version do not consider these devices. To those traditionalists who wonder what is this fellow doing talking about electric toilets; please remember that not all metal boats are built as basic cruisers; even some of the smaller variety, are built as finely fitted yachts. The 'Lavac' toilet is one of several proven units and is available as a manual, (recommended) or more recently as an electric unit (unknown quantity). Make sure, especially in a sailboat, that the plumbing for your toilet is such that it can not back siphon and sink the ship.

You should fit a reasonably sized hand basin. If fresh water is at a premium then the smaller variety saves water. About 9 in / 228 mm diameter is the smallest that can be called a basin. On smaller boats and boats with medium sized head/shower combinations, a convenient arrangement is to have a water saving type shower rose, serve as both the tap for the basin and as a shower head. The flexible supply hose leads through the counter top and self stows under the basin. The rose is drawn out when required as a shower. When using this system, and if hot water is available then a two-tap mixer can serve both shower and basin. On all boats the basin or sink should have a shut off valve or seacock fitted and its location should be familiar to all crewmembers. This advice applies to all inlets, outlets and seacocks.

THE GALLEY

This is an important area of your boat and if you want to keep the cook happy, then you had better get it right! In my books 'Choosing For Cruising' and 'Choosing a Cruising Powerboat' (see appendix 1), I have covered the subject of designing a galley in considerable detail. These books have much more information on all aspects of design than space allows here.

You can arrange the galley benches to suit the available space. It has been found that a 'U' or 'L' shaped arrangement usually works the best. In a sailboat, the stove is best placed outboard, facing inboard. For easiest drainage the sink on a sailboat should be as close to the centre line as practical. Galley benches can be built from 3/4" / 20 mm plywood and covered with Formica, Laminex or other laminated plastic. If weight saving is not critical then tiled bench tops add a nice touch to any galley. Make sure that you round off any corners otherwise the cook will soon be covered in bruises.

Framing for the galley can be 2 in x 1 1/2" timber. The framework will generally be arranged to accommodate the size doors and drawers that are available from the available standard sizes. Unless you are fitting out a Dutch barge or other vessel that is mainly intended for use in inland waters, you are not advised to install the standard kitchen units that are available at the local DIY store or lumber yard.

There are many suppliers of ready-made teak and mahogany door and drawer fronts that you can incorporate into your galley and elsewhere. These items may be more expensive than those you construct yourself, but unless you can produce fine cabinet and joinery work you are advised to at least investigate this option. Resale value of your boat will be considerably affected by the quality of the interior finish of your vessel. Three-ply sliding galley doors with finger holes as openers may be inexpensive and easy to construct but they will add little to the resale value of your boat.

THE GALLEY STOVE

Generally known in the UK as a 'Cooker' and elsewhere as a 'Stove' this appliance will get considerable use in your boat. First you must decide which fuel you will use. The choices include bottled petroleum gas, bottled natural gas (only available in certain areas), diesel fuel oil, alcohol or paraffin (kerosene). This is another subject covered elsewhere in considerable detail, see appendix 1, and we only have space here, to suggest some of the questions and a few of the answers. In time past galley stoves were always 'gimballed' and today most, when installed in sailboats, are still arranged in that manner. Powerboats and stiff sailboats like the Spray types may not require gimballed stoves. Discuss this option with the manufacturer of your chosen appliance.

Today, many if not most, new sail and powerboats are fitted with bottled gas that is commonly known as LPG (liquefied petroleum gas). This gas is available in two main types called, butane and propane. The two types are similar in usage, and each has its advocates. If you choose gas, then you will probably choose the one that is more readily available in your area. Most appliances will burn either type; some may need minor adjustments to the burners to get the best results. If you choose gas as a cooking and/or heating fuel, you must have a certified technician install the system. Also check it over on a regular basis. LPG is a wonderful aid on any boat, but it is heavier than air and can lie in the bilge. Even a small amount of stray of gas, when ignited in the confines of a boat, can cause a catastrophic explosion. You must locate the bottles in their own self-draining locker; fortunately this is easily arranged in most metal boats. Usually two bottles are carried and thus ensuring continuity of supply, when one bottle runs out you switch to the next and refill the other at the first available opportunity. We have had gas in our own boats and I have taken my own advice regarding installation and servicing of the installation and the individual appliances. If you have gas aboard, then a reliable gas detector with one or more sensors must be installed. One sensor is required for each gas appliance that you have aboard. If your gas appliances are grouped in one area then a sensor may be arranged to suit the group.

Diesel galley stoves can be arranged to supply hot water as well as the normal cooking functions, see text.

Paraffin or kerosene stoves, once the mainstay of any galley, have largely given way to LPG gas. If you can stand the smell (although some fuels are now supposedly odour free) and you don't mind the fiddly lighting procedure, then you may find this an ideal fuel for the galley stove. Galley stoves fired with diesel fuel would seem the obvious alternative. Diesel fuel does work well in a properly set up appliance. The drawback is that it takes these stoves some time to reach operating temperature. Perhaps diesel fuel stoves are more suited for use in colder climates. To be practical, you should be able to leave the stove on low heat between meal times.

STOWAGE FOR FOOD AND STORES

This is another area where the person who will actually be working in the galley, should be consulted at the planning stage. The storage lockers or galley cupboards should be arranged to make best use of the available space. The plates, mugs and eating utensils, should be always to hand. Regularly used food such as condiments that do not need refrigeration, should be all is more or less at eye level. Pots and pans will normally be stored in lower cupboards and cleaning and dish washing fluids may be under the sink or in nearby lockers. If you have steps nearby, these make excellent stowage areas when combined with hinged tops. If you lay out your galley in a similar manner to a regular house kitchen, taking into account the obvious space restrictions and with the necessary changes to suit the marine environment, then you will go a long way towards keeping the cook happy.

Under sole stowage for canned goods and other non-perishable foods is a great idea. Try to arrange these lockers, so that the cook is able to access them without having to disrupt the area around the galley. Properly fitted hatches in the sole and 'drop in' plastic bins are most useful. Most general foodstuffs except items that need refrigerating can be stored in these under-sole lockers. All hatches in the sole should be equipped with ring-pulls or finger holes.

Lockers in the galley, and elsewhere, will need to be ventilated. Louvered doors or doors with built in vents or other arrangement will be required to allow air to circulate freely in these areas. You will need a 'trash bin' locker so this can often be arranged on the end of one of the lower galley benches. The bin can be hinged at the bottom and designed to accept a standard medium size garbage bag. Most cruising folks and live-aboards use supermarket sacks as garbage or trash bin liners.

REFRIGERATION

This is another subject too complex to be covered in detail in this text, however there are a few comments that should be made at this time. Firstly avoid most ready built refrigerators that can only be powered by 12 volt DC power; they can consume large quantities of your valuable battery storage capacity. In powerboats you can use gas refrigeration and this is generally very efficient. It does generate a considerable amount of heat, so make sure it is properly ventilated. For more information on this important and complex subject, please see recommended reading in appendix 1.

ICE BOXES

These can useful but need to be very well insulated to be of any value. An 'ice box' that can be used to take one of the freezer conversion kits, is most practical. A freezer compressor that is powered by a take off from the main engine can be a good alternative in a cruising or live-aboard vessels.

This wood burning stove was custom built for Dr Keith and Judy Wolfenbarger and fitted to their steel Roberts 53.

HEATING THE CABIN

For heating the cabin the diesel-fuelled heater has no peer; a drip feed version is ideal for installation in any boat. One per cabin, if you have a large cruiser. These heaters are trouble free and throw out great quantities of heat for a miserly usage of diesel fuel. Dickinson (Canada and USA) and Taylor (UK) are two popular makes but there are several others available in all parts of the world. All fuel-consuming appliances require good ventilation, so keep this in mind when installing heaters and similar items.

Diesel powered; forced air heating can be a troublesome partner aboard any boat. The Eberspacher or similar units need lots of TLC to keep to them operating. This type of forced air heating with multiple outlets, is a great convenience but it can be difficult to maintain.

WATER TANKAGE

This is another area where modern technology has made inroads into our cruising lifestyle. The 'Watermaker' has removed the need forever larger water tanks to be carried on the modern sail or power cruiser. Powerboats and sailboats that are used to cruise locally need to carry only about 3 to 5 days supplies of fresh water. Watering points are now available in all marinas and other havens, so replenishing supplies presents few problems.

Those with long distance cruising in mind will need to give this subject considerable thought. The choices lay between modest tankage and severe economy, large capacity tanks and a better lifestyle. The best solution may be a combination of reasonable tankage, backed up by replenishment techniques including rain collection and using a watermaker.

Although it is possible to build water tanks from mild steel, they do need to be coated inside and we do not recommend this combination for storing fresh water. Aluminum tanks can have various problems as outlined elsewhere, so this leaves stainless steel, sheet or moulded plastic, fiberglass or inflatable tanks.

My choice is either stainless steel or moulded plastic with fiberglass as a last alternative. My experience is that tanks that are fabricated from sheet plastic have not proven successful. All tanks should be fabricated outside the hull and tested against leaks with 3 psi. Take care when testing tanks, I once heard of a builder simply connecting a compressor to the steel tanks; goodness knows how he managed to avoid an almighty explosion. Tanks only need modest air pressure to reveal any leaks. Vetus Den Ouden,

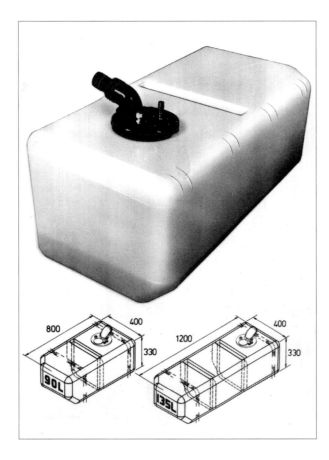

Vetus make a range of molded plastic water tanks in a range of shapes and sizes.

manufacture a fine line of plastic tanks in several shapes and many sizes; these are available with matching hardware and could well suit all but the largest metal boats, see appendix 4.

PUMPS - FRESH WATER

The type of pump you select to dispense your fresh water, will have a great influence on the amount of tankage required. Serious offshore sailboats are usually fitted with manual hand or foot operated pumps. These manual pumps may be in addition to a more convenient electric pumping system. The latter can be turned off during long passages; the manual pumps are then used by all. If your boat is fitted with a gas 'on demand' hot water system, then you will have to install an automatic electric pressure water pump. At least one salt water (or outside freshwater) manual pump should be installed in any boat.

Most powerboats are fitted with automatic electric water pumps as standard equipment. Rarely will a manual back-up, or alternative hand operated system be installed. Electrically operated pressure water pumps are a great convenience, but at least one hand operated back up pump should be installed in any boat. Some of you may prefer to carry extensive

spares for your electric unit. The 'outside' water should be available through a hand-operated pump, or in a powerboat this is often arranged via an electrically powered, deck wash unit.

COMFORTABLE SEATING

It is surprising the number of boats where there is not one really comfortable seat to be had. When planning your accommodation make sure you have given this matter considerable thought and provided a comfortable seat for each member of the crew. In the case of a couple, two really comfortable lounge type chairs are required and the remainder can be normal dinette or settee seating. On all but the smallest metal boats it is possible to arrange two really comfortable seats.

MEASUREMENTS AND SUGGESTIONS

Seats can be too wide as well as too narrow. This may be a problem when designing and building settee/berth arrangements. A settee berth that is wide enough to make a comfortable single berth is too wide as a seat. These problems can be overcome by arranging the back cushions to sit on top of the seat/berth, the cushions can be stowed when the area is used as a berth.

CHART TABLE AND NAVIGATION STATION

Due to the advance in electronic navigational aids especially GPS and GPS linked plotters, the requirement for the chart table has been reduced in importance and size. The chart table is still an important part of any cruising boat and in all but the smallest examples, it should be possible to arrange a permanent purpose built, navigation area. A satisfactory arrangement is to use the inboard end of a quarter berth as a seat and build the chart table just ahead of this arrangement. Not only does this utilise some of the space for two purposes (very important in any but the largest boat) but also it locates the chart table athwartships and places the navigator facing forward; the ideal arrangement.

In most powerboats, the 'chart table' is an area immediately adjacent to the helmsman where the navigational aids are visible and the layout is quite different to that required in a slower moving sailboat, (please excuse my generalising). Persons who are moving from sail to power may have a problem in giving up their purpose boat navigation station that is usually located well away from the helm.

Space at or near the chart table will be required for folded or rolled charts and electronic equipment such as radio(s), GPS and other navigational aids. Even if your boat carries mainly portable navigational equipment, it should have a regular stowage area.

Some navigators prefer to undertake their chart work standing up; others prefer to allocate any spare space to another priority and use the main saloon table for laying out the charts. Given the option, unless you are prepared to have your chart work disturbed by a variety of other activities, then you will be better served with a proper navigational area, no matter how it is arranged.

SAIL STOWAGE

In the not so distant past, the sail locker was one of the more important areas of the vessel and considerable space had to provide for this purpose. Today, many sails are stowed on or adjacent to the areas where they are used. Mainsails are either stowed on the boom, in the boom or inside the mast. Headsails are less in number and are left rolled in place on the headsail furler. Depending on the layout of the rig and what systems are chosen for reefing and stowage, it is important to provide covers for the sails when they are not in use. On sailboats that are used seasonally, the sails (and other selected gear) should be removed and stored ashore during the off season.

There will still be some sails that will need to be stowed aboard when not in use. These sails include spinnaker(s), light weather Genoa and special storm sails. On most sailboats, this will represent a small percentage of the sail wardrobe, but never the less one that requires a place to call home. The sail stowage area can be combined with one of several other areas including the chain locker or workshop area. Or as is often the case they can be stowed up in the forward cabin, on or preferably under the V berths.

Looking forward in the Roberts 434, note the comfortable dinette with drop leaf table. The diesel stove to starboard is a wonderful piece of equipment on any cruising boat, it is more efficient than any other heating device.

Note the comfortable navigation station tucked out of the traffic in the Roberts 434. Forward facing navigation stations are preferred. Many owners will require repeater instruments, which seem to be absent from this area.

Chapter 14
ELECTRICAL SYSTEMS FOR METAL BOATS

Ohms law. . Domestic Batteries. Engine starting batteries. Battery chargers. Generating sets. Estimating your requirements. Electrical installations. Lighting. Monitoring instruments. Testing devices. Solar panels. Wind generators. Inverters.

Here are two simple equations that you should write in your log and learn by heart:

VOLTS multiplied by AMPS = WATTS

and

WATTS divided by VOLTS = AMPS

OHM'S LAW

As you become more involved in studying your boats electrical system you may wish to refer to these Formulas.

VOLTAGE: $E = I \times R$ or $E = P / I$
CURRENT: $I = E / R$ or $I = P / E$
RESISTANCE: $R = E / I$ or $R = E2 / P$ or $R = P / I2$
POWER: $P = E \times I$ or $P = I2 \times R$ or $E2 / R$

E = VOLTAGE in volts. I = CURRENT in Amps. R = RESISTANCE in ohms. P = POWER in watts

Because electrics will play a large part in owning and operating your metal boat, you must learn all you can about this subject. Unless you become well versed in marine electrics, you will need to seek professional help in either fitting or surveying your boatís electrical installations. Whenever you are required to seek professional assistance 'look over the shoulder' of the technician so you can learn to make a similar installation or repair yourself. To increase your understanding of all of these items, make sure you are around when the 'experts' are working on your electrical system. You can gain as much value from asking questions and absorbing knowledge, as you can from having the work performed on your boat. This latter advice extends to any area where you need to employ outside labour.

Make an early decision regarding how many electrical items you install. If your cruising is local or coastal in

nature and your boat is large enough, then you will most likely want to consider having all the same goodies on board that you use at home. Metal boats intended for long distance voyaging may benefit from a simpler and easier to maintain electrical system.

Before you decide on how you are going to satisfy your metal boats electrical requirements, you must decide how many appliances and other electrically driven devices you are going to install. Take the worst case power requirements and make estimates from the literature or the nameplates of the appliances. Estimate how many of these items will be running at one time. Now select the power sources you plan to install; alternator(s), generating set, solar panels, wind generator or other alternatives that will supply the total load. You should be aware that generating sets prefer to be run at least 40% to 75% of their capacity, so you may be forced to actually waste electricity if you over-estimate your requirements!

BATTERIES

In this case we are referring to lead acid wet cell batteries and not the ni-cad variety which have been used on boats, but are generally too expensive to be considered by most owners. Later in this section I will outline some of the claims made for gel cell batteries. You can choose either type with the knowledge that fifty percent of the battery 'experts' will agree with your choice.

In Europe, batteries are sized by quoting amp hours and in the USA the size may be quoted as a 'D' followed by a number. As the numbers are not always consistent between manufacturers, you should enquire further to establish the actual storage capacity of the particular battery in amp hours.

A few examples of the US system of denoting capacity are as follows:

Group 24 = 70 - 85 AH
Group 27 = 85 to 105 AH
4D = 160 -180 AH
8D = 210 - 225 AH

A Golf cart 6V battery is usually 180 - 215 AH.

It is sometimes hard to remember in what order to connect and disconnect the battery terminals. The negative terminal is removed first and connected last.

Traditionally the batteries have been divided into two or more banks, one for engine starting and one or more banks to serve domestic requirements including everything except starting the engine. As batteries have become more reliable, there are some battery 'experts' who argue that it no longer is necessary to divide the battery banks into domestic and starting units. If you have a generating set with its own starting battery, then this can be worked into an arrangement so that in the event of a flat engine starting battery you can fire up the generating set (using its own starting battery) and using the battery charger, you can put sufficient charge into the engine battery to get the engine started and the system recharged. In a worst case scenario, you may be able, via a set of jumper leads, use the generating set battery to start the main engine. Considering the last option it may be worthwhile including a larger than normal battery for use with the gen set.

If you are planning long distance offshore voyaging verses local coastal cruising, your electrical requirements and especially the methods of satisfying those needs will be different. In a coastal cruising situation you will often have access to shore power; this allows you to not only to conserve your battery power, but also enables you to top off your batteries using your battery charger.

You will most likely have more than one battery for domestic use. When this is the case the installation is called a battery bank. It is preferable that all of the separate batteries in the bank, is of similar or preferably the same amp hour capacity. If the sizes vary then the smallest battery may control the system and can halt the charging process when it is fully charged, this can often occur well before its larger companions have reached full capacity.

Generally speaking sailboats have smaller battery requirements than the equivalent sized powerboat. Below are estimates for sailboats. For powerboats add at least 50% to the suggested capacity. These estimates are not recommendations of actual amp hour requirements but rather an indication of the numbers involved.

If you are planning to carry the appliances that many consider as necessities, then you can use these figures as a starting point. Based on sailboat length and assuming there is a crew of 2 to 4 people, you are most likely to require the following domestic battery amp hour storage capacity: (28 ft / 8.53 M 150-250 AH), (35 ft / 10.67 M 400 - 600 AH), (45 ft /13.72 M 800 - 1,000 AH), (55 ft / 16.76 M 1200 - 1500 AH) and (65 Ft / 19.81 M 1,500 - 2,000 AH)

The connections between separate batteries are made in series or parallel; these terms refer to the way in which two or more batteries are connected one to the other. If you require large battery capacity, there is a sensible limit to the size of each individual battery. Unfortunately when considering large capacities it is seldom possible to keep each individual unit to a size easily handled by one person, so give this matter consideration when arranging your batteries. If you have more than one 12V battery and you want to create a bank of batteries, then you would connect these batteries in parallel so they remain and act as a 12V battery. If you want to create a 24V battery (often used on larger pleasure and many commercial boats), then you can connect two 12V batteries in series, or four 6V in series. Golf cart or similar 'deep cycle' heavy-duty batteries are often available in 6V and are becoming more widely used to make up large battery banks where large amp hour capacities (for example 2,000 ah) are required. Most boats will have a number of 12V batteries connected in parallel to make up their 12V domestic battery bank.

Remember that you must balance your battery capacity against your power usage. It takes considerably longer to put back the amperage you take out of the battery than it may to use it. Batteries do not accept recharge at the same speed as they can discharge.

The batteries you choose for domestic storage should be the 'deep cycle' type; these batteries are constructed differently from those used for engine starting. Deep cycle batteries are designed and built to accept a moderate load over an extended period. The plates are thicker, the cases are usually heavier and they are better equipped to accept regular discharges of up to 50 per cent and then be recharged on a regular cycling basis.

A 12-volt battery in operational condition will read more than 12 volts. If using a voltage meter, you take a reading soon after you have discontinued the charging process and your meter will most likely register 13 volts plus. After a few hours (without any discharge due to usage) your battery will read 12.8 volts if fully charged and somewhat less if it has not reached full capacity. A battery that reads 12.2 volts is 50 per cent discharged. A battery that reads 11.6

volts is almost fully discharged and may be damaged beyond further use if left in this condition for long.

Ni-cad batteries have been used as domestic batteries on boats and they were already installed on K*I*S*S when we purchased her. These batteries worked well on this relatively 'low tech' sailboat. Ni-cads are expensive but are reputed to have an extremely long life. It may be worth investigating this option if you are building a new boat, or refitting an existing one.

It is well to remember that ni-cad batteries do need re-cycling on a regular basis and that they also present some health hazard in that they have to be disposed of as a hazardous waste.

Gel Cell Batteries are lead acid batteries and are similar to the common wet cell battery. The differences in the chemistry and construction do provide some unique features. There is no need to add water so the tops of these batteries stay clean. Unlike wet cell batteries, the gel will hold its charge for months when left sitting with no load and no float charge. They can be stored in the off-season without the constant float charge and without fear of freezing. The gel cell battery will accept a higher rate of charge and usually delivers better performance when connected to an inverter than the wet cell variety. The combination of acids in the gel cell prevents sulphation and eliminates the need for battery equalisation. Before you choose this type of battery remember 50% of the experts prefer wet cell batteries!

AGM (absorbed glass mat) batteries are becoming more popular. These batteries hold the electrolyte in a sponge like material. You may want to investigate these batteries if you are initially fitting a new set or replacing an entire bank.

Finally do not confuse gel cell batteries with the so-called maintenance free batteries and water can not be added and these batteries are totally unsuitable for marine use.

ENGINE STARTING BATTERY

In the past it has always been a rule that the engine starting battery should be capable of being totally isolated. One reason is that you may want to leave the domestic battery system switched on to power an automatic bilge pump, alarm or similar device. In some cases you may wish to wire bilge pumping and alarm systems direct to the battery, so they are not accidentally turned off when you leave the boat.

The construction of this battery is different from that of the deep cycle type used for the domestic purposes. The plates are thinner and they are designed to release high power in short bursts. This battery is required to crank your engine and deliver short bursts of power at high amperage. Once the engine is running, the charging from the alternator quickly replenishes the battery.

The above is one explanation why when you check your engine start battery you will often find that it is fully charged. In fact you must be careful not to overcharge this unit; your regulator is designed to prevent this happening. Because this battery seldom gives trouble, (it always cranks the engine and generally performs, as you would expect), it is sometimes neglected. Make sure you regularly check the level of the water (electrolyte), the voltage level and general condition of the battery.

BATTERY BOXES

The first time you are in rough weather should not be the time you decide that your batteries need to be installed in a more secure manner. Batteries complete with fluid weigh around 0.875 lbs (0.4 kg) per amp hour capacity. A 220 amp hour, (8D in USA), battery weighs about 160 lb / 75 Kg. It does not take much imagination to envisage what would happen if one of those monsters breaks loose in a seaway. Batteries need to be installed in a secure manner and the best way is to house them in their own box. A battery box can be built out of 3/4" (20 mm) waterproof plywood and is best lined with fiberglass so that any spills are contained. The box should be bolted to, or otherwise securely fastened to a suitable structural member.

When selecting the location for your batteries remember that during the time you own the boat, they probably will need to be removed or exchanged for new ones. If the batteries are not already fitted with strong handles, make sure you install straps under them so you can remove the batteries from the box. Although many authorities insist on a vented lid to be installed on the battery box; I personally believe that provided the batteries are strapped in place, they are unlikely to jump out of the box and the open top is better for ventilation; more importantly it is one less obstacle to regularly checking the battery fluid levels.

Keep the terminals and top of the case absolutely clean. One reason for the recommended battery box covers, is to prevent accidental shorting out of the battery and electrical system, by some metal article like a spanner or wrench being dropped across the terminals. If you are considering a large battery storage capacity, then you should see if you could locate at least a large percentage of your batteries low in the hull, perhaps in the keel or bilge area. In this case you will need to make sure they are isolated from any possible contact with bilge water.

BATTERY CHARGERS

Most battery chargers are operated on 120, 220V or 240V AC (mains-shore power or are generated via your AC generating set). These units are usually left running when you are connected to either source. There is a great variety of 12V DC battery chargers capable of delivering between 5 and over 100 amps to your electrical system. When you run a 240V AC battery charger on 220V, you will find that it will deliver 80 per cent or less its rated output. The amount of amperage you need from a charger will be calculated at the same time as you are totalling amperage income from other sources such as engine alternator, solar panels, wind generator etc.

Single stage battery chargers only deliver their full output when the battery is deeply discharged. For example, if you are charging a battery via a 30 amp charger and assuming your batteries are 50 percent discharged at the start of the cycle, you will note via your charging gauge that the needle immediately registers 30 amps input. After a period (depending on the capacity of the battery bank), the input amperage needle will drop back to 20,15, and eventually to one or two amp input. This is how most battery chargers are designed to work, they will give your battery as much power as they are designed to deliver until the battery reaches around 80 per cent of capacity and then the input is much slower.

You will note that if you turn on a 12V DC appliance during this period when the charger is not delivering full capacity, then the charge will increase to cover the amount of amperage you are using. I have found this feature to be useful in giving a general estimate the amperage used by a particular appliance.

The internal setting in your battery charger will determine how many volts your charger can deliver; this is usually preset by the manufacturer however it may be possible to alter the voltage. Check with the manufacturer before you start making changes to these settings. If your charger delivers too high a voltage it can cause your batteries to 'boil or gas' and you may permanently damage them. Grossly overcharged batteries have been known to explode so take precautions when working on your batteries. As a minimum safety measure, always wear protective clothing and safety glasses.

EQUALIZING BATTERIES

This method of rejuvenating your batteries is one that should only be considered if you feel comfortable with your system and when you consider you have the experience to handle the process with complete safely. While a battery is being discharged, sulphuric acid in the electrolyte reacts with the lead plates in a chemical reaction, which produces electricity and lead sulphate. When the battery is re-charged, electricity flows back into the battery and causes the reverse chemical reaction, which turns the lead sulphate back into lead and sulphuric acid.

With each discharge and recharge cycle, a small amount of lead sulphate will remain on the plates. If this sulphate is left in place for very long, it will harden and or crystallize and eventually reduce the batteries capacity, increase the internal resistance and destroy the batteries ability to deliver an adequate amount of power. When this occurs, even an equalising charge can not remove the sulphate and the battery becomes useless except for re-cycling purposes.

GENERATING SETS

If you require more electrical capacity than be supplied by batteries and provided by other generating means, and then a diesel powered generating set will be your next option. There are three types of power generating sets capable of making the large quantities of AC electricity demanded by modern appliances. You may select a fully installed diesel powered unit, or a unit that is driven by a power take-off from the main engine, or a portable petrol/gasoline powered unit. There is one additional type of 'gen set' and this unit is unique in that it generates large quantities of 12V DC power as opposed to most units that deliver 120V or 220V AC current. Make sure you turn off all appliances especially the 12V DC ones before you fire up your generating set. When a generating set is first started there can be a surge of power that can harm your appliances.

Sailboat owners, before considering installing these units, you should estimate if your needs can be met by a combination of solar and/or wind generated power combined with the output of the alternator attached to your main engine. Powerboater's will have greater requirements and are not so inclined towards wind generators. Many powerboats have one or two solar panels of sufficient capacity to maintain the battery charge when the boat is not in use.

Although you may use some AC power, most of the electricity generated by a 120V or 220V AC unit is often converted to 12V DC (via battery charger) before it is used on your boat. Perhaps it may be better to start off with a 12V Generating set and only convert the minimum amounts to 120V or 220V AC via an alternator. This 12V gen set is covered later under its own heading.

The portable units are inexpensive but are not suitable for metal sail or powerboats. In most cases they are very noisy. These units introduce petrol/gasoline aboard and are not up to powering the range of appliances that made you consider a generating set in the first place.

For those on a budget, a PTO (power takeoff) generator could be the answer. PTO units have a centrifugal clutch arrangement enabling them to keep generating at varying engine speeds. Units including the M90 Marine Cruising Generator, which is made in the USA, are capable of producing considerable output and units of 3 kW to 6.5 kW (3.75 to 8 KVA) are readily available. These units produce enough power to keep most appliance happy cruising families satisfied.

If you have considered using your main engine and the regular alternator as a primary source of generating 12V DC power, it is well to remember that you should have some load on the engine; in other words it is not recommended to run your diesel engine at low revolutions without some load being applied.

For the larger boats a conventional diesel powered generating set, usually referred to as a ëGen setí, offers power at a reasonable price. These units can supply AC power starting at around 3 KVA up to any size that you could require. The quietest units are powered by a water-cooled diesel engine with at least two cylinders. The entire unit must be either already installed in an well-insulated cabinet or capable of being insulated and contained in a soundproof box.

Most gen sets are reliable and deliver the amount of rated power promised by the manufacturer. The difference between good and best is the amount of sound emitted. Try and hear an example running before you make a final decision. Sound problems can come from the exhaust water rather than from the diesel or the generating unit; it is possible to greatly reduce this noise by using a 'water lift' exhaust system so the water exits the hull below the waterline. Generally speaking these units are quiet, fuel-efficient

and can be tucked away in otherwise unused space in or near the engine compartment. No matter how quiet and efficient your gen set, you will not want to run it more than say two to four hours each day.

ALL 12V DC GENERATING SYSTEM

The generation of large quantities of 12V DC power makes sense when you consider that most appliances likely to be found on even the most completely (electrically) equipped cruising sailboat can be run on 12V DC power. As part of considering this option you would need to be prepared to install a larger amount of battery storage than you would need when using other charging arrangements. Power boat owners because of larger demand, will probably prefer to install a 110 or 220 AC gen set.

There are several 12V DC generating systems now available and one recent development is a combination unit manufactured by Balmar in USA. This unit is arranged to provide constant 12V DC power to operate a water-maker and deep freeze unit as well keep the batteries in a constant state of charge.

All of the major components are readily available and you may wish to custom build a unit to suit your requirements. If you are planning to use an all (mostly) 12V DC system then you will need a battery capacity in the top end of the quoted estimates.

Most cruising boats that have a regular AC generating system fitted need to run 2-3 hours per day. With the all-12V DC system it is estimated that you should only need to run your generating set for the same amount once every two to three days. This factor alone may be sufficient to encourage you to consider this set up.

One disadvantage of the all-12V DC system is that it requires much heavier wiring and fuses. The main requirement is that you must be able to charge larger than usual amounts of 12V DC power so that your batteries can be replenished at a rapid rate. This is necessary to balance the two or three day charging cycle. Your 12V charging system will need to be able to produce between 150 to 300 amps per hour to make the system work; it can be done.

The charging end of the unit will consist of one or more high output alternators coupled with a dedicated suitably sized water-cooled diesel engine. The recommended procedure is to decide how much output you will require to charge your batteries in the desired time. Now match the alternator(s) output to this requirement and then select a suitably sized diesel engine. Between 10 and 20 hp should be sufficient to power the alternator(s). The engine will not require a transmission unit but you will need to have a shaft that can be bolted to the flywheel and this in turn will accept the one or two pulleys used to drive the alternators via a suitable V belt arrangement.

A reliable regulator will be part of this system. The last thing you would want to do is to cook those extensive and expensive batteries. You will need to have the entire unit housed in a sound proof box similar to that used for an AC gen set. The cost of this 12V DC generating set should not exceed the cost of a similarly sized AC (120V or 220V) unit. Your decision can be based purely on the convenience factor and on the requirements of your electrical system. For details of the availability of high output alternators, see appendix 4.

SOLAR PANELS

These are useful in keeping the battery charged when the boat is left unattended. Solar panels have been successfully installed to run all types of appliances including small refrigeration units. Solar panels (when they produce one amp or more) should be run through a regulator so that there is no chance of overcharging the battery. These devices are capable of taking power out of your battery at night; make sure you prevent a reverse flow of current by installing a blocking diode for each panel or bank of panels. Each diode uses 0.4 amp so remember that when calculating input. If in doubt about your abilities in this area, then have the units installed by a competent person.

Solar panels are becoming more efficient and can be mounted on many areas of your boat. You will need to study the position of the sun in relation to the intended location of the panels. If you are able to rotate or angle the panels to take account of the boat position in relation to the sun, then you will have a better chance to optimise the amounts of electricity generated by your panels. You would probably soon tire of adjusting the angle of the panels several times each day so you should calculate a reasonable angle to suit the area where you are operating and settle for around 75 per cent efficiency. When mounting the panels, make sure you allow for air to circulate around the whole unit, otherwise the excessive heat generated will seriously decrease the panel's output.

Once you have made the initial investment the power you receive is free. Most solar panels have a long maintenance free life, usually 10 years or longer. As with most other capital expenses you will need to decide if you will receive a reasonable return on your investment; in the case of solar panels, if you plan to be cruising at least 25 per cent of the time, then they are a good investment. In any case you should install a small unit that is capable of topping up the batteries when you are away from your boat.

Solar panels can produce power from 0.30 amps, which are ideal for battery replenishment when you are away from the boat. One panel per bank of batteries will avoid the need for a regulator in the system. Larger panels can produce up to 3.5 amps which can be arranged to form a charging system ideal for the offshore sailor. If you consider solar power as a serious source of electricity, install several panels designed to produce a total of around 20 amps. Make sure to select solar panels whose rated voltage, at the temperature where you are operating, is at least 14.8 volts (this allows for the blocking diode 0.6 volt loss) to give net voltage of 14.2 volts. This is the voltage required too fully charge lead acid batteries.

WIND GENERATORS

More often used on cruising sailboats than on powerboats. Many experienced cruising people, argue that wind generators are more efficient and cost effective than solar panels. If your boat is intended for serious offshore cruising then why not install both types of generating equipment and you can reap all of the benefits offered by both systems. The thought of those blades whizzing around will ensure that most people consider the safety aspects when deciding whether or not to install one of these units.

To prevent damage to the charging unit and/or to the blades, some types need to be shut down when winds reach 30 to 50 knots. Other manufactures include automatic speed control and shutdown. You should look for these features, as stopping the blades in high winds could be a risky operation. Most generators you will be considering will have blades of around 5ft-(1.52m) diameter. Do not let the above comments put you off considering a wind generator; they are a wonderful source of electricity and the warnings are intended to make sure you treat these wind machines with respect.

Wind generators do make noise; how much noise depends on the model. I have noticed over the years, that they are becoming increasingly quieter. The number of blades does not usually increase the output but it does make for a quieter unit. Try and inspect the various models under operating conditions to see for yourself how much, and what type of noise is involved.

Wind generators will require some maintenance; they are basically electric motors running in reverse so they have all of the same components as an electric motor. Brushes and even bearings will need periodic replacement. Check with the manufacturer on what maintenance procedures are needed and how often replacement parts are required for their particular unit.

INVERTERS

It is well to note that inverters are users rather than manufacturers of electricity; they simply take one form of power and turn it into another, keeping a little for their trouble. The best models only consume around 5 per cent during the conversion process.

There are many inverters available that are capable of converting the 12 or 24 volt power stored in your battery bank into 220/240 or 120 volts AC. They are generally available in sizes ranging from 50 watts to 2,500 watts. If you are intending to run most of your electrical appliances from 120V or 220V/240V AC power supplied by your inverter, then before you purchase, you will need to know the total power requirements of the appliances that you plan to run at any one time. If you have a relatively small sailboat and you are only intending to run one small AC appliance on AC power then a simple strip based 200 watt inverter may suit you best. One of these small units may cost you as little as £100 / US$150 or even less.

For owners of larger live aboard cruising boats it is a common mistake to under estimate your requirements so it is most important that you calculate your expected needs carefully. Allow some room for expanded usage. You will need the 12V DC battery storage capacity to back up this usage and this will temper your appetite for AC appliances. Remember to convert your requirements to the same units, either amps or watts, before you start to estimate your total requirements; see conversion formula at the start of this chapter. There are several manufacturers of these appliances, see appendix 4.

With certain limitations, an inverter that converts 12V to 120 or 220V AC can make life easier for those who want to run AC electrical appliances aboard their boats. In early models the current produced by inverters was not the same as that supplied to your home by the local power authority. The inverter produces a square, stepped or what is generally referred to as a modified sine wave. An on-board generating set and your local power company delivers pure sine wave power. Why do you need to know this? Because the inverter manufactured 120V or 220-volt power may not properly run certain appliances; problems will occur when inverters are coupled with TV or computer screens, radar and similar units. These problems are being addressed and largely overcome but is wise to check with the inverter manufacturer regarding the compatibility of their unit with the appliances you wish to operate. In the past two years there has been a vast improvement in the way inverters operate. You should be able to find one that will suit your requirements and will also give you trouble free service.

When considering which appliances you can run on your inverter, you will need to consider the 'starting' amperage required by many pieces of electrical equipment. An electric drill that operates successfully on 1,000 watts will normally take a considerably larger amount of power during the first few seconds of operation to get going. This is sufficient to create an overload situation and trip out the whole circuit. Because inverter technology is constantly changing, you should investigate the various makes and models to ensure that the unit you select will properly run your AC appliances.

VOLT METERS

To assist in 'managing ' your electrical supply and demand, you will require one or more testing instruments. These will enable you to take inventory of the state of charge of your batteries as well as keep track of the general health of your electrical system.

One of the first items you should acquire is a hand held voltmeter. Most of these instruments not only read volts on the DC and AC scale but also read Ohms and amps. Most units are capable of reading a wide range of voltages from a small percentage of one volt through to 500 volts AC or more. On a cruising boat the main interest will lie in the 12V DC, the 120V AC or 220V AC ranges. Voltmeters are available in two basic configurations, analogue or digital. Like many people I started off with an analogue instrument. However I soon found that the digital version was capable of being read to a more accurate degree. These instruments are relatively inexpensive and good quality ones are available for a little as £15 / US$22, so you can probably afford to own both types. Either of these instruments can be used to test circuits and are the first instrument you would reach for (after you check the fuses!), when any electrical appliance or instrument fails to operate.

For those of us who need to know the exact state of our batteries and associated equipment at all times, there are a number of monitoring instruments that can be permanently installed in the electrical system. These instruments provide instant information on demand.

The E-METER is manufactured in the USA by Cruising Equipment, see appendix 4, and is marketed in the USA and UK under the name of ëHeart Interface Link 10'. The E-Meter is an instrument, which measures most of the battery functions that will be of interest to you. It measures Ampere-hours; voltage, current flow and the time remaining until the battery would be discharged. The amount of energy remaining in the battery can be displayed as an amp hour number on the LED display, or as a percentage of the battery capacity. The meter measures the system voltage and the current are measured via a 500 amp, 50-millivolt shunt supplied with the unit. The time remaining function tells the user how long the battery will last at the present rate of discharge. The meter is powered by the battery system to which it is attached; the drain is so low as to be disregarded in most systems.

Several boating magazines and other interested bodies has extensively tested this meter. The results and comments have all been extremely favourable. The unit comes with extensive documentation so you should have no problems setting it up to work on your boat. Your electrical system will be well served by this device with the constant monitoring of amps, amp hours remaining and your batteries general state of health. All of this for only £188 or US$199

The E-Meter offers a number of optional features that may not be of interest to the average cruising sailor. It has the ability to be connected to a RS232 port, which allows it to communicate with a computer thus enabling data to be recorded as required. Another feature is the ability to be connected to a data-logging device by the same manufacturer; this unit can in turn, be connected to a GPS.

There are many other battery monitoring devices available that enable you to be advised on every battery function. I have featured the E-Meter/Heart Link 10 because it represents such outstanding value for money. There are battery monitors that have even more functions than the E-Meter and you may find these useful.

HYDROMETER

Another measuring instrument that you should have on board is a hydrometer. This device consists of a glass tube with a rubber bulb on one end and a thin tube on the other. Inside is a float marked off in one or more scales designed to give various readings. When used to draw off a small amount of fluid from each cell it gives a reading to determine the amount of charge of the particular cell. If one cell registers a considerably lower reading than another does, then you may well have a problem, not only with that cell but also with the battery. One dead cell will render the whole battery useless and it will have to be replaced.

Many hydrometers also have a scale to measure specific gravity; this scale can be used to test among other things the state of the coolant in your engine heat exchanger system. As temperature can play a part in the operation of your batteries, some hydrometers are fitted with a thermometer. In my opinion this is overkill and there are less expensive ways of determining and factoring in the temperature.

The fluid you draw off the battery when testing with a hydrometer will contain a high sulphuric acid content so be aware that this liquid is capable of burning your skin and eyes so make sure you are adequately protected. Your clothing and fabrics used in the interior of your boat are especially vulnerable to even the smallest amount of battery acid. Always rinse out the instrument in fresh clean water after use; do not put contaminated water down the sink. Always use a separate glass jar for rinsing and dispose of the water in an appropriate manner.

Now that you have some understanding of the complexities of the subject of marine electrics you may wish to study further; the subject is fully covered in several specialised books, see appendix one.

Chapter 15
APPENDAGES, FITTINGS AND ALTERATIONS

Skegs. Rudders. Swim Platforms. Bowsprits. Davits. Tabernacle. Chain plates. Stanchions, Pulpits and pushpits. Bow fittings. Anchor lockers. Hawse pipes. Changing an existing boat. Changing length. Changing cabin structures.

SKEGS

These appendages are usually fitted to sailboats with fin keels and some powerboats. On fin keel sailboats I consider skegs to be preferable to unsupported spade rudders. On powerboats, skegs can often improve the

directional stability. You may want to add a skeg even if your metal boat is not fitted with this feature.

If your sailboat plans call for a separate skeg and rudder, you will need to assure yourself that the arrangement will stay with boat at all times. Skegs are vulnerable and are more easily damaged than a boat that has a longer keel combined with heel supported rudder.

On sailboats where a skeg it fitted, it usually occupies about one third of the total area of the rudder skeg combination. Even though I have been guilty of

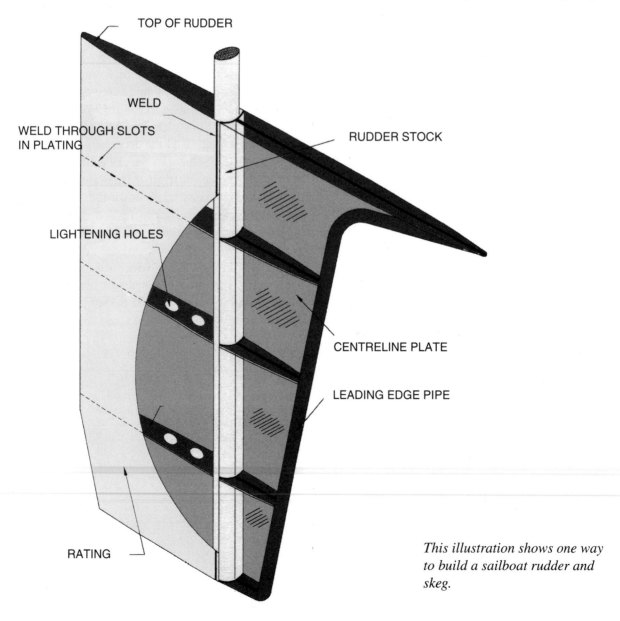

This illustration shows one way to build a sailboat rudder and skeg.

designing single plate skegs and rudders on sailboats I have learnt that this type of arrangement is far inferior to an airfoil shaped appendage. Fortunately if you have a single plate skeg and or rudder, it is a simple matter to add some support fins and outer plating.

Assuming your boat is designed to be fitted with a skeg, it is important that it be built strongly enough to withstand a reasonable amount of rough treatment. It would be possible to design and build a skeg so strong that it would tear the bottom out of the hull before the skeg was severely damaged. This type of overkill may cause you to lose the boat. How strong is strong enough, but not too strong?

Firstly I consider it important that the skeg be built on to the hull after the plating is completed. The skeg should not be a hollow appendage that is open at the top similar to the keel. A keel structure has to be strong enough to withstand anything that the elements

can offer. Most keels on metal boats will survive grounding, unfortunately a skeg is not large enough to have the same strength.

Most metal hulls have a substantial centre line bar on which to weld the centre plate for the skeg. The centre plate can be the same shape as the skeg and be welded directly to the bar. You could have the plate continue up through the hull and then have a number of web floors to reinforce the plate. This latter arrangement is getting over strong and likely to take some of the hull plating with it if ever you have the ultimate skeg damaging collision.

You can see by the foregoing that designing and building a skeg is no simple matter. If you make it too weak, you may lose the skeg; if you make it too strong then you make sustain hull and rudder damage in the event of a serious collision. This is one reason why in some of my latest cruising sailboat designs I am now leaning towards a modern version of the long keel with a heel supporting the bottom of the rudder. Generally speaking, powerboats do not have any of these problems.

The drawing shown here represents my idea of sensible skeg construction. Installing the fore and aft profile centre plate may make it just too strong. I would follow the elements shown in this sketch. In some of our earlier designs, we allowed the skegs to have propeller apertures. Our current thinking is that the security for the propeller comes at too high a price. It is almost impossible to include the cutout without seriously weakening the skeg.

Skeg and rudder pre-built and later welded to hull. Builder D. Johnson of Canada

The leading edge of the skeg can be whole pipe, split pipe or rolled plate. Your plans may incorporate a 'fence' which is like a fin that runs parallel to the DWL and usually extends from the front of the skeg to the aft end of the keel. The skeg can have the leading edge pipe continued around and forward to form the bottom of the fence. The aft edge of the skeg is best constructed using an open face; large diameter split pipe or rolled plate. The aft end needs to be open enough to allow the rudder to swing at least 40 degrees in each direction. The centre line plate will support the airfoil shaped half webs that are arranged each side of the plate. If the centre line plate is omitted, then you can have full width webs attached to the leading and trailing edge of the skeg. The bottom airfoil web is usually 1/2" / 12 mm plate and can support the rudder-bearing cup.

Almost completed rudder for ROBERTS 34 built by Helge Andersson.

Completed rudder and shaft for ROBERTS 34. Note plug in top of rudder for filling rudder with oil.

To install the plating on the skeg, you will need to make slots in the plate so you can weld through the slots and attach the plate to the webs. After fully plating the skeg, you may wish to install a fillet at the top on both sides where the skeg joins the hull. The fillet should measure say 4 in to 6 in / 100 to 150 mm and be installed at 45 degrees between the hull and the root of the skeg. Fair off the forward end of the fillet that will be welded to both the skeg and hull plating.

SAILBOAT RUDDER

Build the rudder in a similar manner to that used to make the skeg. The leading edge of the rudder will be either solid round or a hollow tube of suitable strength to take the strains imposed on and by the rudder. Your plans will indicate the size and type of material recommended for the rudder 'stock'. Take care not to introduce stress into the stock, when welding the webs and the plate to this item. Some builders fit drain plugs to your rudder and skeg, and fill these with oil. The idea is to prevent corrosion in the inside of these appendages. In some publications I have seen concrete recommended as a fill for rudders and skegs; do not follow this recommendation. A fill with foam similar to that used as insulation inside the hull may be of some benefit. My experience with concrete in boats including metal hulls is that it can cause corrosion from inside the hull, so do not include this material anywhere in your metal boat.

You may wish to have an arrangement so you can remove the rudder without removing the skeg bearing or lifting the entire boat. You can arrange flanges bolted together to make the removal of the rudder a simple matter. If you use flanges in the system, make sure they are of sufficient strength and have at least 5 bolts equalling the cross sectional area of the rudder shaft. If you have flanges and bolts, then you must wire the nuts together so there is no risk of the bolts coming loose and allowing the rudder to part company from the boat.

In the bottom cup bearing you may insert one or more metal balls as a bearing surface for the bottom of the rudderstock. If you use this system make sure that the hanging arrangement for the rudder is such that the rudder can not part company from the boat in the event that the balls fail.

POWERBOAT STEERING SYSTEMS AND RUDDERS

Hydraulic steering systems can more easily be interfaced with auto pilot systems and for this and other reasons are generally preferred for most powerboats. This whole question of steering systems and choosing the right system for your boat is covered in my books Choosing For Cruising (sailboats) and Choosing a Cruising Powerboat where more space was available to cover the subject in considerable detail.

Powerboat rudders are usually cast from alloy and the size of the blade and shaft has to be carefully calculated to allow your boat to be steered within a range of speeds applicable to your particular boat. The problem is that the larger rudder(s) that would be ideal for handling the boat at slow speed are not suitable for a boat operating on a plane. It is essential that you have the correct rudder size to suit the type of hull and expected performance characteristics of your particular boat. Consultation with the designer of your boat or better still with a rudder specialist is essential if you are to have a successful match.

SAILBOAT TRANSOM STEPS AND SWIM PLATFORMS

Most sailboats can be improved by the inclusion of one of these features. The platform will need to be designed so it is still clear of the water, when the boat heels to its maximum sailing angle. On sailboats, the swim platform and boarding steps are usually incorporated into the construction of a 'reverse' or 'sugar scoop' transom. If you are building from new, then the whole arrangement can be designed into the stern. If you are planning to add these features to an existing metal boat, then careful thought will be required before you start to alter the transom.

If the aft end of the transom is too high from the water, say over 1 ft 6 ins / 457 mm, then you will need to include a boarding ladder into the arrangement. If you are having a boat designed or altering an existing design to suit your particular requirements it is worth while noting the height of the bottom of the transom above the water. It may be possible to modify the design so a separate boarding ladder is not required.

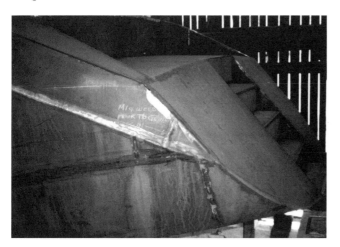

This Roberts 64 sailboat incorporates a set of transom steps

The 'Sugar scoop' stern is fashionable at present. Be careful if you are planning to have one of these added to the stern of your sailboat; I have seen some poorly designed additions that have spoilt an otherwise attractive design.

POWERBOAT SWIM PLATFORMS AND BOARDING LADDERS

In some areas the 'Swim Platform' is referred to as a 'Duck Board'. I confess to not having given this matter much thought until I finally owned a powerboat fitted with one of these appendages and then noticed how the ducks find these platforms an ideal place to roost. This latter fact is not a problem, as the birds seem to know which boats are unused and concentrate their unwelcome attentions on those vessels.

A large percentage of powerboats feature some form of swim platform and most are fitted with a boarding ladder at the stern of the vessel. Anyone familiar with boating will be aware of the usefulness of these features and if you are building a new boat or refitting an existing metal craft, then the design and construction of this part of the hull should receive your serious consideration. I have also seen a set of steps incorporated into the bow of a powerboat. These simple U shaped stainless steel steps were to enable a crewmember to more easily step from the boat to the shore. This arrangement is worthwhile considering if you are planning extensive cruising in the European or other canals.

Recently there has been a trend to carry the hull underwater sections past the regular transom and thus provide a base for the swim platform. This additional underwater volume will need to be considered with the rest of the hull if the boat is to retain its designed fore and aft trim. One way to ensure that there are minimum trim problems, is to use this extended hull volume as liquid storage either as a holding tank or as a way to increase water or fuel capacity. The holding tank option is the most popular solution and dare I say you will have more control as to when and how this form of ballast is discharged.

Another option when considering a swim platform is to have the structure built using a pipe frame that may be permanently left in position or designed to fold upwards when not in use. The fixed version is easier to build and maintain and unless you have some reason, such as marina costs or restrictions where you need to keep your boat a specified overall length, then this is the type I recommend. A pipe swim platform can be built out of 2 in / 50 mm diameter heavy wall pipe and can be an attractive addition to your boat. Suitable spaced 2" x 2" x 1/4" / 50 x 50 x 6 mm angle can be used to support a system of teak planking.

The top of the swim platform will need to be arranged so that it affords easy access for a swimmer or other person wishing to gain access from the water. In some cases, this may involve a calculated guess as to where the final waterline will be located. In any case transom steps or more likely a boarding ladder will be needed to gain access from the swim platform to the main deck.

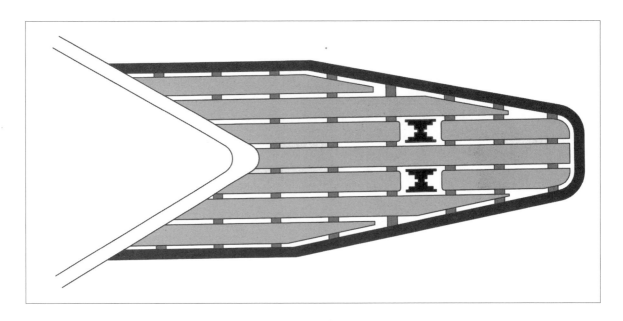

This pipe bowsprit can be easily fabricated from the same metal as your hull and makes an attractive and sturdy addition to any metal boat.

Mr H J Hornicke built this bowsprit on his Spray and combined the arrangement with an sturdy pulpit and additional anchor line reel and jib boom arrangement

BOWSPRITS

Although usually confined to sailboats, short versions of these appendages can often be usefully incorporated into a powerboat hull. Construction would be similar in either case but the sailboat version will need extra strengthening to take the loads imposed by the sailing rig.

The simplest and most effective form of bowsprit on a metal boat is one built using heavy walled pipe to form up a 'U' or similarly shaped structure. The ends of the 'U' are anchored to a suitably reinforced section of the plating near the bow. The illustration shown here will give you a reasonable idea of what I consider to be the basis for a sturdy bowsprit. The structure may incorporate rollers to accept the anchor chain. Your bowsprit should provide and ideal place to stow the anchor. The anchor should be stowed far enough ahead of the bow so as to be out of the way, while remaining ready for immediate use.

In the sailboat version, tangs will be needed to accept the lower end of the forestay. The ideal material from which to build the main pipe structure is 316 stainless steel. The high cost of this material in the sizes and weight required mean that you will probably be using mild steel, aluminum or copper-nickel depending on the metal used to build you boat. It is preferable to use stainless steel for the tangs and other areas of the bowsprit where normal usage would soon wear away the paint and cause maintenance problems in the future.

The working platform of the pipe bowsprit can have 'L' angle installed as supports for the teak decking. Some form of 'bobstay' may be required depending on the strains imposed by your particular sail plan. In some cases where the bowsprit is no more than an extension of the bow/foredeck area and intended to make the handling of anchors and ground tackle as simpler task, then a bobstay may not be required. If the 'U' is wide enough where it is attached to the hull, then side stays may not be required.

DAVITS

These dinghy stowage devices are sometimes seen on sailboats. Davits on sailboats are a mixed blessing where all too often they are of crude design and construction. Davits can increase the available deck area by moving the dinghy out of the way but they may impede the operation of a self-steering wind vane and can cause problems when sailing in a following sea. As davits may sooner or later require some repairs, you may consider it preferable to bolt them in place rather then weld them directly to the deck. There is one type of davit that may be suitable for all types of boats and that is one where the boat is lifted from the water in the normal manner and then 'flipped over' to lay upside down on top of the davits.

I would like to mention the fittings known as 'Snap davits'. These fittings generally are bolted to a swim platform and matching fittings are glued or otherwise attached to the dinghy. The dinghy is positioned so the attachment points match up. The dinghy is then in a position to be pulled upwards and now sits parallel with the vertical transom. The dinghy actually hangs on these snap hinges outside or aft of the swim platform thus allowing reasonable access to the platform. This arrangement is an alternative to fitting regular davits. We have this arrangement on our current powerboat. We are not sure if the disadvantages of restricted access to the swim platform and some restriction of aft vision by the dinghy outweigh its advantages. As they say, watch this space!

Regular davits can be built of mild steel, stainless steel or aluminum and can be constructed of pipe, rectangular tube or sheet metal. If you have a generous budget then it may be simpler to purchase these items ready made. The rest of us will need to decide which design and construction method would best suit our needs. For other reasons your dinghy should be as light as practical so it should not be necessary to build the davits of such heavy construction as to add unnecessary top hamper to your vessel. Try and match the style of the davits to the style of your boat. This in one of the many areas where it is possible to spoil the overall appearance of a boat by adding an ugly item that is there for all to see.

Because of the variety of dinghies likely to be carried, it is impossible to give detailed advice on constructing davits. If you study other boats, which have either off the shelf or custom built units, you should be able to gain sufficient information to enable you to build a set for your boat.

MAST STEPS

No matter whether your mast is deck or keel stepped it will need some form of device to secure the lower end of the spar. Many commercially manufactured masts come complete with a cast aluminum step. This step is fastened to the deck and the mast simply sits in this cup like arrangement. Make sure that your deck-mounted step has the ability to drain the water that lodges around the bottom of the mast.

Examine the mast support post that may be 2 to 3 in / 50 to 75 mm diameter metal pipe to ensure that it is up to the job. You mast under deck support may be in the form of a beefed up bulkhead. Check your plans for details. If you mast is stepped on the keel, check if you have an arrangement that will allow you to alter the rake of the mast (this will change the fore and aft location of the foot).

TABERNACLE

A tabernacle mast step may also be considered. If you mast is not too long or too large, check with the designer regarding this option. This fitting can be manufactured of cast aluminum or fabricated from stainless or mild steel. Naturally the design of the tabernacle will need to match the mast and gear that it is expected to support. When we say that it can be built from 1/4" / 6 mm plate then you will have to determine if that is suitable for your particular situation.

The sturdy tabernacle on this Roberts 53 is in keeping with the rest of this beautifully built boat. A boat built to go anywhere.

CHAIN PLATES AND TANGS

Because of the wear and tear imposed on these items they should be fabricated from 316 stainless steel. If you build chainplates or tangs out of mild steel that is subsequently painted, then you will find that the paint will soon be worn away and corrosion will soon appear. Most other metals, other than stainless, are also unsuitable for making these parts. Just a reminder, when you paint the boat make sure you extend the paint up say 1 to 2 in / 25 to 50 mm on to the stainless fitting; this will prevent any corrosion caused by the proximity of two dis-similar metals. Most chainplates and tangs will be made from plate

of a minimum 1/4" / 6 mm thickness, however consult your plans for exact sizes. Some designs call for the chainplates to be made from solid round stainless steel bar. Watch for crevice corrosion reread the section of stainless steel, its strengths and weaknesses should be kept in mind when using this material.

Avoid chain plates that are simply welded to the outside of the hull; these look crude and also they are corrosion traps in that they are welded on top of another metal. In my opinion, welding even similar metals one on top of the other is bad practice and

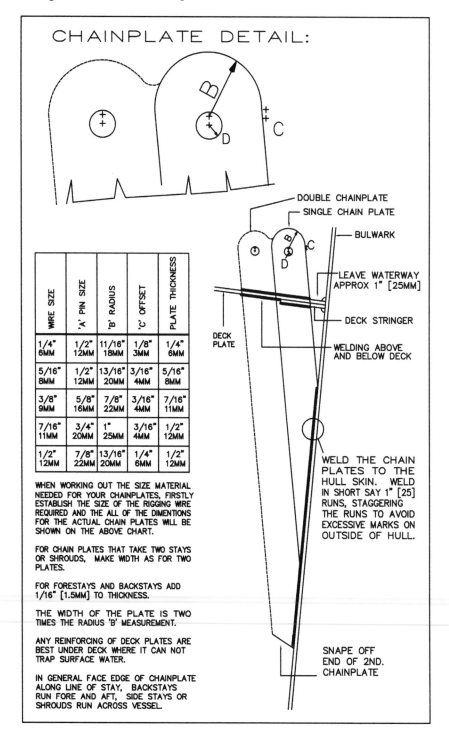

CHAINPLATE DETAIL:

WIRE SIZE	'A' PIN SIZE	'B' RADIUS	'C' OFFSET	PLATE THICKNESS
1/4" 6MM	1/2" 12MM	11/16" 18MM	1/8" 3MM	1/4" 6MM
5/16" 8MM	1/2" 12MM	13/16" 20MM	3/16" 4MM	5/16" 8MM
3/8" 9MM	5/8" 16MM	7/8" 22MM	3/16" 4MM	7/16" 11MM
7/16" 11MM	3/4" 20MM	1" 25MM	3/16" 4MM	1/2" 12MM
1/2" 12MM	7/8" 22MM	13/16" 20MM	1/4" 6MM	1/2" 12MM

WHEN WORKING OUT THE SIZE MATERIAL NEEDED FOR YOUR CHAINPLATES, FIRSTLY ESTABLISH THE SIZE OF THE RIGGING WIRE REQUIRED AND THE ALL OF THE DIMENTIONS FOR THE ACTUAL CHAIN PLATES WILL BE SHOWN ON THE ABOVE CHART.

FOR CHAIN PLATES THAT TAKE TWO STAYS OR SHROUDS, MAKE WIDTH AS FOR TWO PLATES.

FOR FORESTAYS AND BACKSTAYS ADD 1/16" [1.5MM] TO THICKNESS.

THE WIDTH OF THE PLATE IS TWO TIMES THE RADIUS 'B' MEASUREMENT.

ANY REINFORCING OF DECK PLATES ARE BEST UNDER DECK WHERE IT CAN NOT TRAP SURFACE WATER.

IN GENERAL FACE EDGE OF CHAINPLATE ALONG LINE OF STAY, BACKSTAYS RUN FORE AND AFT, SIDE STAYS OR SHROUDS RUN ACROSS VESSEL.

DOUBLE CHAINPLATE

SINGLE CHAIN PLATE

BULWARK

LEAVE WATERWAY APPROX 1" [25MM]

DECK STRINGER

DECK PLATE

WELDING ABOVE AND BELOW DECK

WELD THE CHAIN PLATES TO THE HULL SKIN. WELD IN SHORT SAY 1" [25] RUNS, STAGGERING THE RUNS TO AVOID EXCESSIVE MARKS ON OUTSIDE OF HULL.

SNAPE OFF END OF 2ND. CHAINPLATE

welding stainless on top of mild steel or other metals is dangerous. Make sure the chain plate angle is in line with the load of the shroud or stay. Check fore and aft angles and loads, as well as the obvious athwartship ones. All loads of this type should be in sheer and avoid all twisting or bending loads.

CLEATS

Make sure your cleats are adequately sized to handle the lines that they are intended to accept. Cleats may be made of aluminum or stainless steel. Painted mild steel cleats would corrode due to the paint being worn off when the cleats are in use. Try to position them in such a way as to minimise the chances of stubbing your toe. In many cases cleats have to be in a certain location, but you can usually manage to avoid placing them in the most dangerous places. Fastening the cleats to decks coamings and cabin tops should be a simple matter of welding them in place.

You should always use 316 stainless steel when making these items. It is worth taking the fabricated cleats to a metal shop and having them polished, as the finish will be long lasting. One of the many advantages of building a metal boat is the fact that you can weld most cleats and fittings directly to the deck or other surface. Your plans may include the exact locations of the sail handling cleats or you may confer with your rigger and or sail maker for suggestions in this area. In a sailboat you will have a variety of cleats including ones to accept the various sheets and halyards.

Both sail and powerboats require mooring cleats and these should include one each side in the following locations: one near the bow, one midships and one near the stern. The midship pair are sometimes omitted and this is a pity because these are often the most useful. If your boat is over 40 ft / 12.19 M, then you may require additional mooring cleats. It is always advisable to install a substantial cleat on the foredeck; this cleat can be used for towing as well as other purposes. Even if you have a substantial anchor winch, the centre line cleat can be used when laying additional anchors. Always make sure that any cleats bits or other fittings that are welded directly to the deck or superstructure are fully welded to the surface. Do not leave gaps where moisture can creep underneath and start a pattern of corrosion that can result in failure of the fitting and severe corrosion of the deck or other surface. The foregoing advice applies to all fittings welded to a deck, coaming or cabin top.

A thickened section of plate under the cleat or other fitting may be required and in any case this is just good practice.

BITTS

On our boat we prefer mooring bitts to cleats. Cleats are fine for sail handling and control but when you have the weight of the entire boat plus a surging action wanting to separate a mooring line from your

Example of well made stainless steel mooring bollard

boat, then a well built set of bitts is preferred. Six of these fittings should suffice on boats up to 55 ft / 16.76 M, one pair up near the bow, one pair amidships and another near the stern. These bitts make the best termination for your mooring lines and will provide a perfect arrangement should you decide to take your sailboat through some of the canals and waterways of Europe, the USA and elsewhere. As with all stainless fittings that you can weld directly to the boat, do not forget to paint 1 to 2 in / 25 to 50 mm up the sides of the stainless fitting to ensure no corrosive action will take place between dissimilar metals.

BOLLARDS

Bollards are deck fittings featuring a tubular base with a solid pin set at right angles to form a fitting that is something of a cross between a cleat and a set of bitts. On advantage of these fittings is that as they are a popular power boat item, they are easy to obtain ready made in stainless steel. Of course you can make your own from tube and solid rod. As with many fittings, you may decide to purchase one as a pattern and then make as many as you require thus saving yourself a great deal of cash.

STANCHIONS AND GUARDRAILS

Stanchions and guardrails as well as pulpits and pushpits are best fabricated from stainless steel, however if the cost is too daunting then galvanised and painted ones will be the next best thing. Some builders construct stanchions and chain plates as a combination fitting. In my opinion it is better to separate these items as, they need strength in different areas. There is much discussion as to whether you should weld the stanchion directly to the deck or mount it on a plate that is in turn bolted in place. Other experts suggest that an oversize pipe socket to accept the stanchion can be welded to the deck. My opinion is that provided that the stainless variety, as mentioned earlier, are painted at the attachment point, then these and mild steel stanchions are best welded directly to the deck.

If you wanted to have the ultimate connection, then you could have 2 1/2" / 35 mm square or disk of 1/4" / 6 mm plate bevelled on the edges so the thicker portion stands proud of the deck and then welded in place. The stanchion is simply welded to this thicker, reinforced and raised plate. The water will naturally run off the area of the stanchion/deck join and minimise the chance of corrosion.

If your boat is large enough you may wish to consider guard rails as opposed to stanchions and wire lifelines. Any sailboat over 40 ft / 12.19 M should be able to 'carry' these. Any powerboat of even smaller size seems to look right when fitted with guardrails. To look right, the rails should be a smaller diameter than the stanchions. Rails of about 75 percent of the stanchion size seem about right. The diameter of the stanchions will depend on the size of boat. Any 'security fence' around the perimeter of your decks that is less than 28 in / 711 mm high is dangerous. You need stanchions that are 36 in / 914 mm high and this is perfect for security but would look too high on some boats. If possible combine your stanchions with at least a low bulwark, and this will keep the 'apparent overall height' of the stanchion/bulwark within reasonable limits. Don't forget access in your stanchion arrangements. You should have a 'gate' each side near the most obvious exits from your side decks.

If you opt for stanchions and wire lifelines, make sure you have either small diameter pipe fitted through the stanchions to carry the wire or use some method to avoid water getting into the stanchion and causing corrosion at the base. Use flexible stainless steel wire for lifelines, galvanised wire will not last long. The 'off the shelf' plastic coated variety is dangerous.

These pulpitt rails were made by the builder of this Roberts 44.

PULPIT AND PUSHPIT

The pulpit and pushpit can be built of the same metal as the stanchions but use a slightly larger diameter pipe. You can study other boats as to the latest trends and design of these items. The pulpit is best arranged with an opening in the most forward area so you can exit and enter the bow when moored 'bow to' as is necessary in some areas. This arrangement will combine well with a short bowsprit or platform. The pulpit can be a little higher than the guardrails without spoiling the overall 'line' of the hull.

The pushpit or stern pulpit needs a gate for aft access to the boarding ladder or swim platform. Before designing and fabricating this safety feature, study other boats similar of size and style to your own.

BOW FITTINGS

These can be fabricated from 316 stainless steel and if you are fortunate, your plans may include specific details on how to construct this item. On a sailboat, the bow fitting will most likely include tangs for the forestay and a position to attach the furler or tack of the jib.

Depending on the arrangement for your boat, you may also incorporate rollers, one for the anchor chain and another for anchor line. If you wish to stow the anchor under the bow roller then a 'Bruce' or a 'CQR' may be arranged in that manner.

ANCHOR LOCKER

You will want to decide if you want the self-draining variety, that is one where the drains are at the bottom of the locker and where the locker is sealed off from

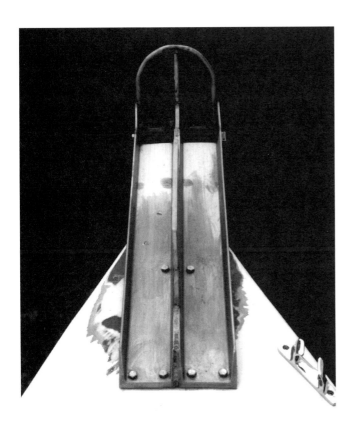

This sturdy stainless steel bow fitting is up to the job however the fairlead looks a little undersize for this boat.

HAWSE PIPES

Formally the preserve of larger vessels, hawse pipes are now often seen on power boats as small as 30 ft / 9.14 M. If you carry only one bow anchor and your hawse pipe is only on one side this can be a problem when anchoring under certain wind and sea conditions as the chain can chafe the bow. In a smaller boat the hawse pipe should be located in the bow itself and placed on the centre line. Where you are able, have an anchor locker with a bulkhead down the centre line and then carry two bow anchors, each in their own hawse pipe. This arrangement is worth considering, especially on a larger powerboat. Make sure the actual hawse pipe is large enough for the chain, about 3 to 4 times the diameter of the chain should be about right. Do not install a hawse pipe so that the chain has to make any difficult bends before it self stows in the chain locker.

When you boat is fitted with one or more hawse pipes, you will need to make some provision for preventing the anchor from damaging the hull paint-work or even scoring the hull itself. A light stainless steel plate is usually placed around the area where the anchor will reside. In addition you should fit a floating ring that stows permanently over the chain and lays between the anchor and the hull.

Especially in a sailboat, I would favour a small bow platform or bowsprit and then the anchor and chain would be more accessible at all times. If you have one or more hawse pipes then you will only be able to carry an anchor similar to the one shown here.

CHANGING AN EXISTING BOAT

In this section I want to discuss the possibility of altering a boat you already own or one you can acquire at the right price. Here the definition of changing means to shorten, lengthen or maybe even widen an existing boat. In my opinion widening a boat is almost impossible, so unless you have some information that has eluded me all these years, then you had best put that idea aside. If you are thinking of changing your boat, then it is simpler to make these alterations to a boat built of metal than it is to make similar modifications to one built of fiberglass or timber.

It is uncommon to consider shortening an existing powerboat so I will confine my remarks to the possibility of lengthening a sail or powerboat. Steel aluminum and copper-nickel all present about the same amount of difficulty, so they can be considered at the same time. There is one exception to the above statement. This concerns the shortening of barges and

the rest of the boat. Water can drain out; it can also flush in through the drain holes. I prefer a locker that drains via a pipe to the bilge where the bilge pump is located.

Many cruising boats carry two anchors in the forward anchor locker however very few are divided so that the anchor line and or chains do not become mixed between the two anchors. Generally the main anchor, plough or ëBruceí style (sorry no relation!), is kept stowed on bow rollers or small bowsprit and ready for use. The secondary anchor, usually a ëDanforth typeí is stowed in the locker along with its rope and/or chain. Some anchor lockers are arranged so that the chain runs through a tube down towards the centre of the boat. This puts the weight where it can contribute to the stability of the vessel. If you decide to arrange your anchor chain in this manner, make sure that you can gain access to assist the chain to stow neatly. Also ensure that it can not get loose in the event of a knockdown. In the case of a third anchor, you may want to consider carrying this at or near the stern, where it can be useful in situations where you wish to anchor fore and aft.

similar vessels. Many Dutch and other European working barges are shortened when they are converted from commercial to pleasure usage.

LENGTHENING A POWER BOAT

Over the past century, thousands of large metal powerboats have been lengthened. This usually occurred when their current or new owners decided that it was less expensive and/or otherwise more desirable, to increase the size of the boat as opposed to buying or building a new vessel.

There are many factors to be considered before you commit to changing the dimensions of your metal powerboat. Firstly when to make the addition. Many owners often mistakenly believe that to increase the length, it is just a matter of adding a few feet to the stern. While many boats are lengthened in this manner, it is worth exploring all the options before making the final decision on how you will tackle the project.

If you opt for extending the stern here are a few items you will need to consider. Will the engine room need to be moved? How about the rudder(s), how will they be affected. Steering location; will the new longer hull be harder to steer from the current steering station. How will the hull lines be continued and how will this affect the handling. Will the fore and aft trim of the vessel be affected and how can we overcome any problems in any of these areas. Many of these factors will need to be discussed preferably with the original designer or if that is not possible then you should seek the help of a suitably qualified naval architect.

The reason that extending a powerboat by lengthening the stern is such a popular option is that usually it means that the interior accommodation, electrics and plumbing can be similarly extended without disturbing the existing arrangements.

LENGTHENING A SAILBOAT

On reflection, I consider it easier to increase the size of a powerboat as opposed to lengthening a sail driven vessel. Here we have a whole new set of factors to consider the position and length of the keel, the amount and location of the ballast, the location of the auxiliary and the possible increase in the size of the rig. These are all factors that need consideration when increasing the size of a metal sailboat. If your plan changes are in these areas, you will need the services of the original designer. It is my opinion that lengthening a sailboat is probably not worth the trouble.

CHANGING CABIN STRUCTURES

This is one area where you may be able to improve your existing boat. Firstly on no account raise the overall height of the cabin structure without seeking professional advice. You may totally destroy the handling and performance of your vessel if you raise the cabin top beyond sensible limits. The most common change made to cabins is the addition of a pilothouse. While this can be a worthwhile addition for many boats, it is one that needs to be carefully designed before changes are made. Keep it light and keep it low! Pilothouses are discussed elsewhere.

Metal boats especially traditional types like the Sprays are ideal for saving money. You can make all your own fittings and they don't look out of place. Ulrich Kronberg made all the fittings for his Spray 40 including the parrel balls pictured here.

Chapter 16
COPPER-NICKEL

A special report on Copper-nickel - Pretty Penny by C. A. Powell consultant metallurgist, with notes by R. Bruce Roberts-Goodson

INTRODUCTION

The Pretty Penny was designed and commissioned by Alan Beckett, an engineer and sailing enthusiast, whose aim was to create a maintenance free sailing yacht. The material chosen for her construction was 90-10 Copper-nickel. She was built by Arma Marine Engineering Co Ltd in the UK and launched in 1979. In October 1995, 16 years after she was built, she was hauled to be thoroughly surveyed for the first time since her launch. An invitation was issued to the writer to examine the boat. This report collates the

Photographs taken Nov.1995 of 'Pretty Penny' unpainted Copper-Nickel sailboat, launched in 1977 and showing no fouling apart from a few isolated barnacles in propeller aperture, after 18 years on tidal mooring.

information available about the vessel, recent surveys about her condition and comments on her overall performance.

DESCRIPTION

The boat is 31 ft / 9.45 M, LOD and 9 ft / 2.74 M Beam and had a draft of 5 ft 1.52 M, and a gross tonnage of 7.66 tons. The framing, hull and superstructure plating were fabricated using 90-10 copper-nickel. The hull is slightly magnetic which indicates not all the iron and alloy composition is in solution. The hull is plated in 1/8" / 3 mm plate and the same materials were used to form the L angle framing material.

This boat has never been painted inside or out. The life rails, pulpit and propeller shaft was in stainless steel. The propeller is a regular off the shelf bronze version so the exact composition of the metal is unknown. The deck was originally covered with Trackmark but the adhesive failed and this was replaced with regular marine deck paint.

PERFORMANCE

Since the launch, she has been afloat continuously and moored for the greater part of the time in the River Swale, at Uplees off the Thames estuary. For the first three years she remained free of fouling but since then her owner has found it necessary to scrub her at least once a year. For the most part, the form of fouling was weed and barnacles, mainly concentrated at about 6-12 in / 150-300 mm below the waterline and quite easily removed by a scraper. She has a 10-hp Volvo single cylinder engine and sails well with a clean bottom managing 5 knots in force 4-5 conditions.

CONDITION AFTER 16 YEARS

In October 1995, the yacht was removed from the water for the first time since her launch 16 years ago and inspected at Conyer Marine, at Teynham, Kent. Prior to inspection, Mr Beckett cleaned the hull for the first time during the year, there was a grass layer but hardly any barnacles were noticed. The grass was loosely adherent and a piece of wood cleaned this away in a few minutes. The yacht has been sailed very little during the past 12 months. It is worthy to note that the surveyor concluded that the craft could be considered in 'almost new condition with the hull plating in the same condition as when she was originally built.'

The owner noticed some seepage from a small hole on the stem at the waterline and cured it at the point

of the leak and fitted a washer. Concerned that he might be getting thinning of the hull around the waterline, he asked a firm of specialists to take ultrasonic measurements of the hull around the waterline. This survey report showed that there appeared to be some thinning of the original 3-mm down to 2.7 mm at the waterline on the main part of the hull and 2 mm near the bow. The owner speculated that some of the material in the bow area was lost by over zealous grinding during the construction stage.

C.A. Powell was invited to examine Pretty Penny by then cradled at Iron Wharf boat yard, Faversham and visited her on 8th November. The hull was indeed in excellent condition and had amazed the boat yard staff when they became aware that the boat had been in the water continuously for the past 16 years. Photographs of the hull are included elsewhere in this book. The stainless steel rails and rigging seemed in excellent condition and are still looking bright and shiny. There did not appear to be any galvanic problems with the copper-nickel connections.

COMMENT BY C.A. POWELL

Overall the Pretty Penny was in excellent condition and Alan Beckett seems pleased with her performance. The hull remains a unique testimony to the corrosion performance of copper-nickel in a marine environment over 16 years, both above and below the water.

Aesthetically, the copper colour above the waterline might not appeal to all when compared to painted vessels. The original concept was to produce a maintenance free hull and without doubt this area is in perfect condition. (See notes by Bruce Roberts-Goodson later in this chapter.)

When considering the water line and ignoring the grinding effects during fabrication, the corrosion rate of the hull at the bow averaged .019 mm per year. General corrosion rate for immersed copper based alloys given for guidance is generally in the range 0.025 -0.0025 mm per year. In practice, immersed corrosion rates would be expected to reduce with time as the surface films matured.

The thinning near the bow appears to be in excess of the norm and as the speed of the vessel would not suggest the possibility or erosion. The thinning at the waterline and particularly at the stem and bow has been noticed in other boat studies for copper-nickel and will need to be examined more closely in future and verified. It is however a useful observation for perhaps incor-porating greater thickness for the bow waterline area in future boat design. (See notes by R. B. R-G).

The anti fouling behaviour is not ideal being fouling free for 3 years and then requiring a scrubbing once a year. The vessel is not very actively used latterly and such behaviour is in line with observations of fouling build up in quiet waters in test work carried out at the LaQue Centre for Corrosion Technology by Efird. The sailing speeds may also have been too low to effectively remove the fouling once it had occurred. It is encouraging to note that the fouling once formed was easily removed by using a wooden scraper.

NOTES BY THE AUTHOR - R B. R-G:

I have long been aware of the existence of Pretty Penny having sailed in the general area of the Swale River over a number of years. It was a pleasant surprise when I learned that she had been hauled and I was invited to inspect her at nearby Iron Wharf boat yard. During my visit I was fortunate in being able to discuss with the owner the design and construction of this vessel.

My observations of the exterior of the hull were in line with those outlined earlier so I will not repeat them except to say I was most favourably impressed with the general condition of the vessel considering the age and the fact that it had been under-used for a considerable time. It is common knowledge in our profession that generally speaking; the more that a boat is used the better condition she is likely to sustain.

Regarding the thinning of the plating near the bow and to a lesser extend on and near the waterline, it is my contention that the latter was a known natural wastage of the material but that the thinning near the bow was probably due to grinding during the construction. In any case a very simple remedy to this known wastage factor is to use a slightly thicker material at the waterline and bow areas, see my comments in later paragraph.

INTERIOR FRAMING

On being invited to inspect the interior and make a detailed study of the construction techniques used to build the hull decks and superstructure my enthusiasm grew as I inspected each detail of the methods used to frame and plate the vessel. Fortunately Mr Beckett at least in things boating is something of minimalist, so the interior framing was not covered and this made a detailed inspection possible. The framing was angle that had been simply bent from strips of the same material as was used to build the hull, namely 1/8" / 3 mm plate. I was very impressed with this boat and it together with other experiences with this material has inspired me to prepare preliminary calculations on existing designs to enable them to be built in copper-nickel.

OTHER COPPER-NICKEL BOATS

Sanford Marine of Richmond California built one copper-nickel boat that I would like to hear more about. In 1988 this company built the lower portion of what appears to be a composite sailboat out of 90-10 copper-nickel. The report goes into some detail about the construction of the lower sections of the hull and keel. The copper-nickel tanks were all

No matter which material you choose you will find that the method of building the hull upside-down has much to recommend it. Here we see a Spray 38 being built in UK

integral. It appeared from the text and the photographs that the topsides and the remainder of the boat were to be built in a different material. But what material?

That is the question I would like answered. Can you help? Below are listed some other copper-nickel boats some of which I have additional information but others are unknown to me. Besides those listed there are several projects in various countries, this writer will welcome any information. Some of the larger vessels listed below are fishing trawlers and I have a considerable amount of information about those. Again any information you the reader can supply will be gratefully received and reported in future editions of this book.

VESSEL	LENGTH	LAUNCHED	BUILT	HULL (MM)	HOME PORT
Asperida 11	16M/52'-6"	1968	Holland	4mm	USA
Illona	16M/52'-6"	1968	Holland	4mm	Caracas
Copper Mariner	22M/72-'2"	1971	Mexico	6mm	Nicaragua
Pink Lotus	17M/55'-9"	1975	Mexico	4mm	Sri Lanka
Pink Orchard	17M/55'-9"	1975	Mexico	4mm	Sri Lanka
Pink Jasmine	17M/55'-9"	1975	Mexico	4mm	Sri Lanka
Pink Rose	17M/55'-9"	1975	Mexico	4mm	Sri Lanka
Sieglinde Marie	21M/68'-10"	1978	UK	6mm	Caribbean
Pretty Penny	10M/32'-10"	1979	UK	3mm	UK
Akisushima	10M/32'-10"	1991	Japan	4mm	Japan

Radius chine hulls like the Roberts 432 pictured here are ideal candidates for building in copper-nickel. If you want maintenance free boat that will literally last forever, then this material may be your choice.

ROBERTS 310
PILOT HOUSE VERSION

Pilothouses can be added to alomost any sized sail or powerboat. Center cockpits and pilot house combin-ations should not be considered for boats under 33ft/10.00 M LOD

Chapter 17
SAIL DESIGNS FOR METAL

Tom Thumb 26. Roberts 28. Roberts 310. Roberts 345. Spray 33. Spray 36. Roberts 370. Roberts 392. P.C.F. 40. Centennial Spray 34/36/38/45. Spray Pilot house 40. Roberts 420. Roberts 432. Roberts 434. New York 46. Roberts 532. Roberts 58. Spray 55. Roberts 64. New York 55. New York 65 .Trader 65

The displacements shown for these designs are for **Loaded Displacement**, and include allowances for fuel, water and stores as well as the crew and their personal gear. All of the designs mentioned are available as stock plans. The plans consist of many sheets of large scale, well detailed drawings with copious written notes. These designs are available with a variety of superstructures, keels and sail plans. This allows you to customize your own version from the standard set of stock plans. Also included are full size patterns for the frames, stem, deck beams and other important parts of the construction.

Most of the designs featured in this section have been built in considerable numbers and consequently are well proven boats that can be recommended for family sailing and long distance cruising.

Additional information and study plans for these and other designs that are suitable for building in Aluminium, Copper-nickel or Steel is available from any Bruce Roberts Design office (see appendix 4).

Roberts 432: *This multi-chine steel version is now a successful charter boat in the Mediterranean*
SEE MORE ON OUR WEB SITE
http://www.bruce-roberts.com

Roberts 434 *built in Riga Latvia as a hull and deck kit for a Swedish client who completed the boat.*

HISTORY OF THE ROBERTS SPRAY SERIES:

The story of Captain Joshua Slocum and his sloop, *Spray, is* standard reading for any cruising yachtsman and the Captain's book, Sailing Alone Around *The World,* makes fine reading. Over the last 100 years, it has been the inspiration for many of those who go to sea in small boats.

Some years ago, our design office was approached by a Spray enthusiast who wanted to know if we could prepare plans for the Spray to be built in fiberglass. It so happened, while we were considering this request, another approach was made by an English yachtsman who had just completed a voyage from England to Australia and who wanted plans for a cruising vessel similar to the *Spray.*

It was a challenge; so we researched and came up with sufficient information to convince us that the proposition was practical. Work was started on the plans. About this time, we were fortunate in securing a copy of Ken Slack's book, In *The Wake Of The Spray,* which provided a wealth of information. Ken, an Australian, had included a detailed analysis of most aspects of the *Spray,* which was of great help. Much of the information in Ken's book is now included in Bruce Roberts-Goodson's book *SPRAY THE ULTIMATE CRUISING BOAT.*

For those of you who are not already familiar with the original *Spray,* perhaps this is a good time to recap some of the exploits of this fine boat, and lay to rest some of the misconceptions and half-truths that have been written about her over the past 100 years. In 1892, Joshua Slocum at age 51, was given an aging and decrepit sloop the *Spray.* The Captain spent the next few years rebuilding the vessel. He removed the centerboard and replaced almost every piece of timber in the hull and deck. All of the materials used were collect around Fairhaven, Massachusetts, where the vessel had lain in a field for several years.

The *Spray's* lineage is clear when one examines photographs of old and still-sailing examples of the North Sea fishing boats than have worked off the coast of England and France for at least 150 years. Slocum's *Spray* was reputed to have served as an oyster dragger off the New England coast. Slocum sought to improve the sea-worthiness of his acquisition by adding freeboard, so that the vessel would be better suited to the deep water sailing that he obviously had in mind.

After a year of commercial fishing on the Atlantic coast and generally proving the worth of his new boat, Slocum decided to undertake a voyage that even today is not undertaken lightly. Slocum's trip proved a resounding success. Not only did he achieve what he set out to do, that is, circumnavigate the world singlehanded, but he proved the many fine features of the *Spray* and that is what we are considering here.

Building replicas of the *Spray is* certainly not new. Although ours were to be the first foam/glass versions many copies of the *Spray* had already been built in other materials. The first known replica was built in Rochester, England in 1902. This slightly enlarged Spray 42 feet overall was built by Gill of Rochester and sold abroad to a German buyer. The history of this replica makes interesting reading. She was renamed *Heimat* and was sailed extensively in European waters, making voyages to Norway, and spending a lot of time sailing in the Baltic. During the course of her career, *Heimat* became *Jurand,* and was sold to two Polish owners. Her history extends right through into the Second World War when she was captured by the German navy and used as a training school for the Luftwaffe. She was re-captured at the end of the war by the R.A.F. It is believed she was then towed back to England, where she disappeared into obscurity. Another replica was the *Pandora,* which was built in Perth, Australia, in about 1908. This vessel sailed from Australia to New Zealand and then on to Pitcairn and Easter Island. From Easter Island, the Pandora sailed for Cape Horn, arriving off the Horn in January 1911. A week later, she was struck by a huge wave that rolled her over completely. It is an interesting point to note that the vessel was self-righting. She did come up the right way after being capsized. In the Faukland Islands, repairs were made to the Pandora and she crossed on to St. Helena, and on to New York. Several other Spray replicas have been built in Australia, and this is not surprising considering that Slocum spent a considerable amount of time in both Melbourne and Sydney. The *Spray* caused a great deal of interest in the yachting fraternity in those cities.

In the United States, many replicas have been built. The late John G. Hanna, well-known naval architect of Dunedin, Florida, designed modified versions of the Spray, which were built in sizes ranging up to 100 feet. Another well-known U.S. boatbuilder/designer Captain RD (Pete) Culler, built two Sprays, one for his own use, and another for Gilbert Klingel. Captain Culler owned his Spray for 23 years and in various writings, both he and Mrs.Culler spoke very highly of the Spray's sea-worthiness and comfort.

The list of successes and virtues of the many Spray replicas that have been built is far too long to be listed here. In fact, some of the voyages and comments of owners and builders of Sprays make almost as interesting reading as does the voyage of the original.

It is a fact that the Spray as Slocum sailed her, would be most unacceptable to the cruising yachtsman of today. Firstly, Slocum's accommodations were basic. He had the after-cabin fitted out with two berths, a sea chest, and book racks. The forward section of the vessel was used as a cargo hold, and nowhere were there provisions for the modern cooking and toilet facilities which are considered essential by today's yachtsmen.

Because of the volume provided by the Spray's hull, it was a simple matter to arrange several alternate accommodation plans to allow for the varied tastes of today's cruising fraternity. During the design stage, it was decided that instead of having the over-sized cut-water at the bow, it would be preferable to fair in the forward sections above the waterline, and hopefully to improve the appearance. These minor changes would in no way adversely affect the sailing performance of the design.

Since those early days we have gone on to design many new versions of the Spray including those shown in this publication. The round bilge Steel Spray replicas are now very popular.

SPRAY 33

There are over 400 examples already on the water and cruising throughout the world. This design is a smaller versions of the original Spray and share many of the same features. Either can be built in Steel, Aluminum or Copper-nickel. These designs are available in double chine or round bilge hull form. A large variety of deck layouts including centre cockpit, aft cockpit and pilot house versions are available for these boats. Below is a photograph of Maureen Jenkins, who recently sailed her Spray 33 single-handed to the Azores

Available sail plans for the Spray 33 include Bermudian cutter and ketch, Gaff cutter, schooner or ketch, or Junk schooner. The exploits of many previously built examples of these Sprays are detailed in 'Spray the Ultimate Cruising Boat'

LOA:	37'-8" / 11.48 M
LOD:	32'-11" / 10.03 M
LWL:	26'-7" / 8.13 M
BEAM:	12'-0" / 3.66 M
DRAFT:	4'-0" / 1.22 M

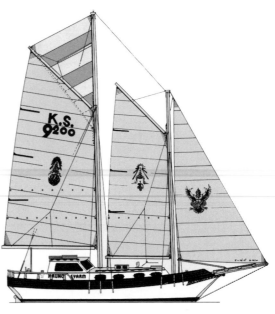

SPRAY 36

LOA:	41'-0" / 12.50 M
LOD:	36'-10" / 11.22 M
BEAM:	12'-0" / 3.66 M
DRAFT:	4'-0" / 1.22 M
DISPLACEMENT:	24,400 LB / 11,068 KG
HULL FORM:	CHINE or ROUND BILGE

The Spray 36 is a very popular design and over 300 hundred examples are currently sailing in various parts of the world. We have long since lost count of the number of circumnavigations that have been made in this Spray's built to this design.

There are many different versions of this boat, check with your nearest Bruce Robertst Design office for details.

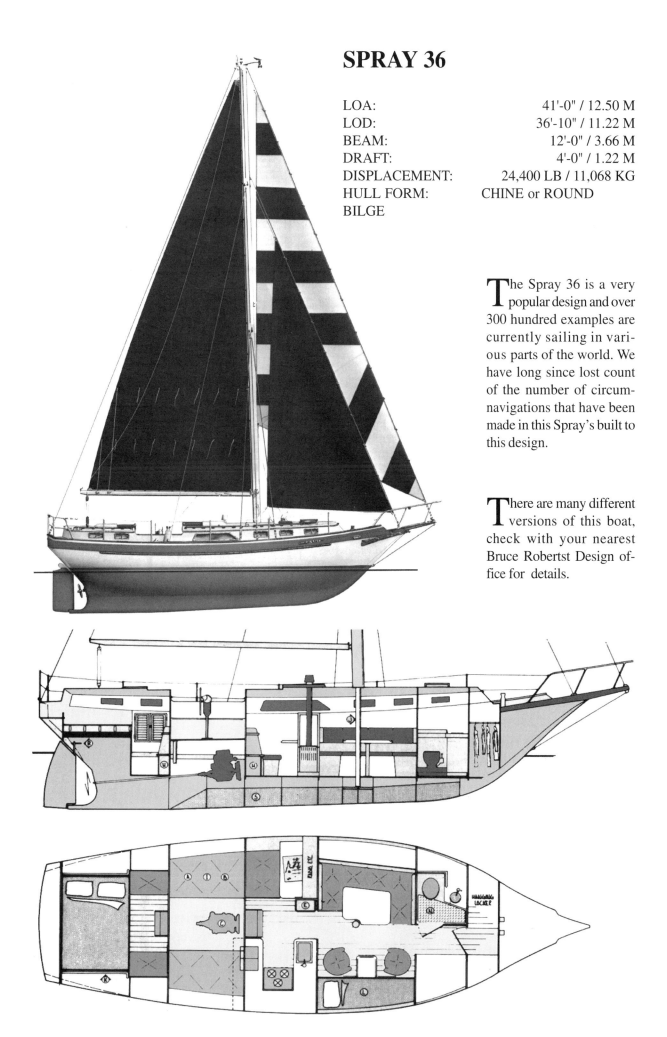

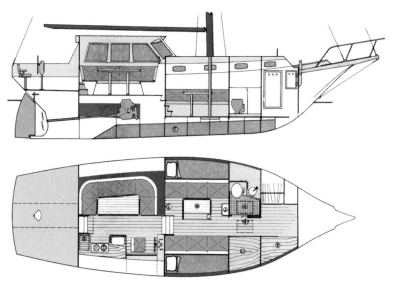

SPRAY 36 B

MULTI CHINE
STEEL ALUMINUM
OR COPPER-NICKEL.

LOD	36'-10" 11.23 M
LWL	30'-0" 9.14 M
BEAM	12'-0" 3.65 M
DRAFT	4'-0" 1.22 M
DISPL	24,400 LB 11,068 Kg
BALST	8,400 LB 3,810 Kg

This aft cockpit version combined with a generous sized pilot house offers many alternate lay-out possibilities. Using the Super Study Plan package you can design your own interior accommodation.

SPRAY 36 C

MULTI CHINE
STEEL ALUMINUM OR
COPPER-NICKEL.

LOD	36'-10" 11.23 M
LWL	30'-0" 9.14 M
BEAM	12'-0" 3.65 M
DRAFT	4'-0" 1.22 M
DISPL	24,400 LB 11,068 Kg
BALST	8,400 LB 3,810 Kg

Over 300 completed. The 'C' version of the Spray 40 has been so popular that we received many requests for a similar arrangement for the smaller Spray 36. There is a great photograph of David Sinnett-Jones 'Zane Spray' in the book *SPRAY The Ultimate Cruising Boat.* The same book details David's single handed **round the world voyage** as well as his Atlantic crossings in the SINGLE HANDED TRANS-ATLANTIC RACE.

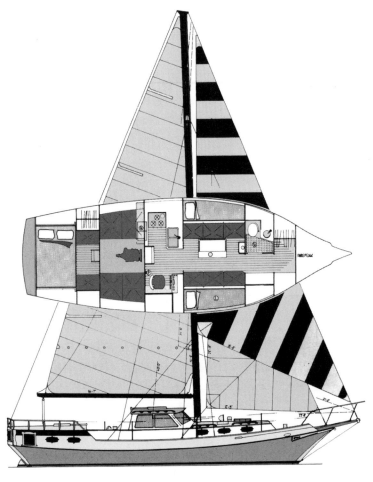

If you are seeking the maximum family accommodation while retaining the excellent sailing qualities of the Spray then this version may be just for you.

Note the 4 ft / 1.22 M draft, this is one of the shallowest fixed keel cruising boats available that really sails!

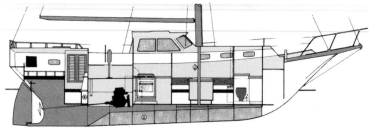

Centennial Spray 34

ROUND BILGE STEEL

To celebrate the one hundredth anniversary of Slocum's record-setting voyage, we are designing a new **'Centennial Spray'** series.

These boats embody all of the desirable features of the Spray plus incorporate the improvements we have discovered over the past 30 years of designing, building and sailing these boats. Sprays are available from 34' to 75' and these boats are in correct proportions to the original Spray.

These new Sprays have been designed to be built using **Round bilge steel Aluminum or Copper-Nickel.** At present they are available for the materials as indicated for each plan.

The **Centennial Spray 34** is rigged as a gaff schooner however any rig can be used to power this boat. Custom accommodation arrangements may be drawn to your requirements. Center cockpit, pilot house and other similar arrangements are available for these new designs.

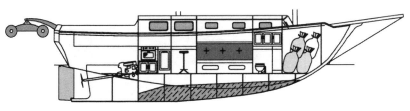

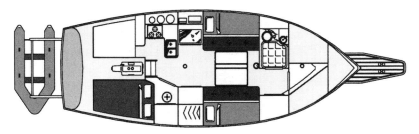

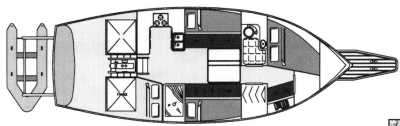

Specifications Centennial Spray 34

LOD .... 34'-9" 10.59 M
LWL .... 30'-11" 9.45 M
BEAM .... 13'-0" 3.96 M
DRAFT .... 4'-9" 1.45 M
DISPL. .... 27,000 LB 12,247 KG

Centennial Spray 36
ROUND BILGE STEEL

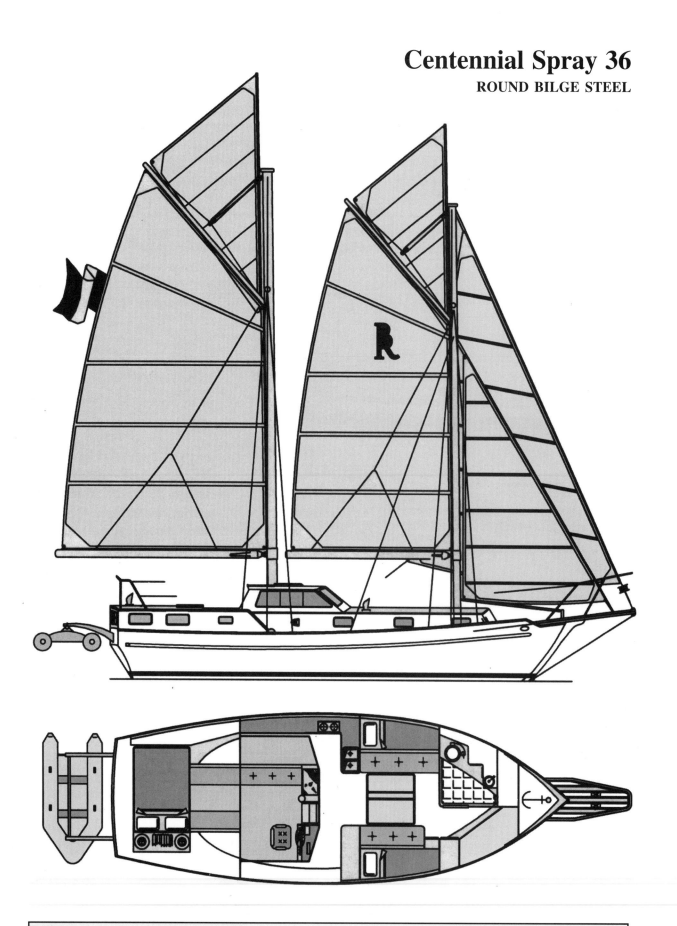

LOD	36'-4"	11.05 M
LWL	32'-4"	9.85 M
BEAM	13'-0"	3.96 M
DRAFT	4'-3"	1.30 M
DISPL	28,000 LB	12,700 K
MATL		RB STEEL

The CS34 is designed for Round bilge STEEL plans are also available to build in Aluminum or Copper-Nickel. The large scale building plans and full size patterns include all information to build this boat including patterns for casting the ballast.

CENTENNIAL SPRAY 38

LOD	38'-6" 11.73 M
LWL	33'-1" 10.08 M
BEAM	14'-1" 4.29 M
DRAFT	4'-10" 1.47 M
DISPL	35,638 LB 16,174 KG
SAILS	1,007 SQ FT 93.55 SQ M

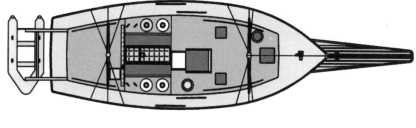

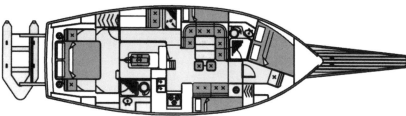

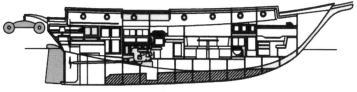

The Centennial Spray 38 is designed for Round bilge steel and Wood/Epoxy construction.

Already several sets of plans and full size patterns have been sold to experienced builders so we expect to see a number of this design in the water before too long. An option would be to fit this hull with a pilot house. You could choose between a center or aft cockpit configuration. The possibilities are endless.

Semi-custom plans can be made available to build in fiberglass or wood/epoxy, enquire at your local Bruce Roberts Design office.

The Centennial Spray 38 shown on the right was built in Sweden by Tekno Material and is one of several Bruce Roberts designed boats built by that company.

SPRAY 38

MULTI CHINE STEEL, ALUMINUM OR COPPER-NICKEL

LOD .... 38'-10" 11.84 M
LWL .... 31'-8" 9.65 M
BEAM .... 13'-0" 3.96 M
DRAFT .... 4 FT/5 FT 1.22 / 1.52 M
DISPL .... 29,000 LB 13,154 KG

The Spray 38 was designed to be a slightly smaller and lighter version of the Spray 40 and plans and full size patterns are available to build this version in multi-chine steel or aluminum.

Over 100 Spray 38s have been completed and several have made extensive voyages, see 'Spray The Ultimate Cruising Boat' for details.

The Spray 38 also has other versions included with the plans and study plans. **Super Study plans** to build this boat in all metals and include some construction sheets.

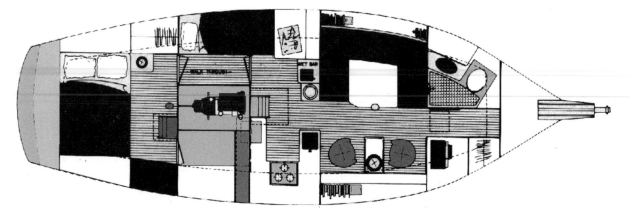

SPRAY 40 A

LOD	40'-0"	12.19 M
LWL	31'-11"	9.73 M
BEAM	14'-4"	4.37 M
DRAFT (Regular)	4'-2"	1.27 M
DRAFT (Deep)	5'-0"	1.52 M
DISPL	35,480 LB	16,257 Kg

Back in 1968 the Spray 40 was the first of our Spray replicas and was designed for Charlie Jupp and John Haskins both of whom built fiberglass Spray 40s at Marine Park Brisbane Australia.

There are now over 1,000 Spray 40s cruising in all parts of the world. If you would like to read about these and some of the other hundreds of Sprays currently in service then we recommend you read 'SPRAY The Ultimate Cruising Boat' where you will find details of hundreds of Sprays.

You can build the Spray 40 in **STEEL, ALUMINUM OR COPPER NICKEL.** Many have been built in each material. No matter where you cruise in your Spray you will meet many other owners and this establishes a comradeship unequalled in the boating world

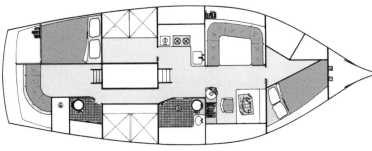

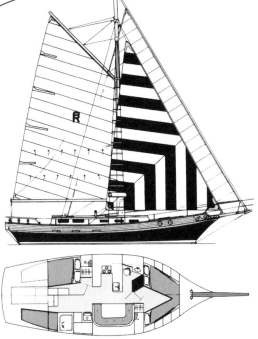

SPRAY 40 B

165

The Spray 40 'C' version is one of the most popular of the Spray range and hundreds are cruising in all parts of the world. This boat can be built in Steel, Aluminum or Copper-Nickel.

SPRAY 40 C

LOD	40'-0" 12.19 M
LWL	31'-11" 9.73 M
BEAM	14'-4" 4.37 M
DRAFT	(Regular) 4'-2" 1.27 M
DRAFT	(Deep) 5'-0" 1.52 M
DISPL	35,480 LB 16,257 Kg

NEW Spray 40 Pilot

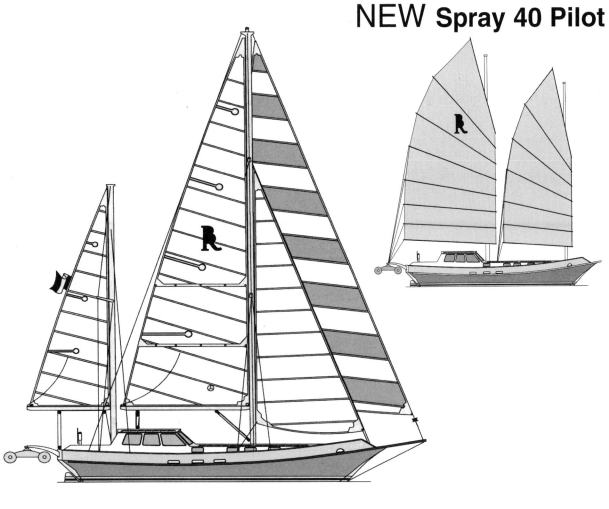

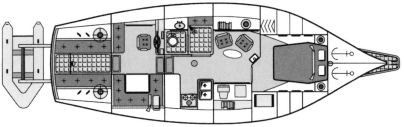

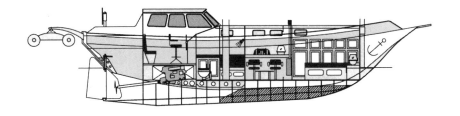

This new design has the same basic dimensions as the regular Spray 40.

The plans and full size patterns are available for steel multi chine.

Any rig that is available for the regular Spray 40 can be used on this version.

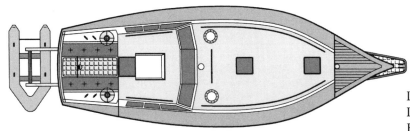

LOD	40'-0" 12.19 M
LWL	31'-11" 9.73 M
BEAM	14'-4" 4.37 M
DRAFT (Regular)	4'-2" 1.27 M
DRAFT (Deep)	5'-0" 1.52 M
DISPL	35,480 LB 16,257 Kg

CENTENNIAL SPRAY 45
Round bilge Steel or Wood/Epoxy

Specifications Centennial Spray 45

LOD .... 45'-6" 13.87 M
LWL .... 40'-9" 12.42 M
BEAM .... 15'-6" 4.72 M
DRAFT ....5'-0" 1.53 M
DISPL .... 49,000 LB 22,226 KG
SAILS ..... 1,007 SQ FT 93.55 SQ M

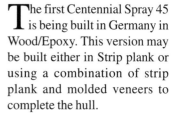

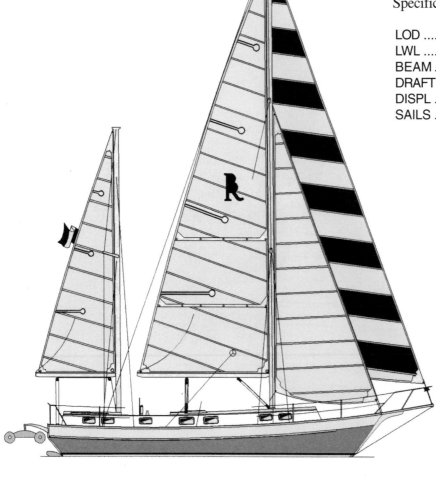

The first Centennial Spray 45 is being built in Germany in Wood/Epoxy. This version may be built either in Strip plank or using a combination of strip plank and molded veneers to complete the hull.

The Round bilge metal version may be built in Steel, Aluminum or Copper-Nickel or a combination of these metals. For instance many metal boats are built using steel for the hull and aluminum for the decks and superstructure.

Because of the large amount of room available in this design it lends itself to custom lay-outs. A pilot house version would make an ideal long distance cruising vessel providing shelter from the extremes of hot and cold weather that one encounters in many parts of the world.

A variety of rigs would be suitable for both this design and the the smaller Centennial Spray 38 so if you have a particular rig in mind then please contact any Bruce Roberts design office and let us know your ideas.

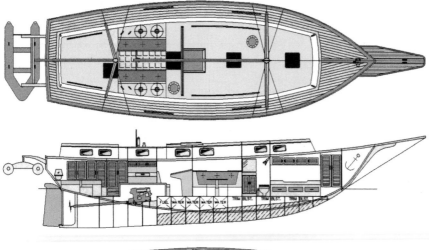

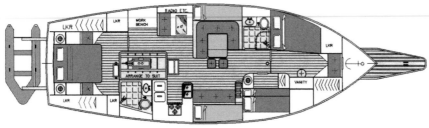

CENTENNIAL SPRAY 45

NEW VERSION B

Round bilge Steel, Aluminum or Copper-Nickel

LOD .... 45'-6" 13.87 M
LWL .... 40'-9" 12.42 M
BEAM .... 15'-6" 4.72 M
DRAFT ....5'-0" 1.53 M
DISPL .... 49,000 LB 22,226 KG
SAILS ..... 1,007 SQ FT 93.55 SQ M

The Round bilge metal version may be built in Steel, Aluminum or Copper-Nickel or a combination of these metals. For instance many metal boats are built using steel for the hull and aluminum for the decks and superstructure.

Because of the large amount of room available in this design it lends itself to custom lay-outs. A pilot house version would make an ideal long distance cruising vessel providing shelter from the extremes of hot and cold weather that one encounters in many parts of the world.

A variety of rigs would be suitable for both this design and the the smaller Centennial Spray 38 so if you have a particular rig in mind then please contact any Bruce Roberts design office and let us know your ideas.

Spray 55
Staysail Schooner

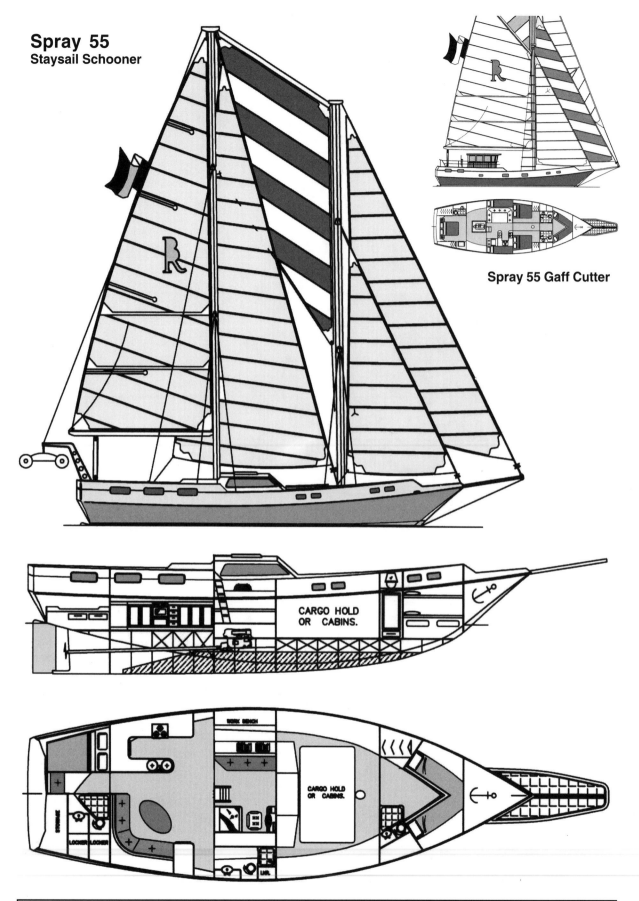

Spray 55 Gaff Cutter

CARGO HOLD OR CABINS.

WORK BENCH

CARGO HOLD OR CABINS.

LOA	55'-0" 16.70 M
LWL	46'-6" 14.17 M
BEAM	18'-0" 5.48 M
DRAFT	5'-3" 1.60 M
DISPL	5,000 LB 34,020 K

Plans are available for multi-chine Steel, Copper-Nickel or Aluminum Construction.

Bruce Roberts design office has prepared plans for many commercial and charter vessels so this Spray design was prepared with special interest. Other versions available.

ROBERTS 345

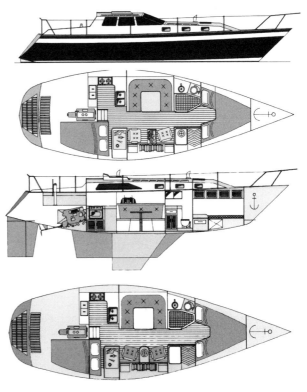

Over 200 of this design have been builtin several different configerations. This boat can be rigged as a sloop, cutter or ketch. A variety of keel and general arrangement combinatons, make this a very versitile design.

LOA	34'-5" / 10.50 M
LWL	28'-9" / 8.76 M
BEAM	11'-7" / 3.52 M
DRAFT	4'-3" - 5'-9" / 1.3 - 1.75 M
DISPLACEMENT	10,500 LB / 4,762 KG

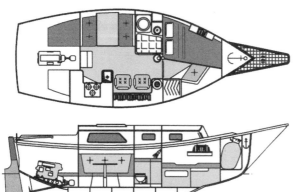

TOM THUMB 26

Developed from and effectively replacing the TT24, this larger version offers an incredible amount of living space for its size. The Tom Thumb 26 can be built in either Steel, Aluminum or Copper-nickel or a combination of any of these metals. Designed to be built using the 'frameless' construction techniques, this boat would make an ideal first project. This is a 'go anywhere boat' and capable of voyaging anywhere the crew can take her. The plans include alternate accommodation plans, a choice of rigs including, Bmu. Sloop, Gaff cutter and a cat rigged version.

LOA	.25'-11"	7.92 M
LWL	23'- 9"	7.24 M
BEAM	10'- 4"	3.15 M
DRAFT	4'- 0"	1.22 M

ROBERTS 310: Photos above and right show an R310 built by Ulysse Girouard in Canada. The R310 can be built in M/Chine, R/C Steel or Aluminium,

ROBERTS 28

ROBERTS 310

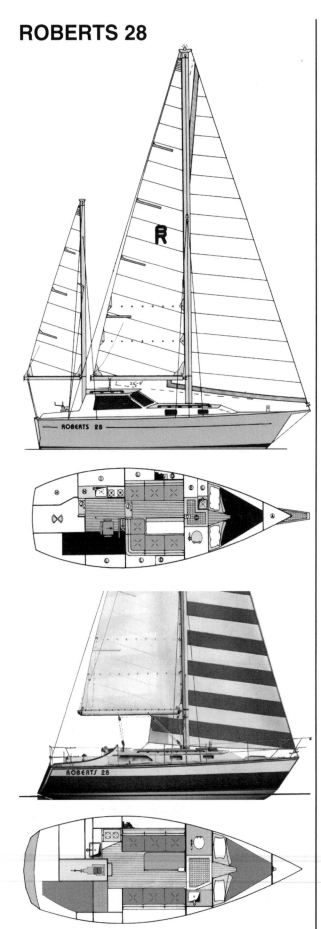

Pilot house version B

Trunk Cabin version A

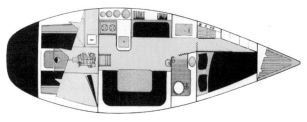

LOD	31'-0" / 9.45 M
LWL	25'-6" / 7.77 M
BEAM	10'-6" / 3.20 M
DRAFT	3'-6" - 5'-6" / 1.07 - 1.66 M

Designed for M/C Steel, Aluminum or Copper-Nickel, this popular design can be built as a regular or pilot house version.

MULIT-CHINE or R/C STEEL or ALUMINUM OR COPPER-NICKEL...... Over 100 of this design have been built in several different configurations. This boat can be rigged as a sloop or cutter combined with a variety of general arrangements. The Roberts 310 is a VERY fast boat.

ROBERTS 36

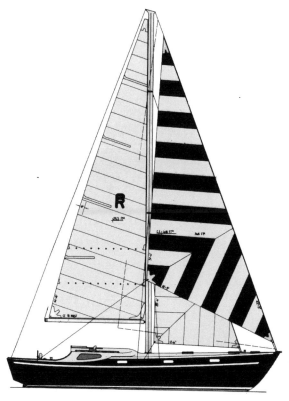

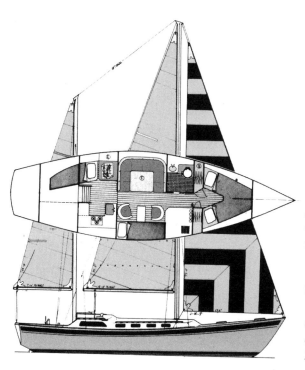

L.O.D	36'-9" [11.20]
L.W.L	28.9' [8.76]
Beam	11'-0" [3.35]
Draft	.4'-0" - 4'-9" [1.22 - 1.48]
Displ	18,000 LBS. [8,164 KG]

This design was drawn in 1971 and over 2,000 examples can be found in service around the world. You can build the LONG KEEL Roberts 36 in MULTI-CHINE STEEL, COPPER-NICKEL or ALUMINUM.

Many examples of this design have made numerous ocean crossings and several have completed complete circumnavigations. This is a great family boat and one that is ideal for both local and long distance cruising.

There are three basic versions Raised fore-deck, Pilot house / raised fore-deck and Aft cockpit / trunk cabin configeration. Any of the basic versions can be rigged as a cutter or ketch. We can design other rigs such as the Lug / Junk schooner or whatever your heart desires.

ROBERTS 370
VERSION A

This is one of our most popular designs and there are over 1,000 examples sailing in all parts of the world. As you can see by the information on this and following pages there many options and combinations that you can choose when you build this cruising sailboat. Designed as a performance cruiser while retaining those features popular with families, the R 370 is truly a boat that has something for everyone.

Big enough to be used as a live-aboard, fast enough to win Club championships, rugged enough to undertake World cruising and versatile enough to be built in any of the popular boat building materials; this could be the boat for you. There is even a **DROP KEEL** version, this may suit you if the waters are particulary shallow in the areas where you plan to cruise.

LOD	37'-2" 11.32 M	DISPL.	18750 LBS 8,512 Kg
LWL	31'-8" 9.66 M	BALST	8,000 LBS 3632 Kg
BEAM	12'-4" 3.76 M	AUX. PWR.	20 TO 50 HP
DRAFT-SHOAL	L4'-9" 1.45 M	SAIL	SLOOP, CUTTER, KETCH
DRAFT-DEEP	6'-6" 1.98 M	BALST	. LEAD OR SCRAP STEEL

SEE MORE ON OUR WEB SITE
http://www.bruce-roberts.com

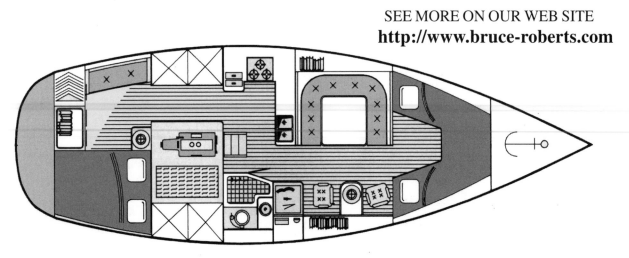

ROBERTS 370
VERSION B

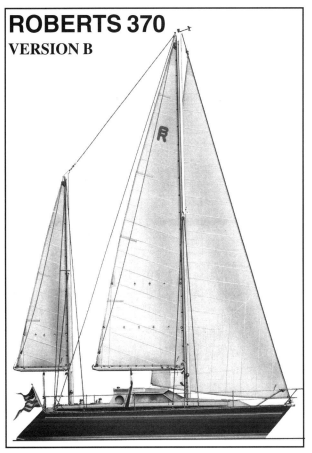

ROBERTS 370
VERSION C

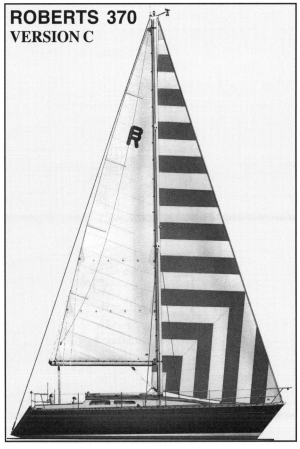

ROBERTS 370
VERSION B

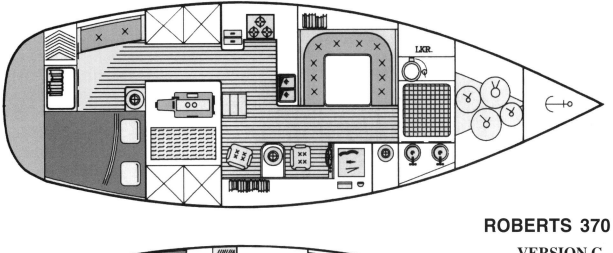

ROBERTS 370
VERSION C

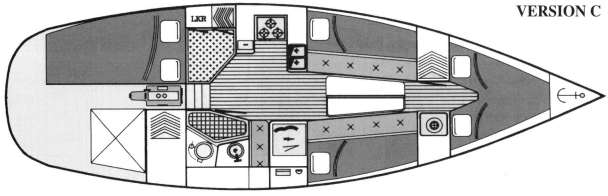

NEW ROBERTS 370E

LOD	37'-2" 11.32 M
LWL	31'-8" 9.66 M
BEAM	12'-4" 3.76 M
DRAFT-SHOAL	4'-9" 1.45 M
DRAFT-DEEP	6'-6" 1.98 M

M/C Steel, R/C Steel, Copper Nickel or Aluminum.

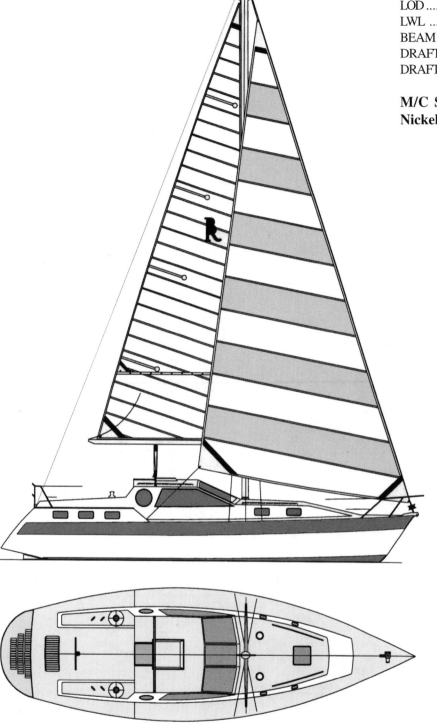

In this a new version of the popular Roberts 370E we have installed a vertical transom just aft of the double berth and incorporated a *Sugar Scoop* stern. The boat is still 37ft LOD but has much more room at the head of the double berth. If you require a cockpit well as opposed to the flush poop deck (without cockpit) then the accommodation could be re-arranged to suit this requirement.

Big enough to live-aboard, fast enough to win Club championships, rugged enough to undertake World cruising and versatile enough to be built in any of the popular boat building materials; this could be the boat for you.

There is even a DROP KEEL version, this may suit you if the waters are particulary shallow in the areas where you plan to cruise.

ROBERTS 392

This design is a companion to the Roberts 39 which until now has been available only in multi-chine hull form. Due to the great demand for radius chine steel and aluminum plus fiberglass plans for the Roberts 39 we have designed the Roberts 392 to meet your requests.

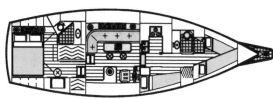

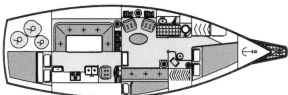

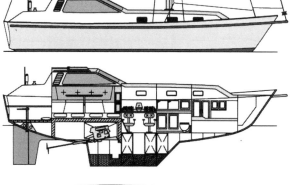

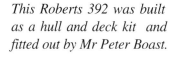

This Roberts 392 was built as a hull and deck kit and fitted out by Mr Peter Boast.

L.O.A	39'-9" [12.15]
L.W.L	34.0' [10.37]
Beam	13.0' [3.96]
Draft.	5.66' [1.73]
Displ	26,957 LBS. [8.219 KG]

The low profile cutter rig shown over the 'B' version can be used with any deck and superstructure combination available for the Roberts 392. We offer a tall cutter and ketch rig as well as the low profile version shown above.

P.C.F 40

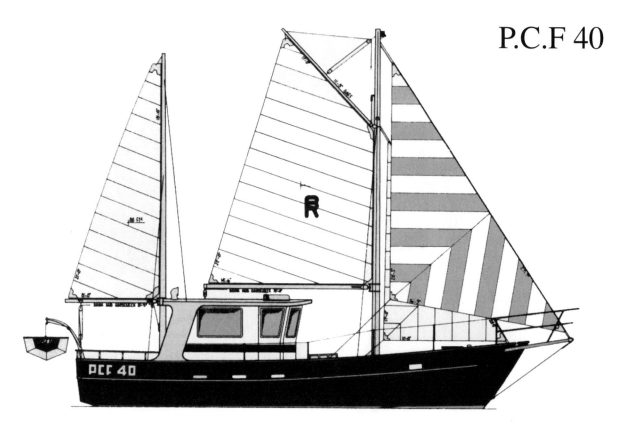

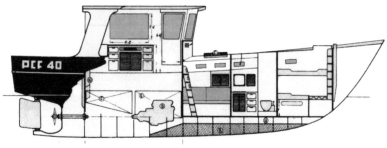

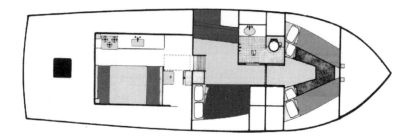

It has long been our contention that boat fashions may change but the sea does not! A good design will endure. The PCF 40 has great potential as a family or fishing boat and is suitable for anyone who wants a comfortable, sensible coastal cruising vessel. The accommodation could be expanded.

If you are looking for a lower profile, then the pilot house could be reduced in height by lowering it into the main deck; not a problem with this design as there is adequate height in the engine compartment to accept any power plant you are likely to install in this displacement hulled vesssel, say 50 to 100 HP

Build the P.C.F. 40 in Steel, Aluminum or Copper-Nickel.

LOD .... 40'-0" 12.19 M
LWL .... 35'-0" 10.67 M
BEAM .... 13'-0" 3.97 M
DRAFT .... 4'-3" 1.30 M
DISPL. ... 31,000 LB 14.06 Kg

ROBERTS 420

Alternate sail plans available

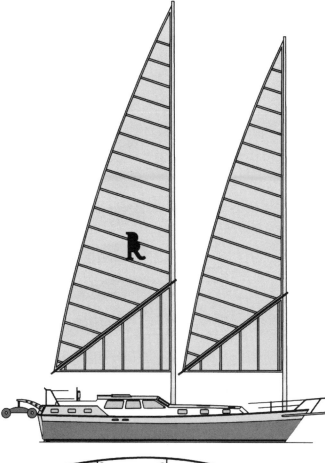

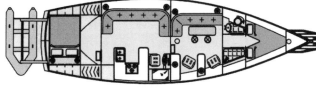

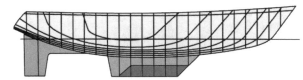

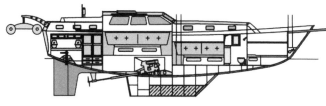

The Roberts 420 was created as a custom design for a client who found one of our designs (in this case the Roberts 392) attractive but had some ideas of his own. Occasionally a person will have requirements that are specific enough to warrant the *relatively* small additional expense involved in commissioning custom plans.

Designed to be built in radius chine steel, this boat can also be built of aluminum or a combination of these two metals.

Over the past ten years we have been refining our radius chine hull techniques which are now widely accepted as the optimum method of building a round bilge metal boat. As we have received more feed-back from owners of boats already in service, we have been able to refine these hulls and building techniques to provide you with designs that offer high performance, combined with all of the features you consider desirable in a cruising sailboat.

As the design developed it became apparent that this boat was taking on the appearance and characteristics of a smaller version of the hugely popular Roberts 53 G; this fact alone should ensure this boat a great future.

Most sailboats in the forty foot range are suitable for either single or twin masted rigs so it is up to the individual owner to make a final choice; with this design we will offer sail plans for a cutter, or ketch as well as the cat schooner rig as shown.

For those of you who like to create your own design and have it drawn as a custom plan, I have included a profile of the Roberts 420 lines featuring an alternate stern. I would welcome your thoughts on this concept.

LOD	42'-9" 13.03M
LWL	36'-6" 11.12M
BEAM	13'-0" 3.96M
DRAFT	5'-8" 1.73 M
DISPLACEMENT	31,455LB 14,267KG
BALLAST.	8,000LB 3,629 KG
SAIL AREA	904 S/F 84 S/M

ROBERTS 432
Versions A and B

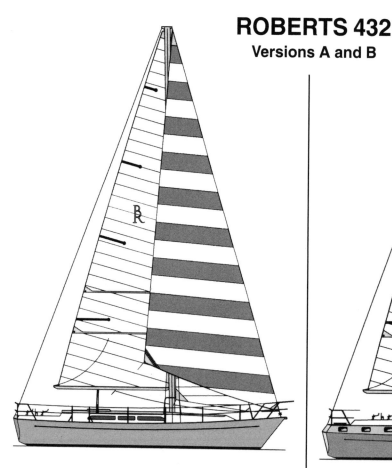

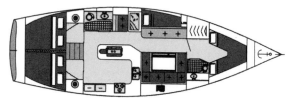

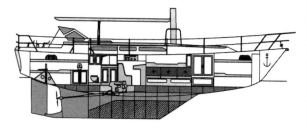

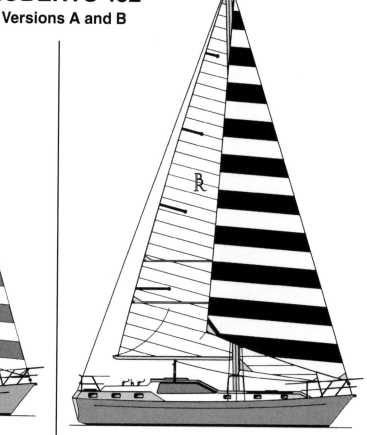

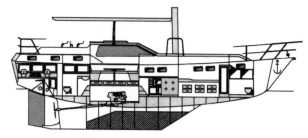

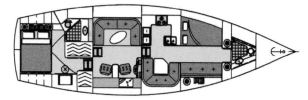

It is now several years since this design replaced the Mauritius and Norfolk 43. Both those earlier designs enjoyed enormous popularity and we kept them in the range for over twenty years. There are few sailboat designs that have enjoyed such long-standing popularity. Now we have the Roberts 432.

This design is ideal for building in Steel, Copper-nickel or Aluminium. As usual with our designs, there are a number of versions featuring a variety of accommodation and sail plans. The long keel con-figuration combined with a heel supported rudder featured in this design, represents our latest thinking in a modern sailboat suitable for serious offshore cruising.

The Roberts 432 features our latest thinking on the LONG KEEL confijgeration. Alternate tran-som shown.

LOD:	43'-11" / 13.4 M
LWL:	38'-0" / 11.6 M
M:	13'-6" / 4.10 M
SHOAL DRAFT:	5'-3" / 1.60 M
REGULAR DRAFT:	6'-0" / 1.80 M
DISPLACEMENT:	29,850 LBS / 13,539 KG

DOUBLE OR RADIUS CHINE, ROUND BILGE

ROBERTS 434

Version D

Several other versions available.

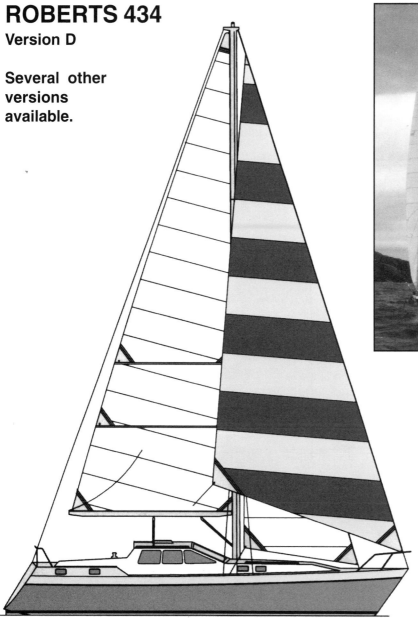

This beautiful **ROBERTS 434** was built in Belguim by Louis Delbaere.

There are over 500 Roberts 434 sailboats already completed and in service around the world. Many of these boat have completed circumnavigations includingone sailed single handedly by Major Pat Garnett who completed his 27,000 mile / 43,450 Km circumnavigation in only 218 days.

For those that prefer the medium fin / skeg arrangement, this makes an excellant cruising boat and it can be built in either Steel, Aluminium or Copper-Nickel.

There are many different accomodation arrangements, a choice of sail plans and various keel configerations.

LOD:............... 43'-4" / 13.32 M
LWL: ....36'-8" / 11.18 M
BEAM: ....13'-6" / 4.10 M
SHOAL DRAFT: 5'-0" / 1.52 M
DRAFT: ....6'-0" / 1.83 M
DISPL: 29,859 LB / 13,544 KG

HULL OPTIONS : DOUBLE CHINE, ROUND BILGE, AND RADIUS CHINE.

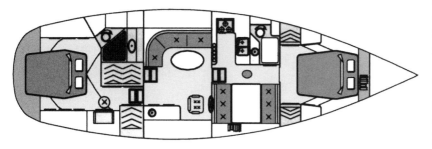

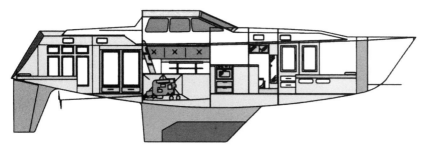

NEW YORK 46

VERSION B

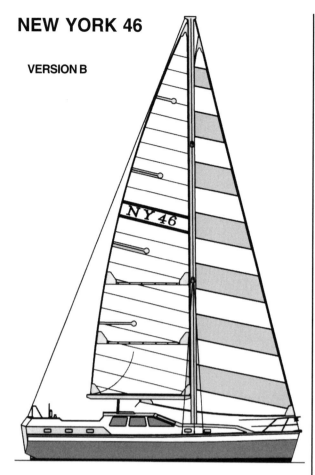

NEW YORK 46

VERSION C

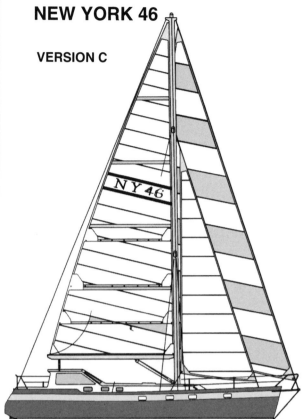

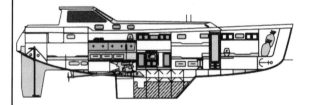

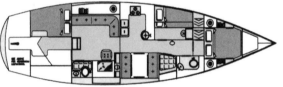

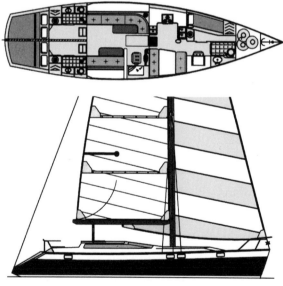

VERSION A

SHOAL DRAFT VERSIONS AVAILABLE.

LOA	46'-10" [14.28 M
LWL	43'- 5" [13.24 M]
BEAM	I3'- 1" [3.99 M]
DRAFT	7'- 6" [2.29 M]
DISPL	42,972 LBS [19,492 KG]
BALLAST	12,750 LBS [5,783 KG]
SAIL AREA	1,200 S.F. [111 S.M.]
AUX. POWER	85 HP
D/L RATIO	235
S/A DISPL...RATIO	16.5

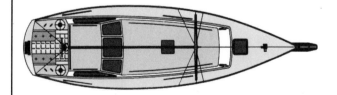

Smallest of the New York series, this very modern design is available in a variety of arrangements and appeals to those who are interested in fast cruising. This boat combines a fast hull with the ability to carry sufficient stores to qualify her as a proper cruising boat. There are several accommodation and deck layouts to choose from and a variety of sail plans have already been designed to suit this boat. Ideal for building in Aluminium, Copper-nickel or Steel, the New York 46 is well worth your consideration.

NEW YORK 55
VERSION A

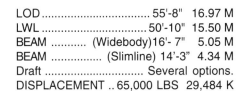

LOD .... 55'-8" 16.97 M
LWL .... 50'-10" 15.50 M
BEAM .... (Widebody)16'- 7"   5.05 M
BEAM .... (Slimline) 14'-3" 4.34 M
Draft .... Several options.
DISPLACEMENT .. 65,000 LBS 29,484 K

This aft cockpit / low pilot house configuration is available for both the New York 55 and 65 (not shown). When you order the Super Study Plans for NY55 or NY65 you receive all versions A and B etc. All sail plans, all accommodation plans, materials lists, some construction sheets for each material and a wealth of additional information about your chosen design is included in each Super Study Plan.

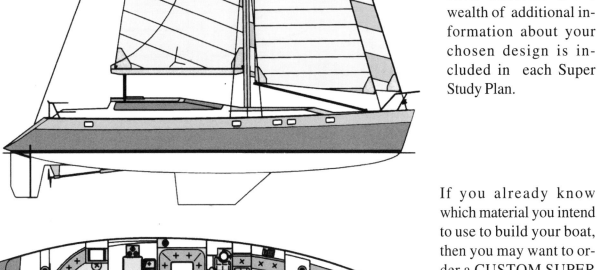

If you already know which material you intend to use to build your boat, then you may want to order a CUSTOM SUPER STUDY PLAN (Add $10) and we will include extra construction sheets pertaining to your chosen material.

You can build this boat in RADIUS CHINE STEEL, RADIUS CINE COPPER NICKEL or RADIUS CHINE ALUMINUM.

The first plans to be drawn for this design were for the fiber glass version, currently being built for a customer of French nationality who lives in Cyprus.

Already other versions of this sail boat are available in radius chine steel and aluminum,

We have refined this hull design using the latest versions of yacht design software. This is a very fast boat and one that will make extended passages with maximum speed and comfort.

This is a large boat with a relatively low displacement length ratio of 220. This boat is VERY fast.

NEW YORK 55
VERSION B

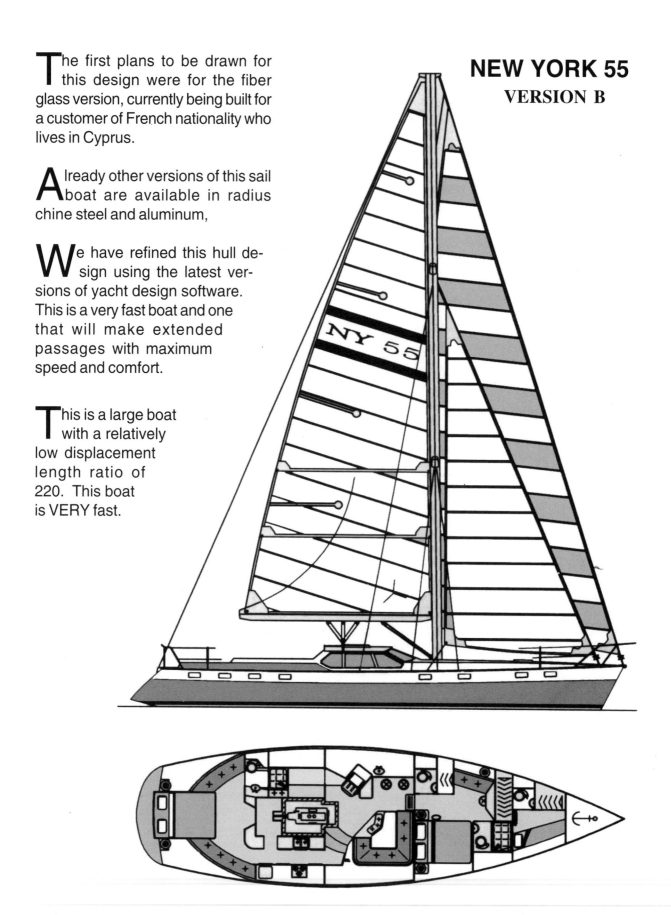

LOD	55'-8" 16.97 M
LWL	50'-10" 15.50 M
BEAM (Widebody)	16'- 7" 5.05 M
BEAM	(Slimline) 14'-3" 4.34 M
Draft	Several options.
DISPLACEMENT	65,000 LBS 29,484 K

There is also a 'Slimline' version. The beam is narrower at 14'-3" / 4.34 M. All Study Plan Packages show all versions.

The first plans to be drawn for this design are for the round bilge aluminum version. Other versions will be drawn as required.

LOD .... 73'-0"   22.25 M
LWL .... 66'-3" 20.20 M
BEAM .... 16'- 7"   5.05 M
Draft .... Several options.
DISPLACEMENT ...... 105,000 LBS 47,628 K

NEW YORK 73

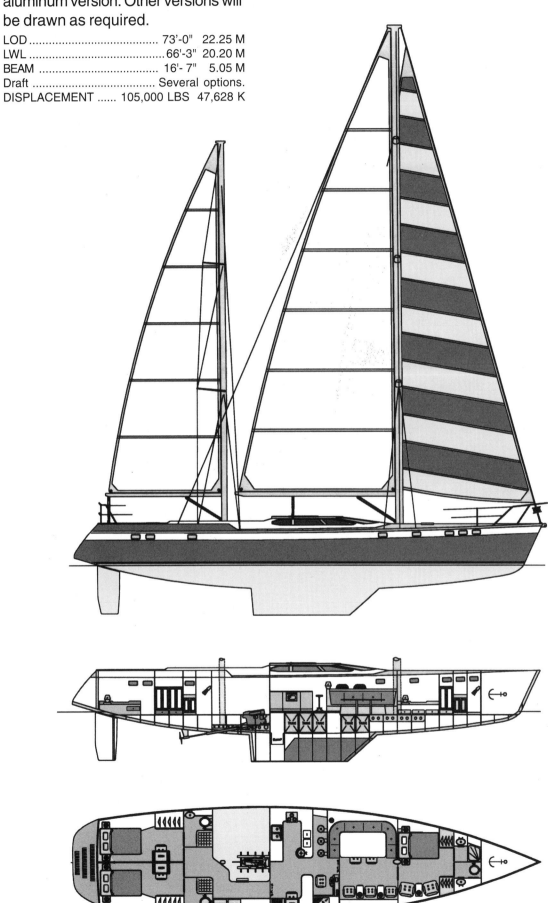

ROBERTS 532
STEEL, COPPER NICKEL OR ALUMINUM.

Above is shown the long keel configuration that is now available as an option for the Roberts 532 Radius chine version.

Designed to supersede the popular Roberts 53 (the design that will not go away !) the Roberts 532 is available with a long cruising keel as well as the original long fin and separate skeg and rudder combination shown on the left. Both keel arrangements work well. You can build this up-to-date cruising boat in Steel, Aluminum or Copper-nickel or a combination of these metals.

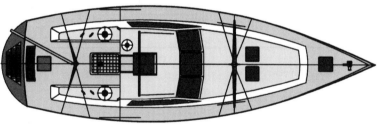

This is an ideal boat to build if you are seriously considering charter work and numerous variations are possible. The interior shown here can make a good starting point.

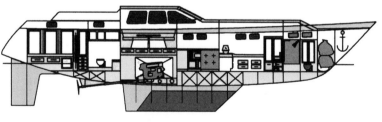

Already several examples of the Roberts 532 are in service and these have proven extremely popular with their owners. Because this is a relatively new design there have been few re-sales however if you consider the great prices that have been realised by owners of the Roberts 53 you will know that you can expect to do as well.

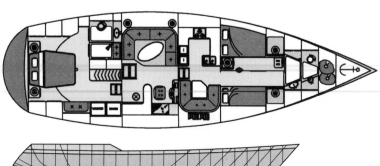

LOD .... 53'-6" 16.3 M
LWL .... 44'-5" 13.5 M
BEAM .... 16'-0" 4.9 M
DRAFT 5'-6" - 7'-0" 1.66 - 2.13 M
DISPL .... 55,000 LB 24,950 Kg
BALST. .... 16,600 LB 7,484 Kg

ROBERTS 58

R/C Steel Copper-Nickel or Aluminum.

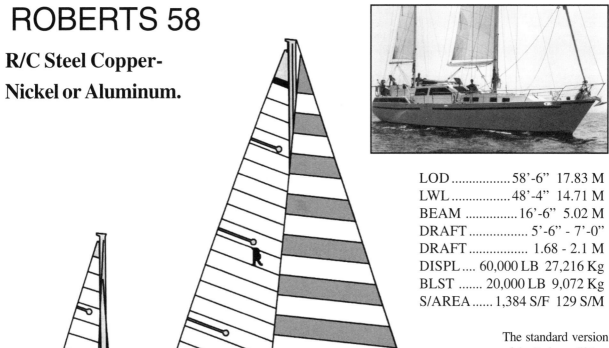

```
LOD ................ 58'-6"  17.83 M
LWL ................ 48'-4"  14.71 M
BEAM ............... 16'-6"  5.02 M
DRAFT ................ 5'-6" - 7'-0"
DRAFT ................ 1.68 - 2.1 M
DISPL .... 60,000 LB  27,216 Kg
BLST ....... 20,000 LB  9,072 Kg
S/AREA ...... 1,384 S/F  129 S/M
```

The standard version of the Roberts 58 has a draft of 7'-0" / 2.1 M but this could be reduced by using a centerboard, drop keel, wing keel or a specially designed 'Wedge Keel" similar to the one we has successfully used on the Roberts 434.

The accommodation plans could be rearranged to make this into a great charter boat with twin double cabins both fore and aft; this would provide accomodation for up to 10 guests and crew.

The Super Study Plan package for this boat covers the various material options and includes some construction sheets and material lists for each. There is enough information in ALL our study plan packages to enable you obtain quotes from builders and suppliers.

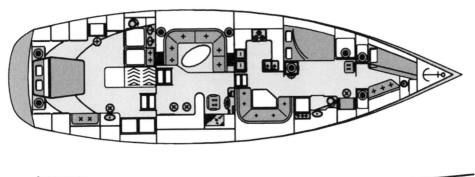

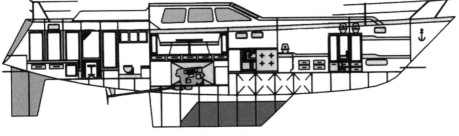

ROBERTS 64

M/C or R/C Steel, or Aluminum

Over 200 examples of this design are already cruising and many are used as professionally crewed charter boats. A still greater number are currently being built by both amateur and professional yards worldwide. The few Roberts 64's that have come on the market have been snapped up by keen buyers. A great boat for charter.

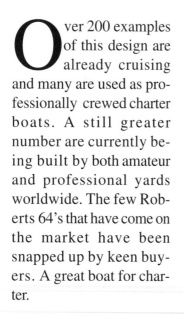

This radius chine Roberts 64 was built by Richard White and family of Quebec Canada. Richard has kept us updated throughout the building of this boat.

LOD	64'-0" 19.50 M
LWL	52'-6" 16.00 M
BEAM	16'-2" 4.93 M
DRAFT	7'-6" 2.29 M
DISPL (FG & ALU)	65,850 LB 29,869 Kg
DISPL (STEEL)	79,150 35,901 Kg

NEW YORK 65
Widebody Version B

L.O.A ....65'-0" 19.81 M
L.W.L.........................60'-8" 18.53 M
BEAM (Slimline) ....12'-6" 3.81 M
BEAM (Widebody)....16'-0" 4..88 M
DRAFT.............................VARIOUS

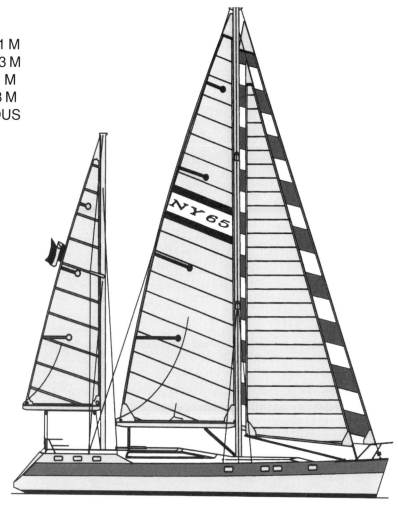

This boat can be built in either Radius Chine STEEL, ALUMINUM OR COPPER NICKEL.

There are several versions available including a slimline model and also a variety of sail plans including cutter or ketch.

There are a variety of accomodation layouts available and special custom designed arrangements are possible.

The versions can be varied depending on the building material, draft limitations and any client options and requirements.

The construction methods include: radius chine aluminum, radius chine steel and any one of the fiberglass methods. There are several different arrangements available.

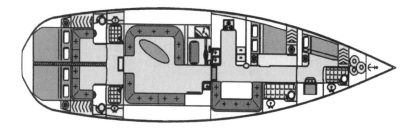

This is a sailboat that can be modified to suit a variety of sailing lifestyles. Both slimline and wide body versions are available.

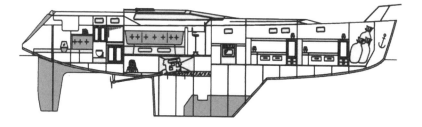

The prototype is the Omani 65 which is being built in the Middle East to be sailed single-handed non-stop around the world to establish a new record.

The **New York 65** is for fast family sailing and offers a variety of accommodation options and many other layouts are possible.

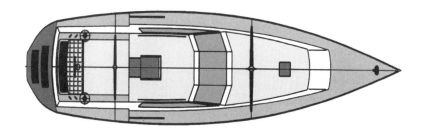

TRADER 65
Radius chine Steel or Aluminum

Designed as a combination Crewed charter / Cargo carrying vessel for an experienced cruising couple, this boat has already found many other admirers.

The Trader 65 could be fitted with a variety of rigs including, Bmu Ketch, Cat Ketch or Schooner or Lug / Junk Ketch or Schooner.

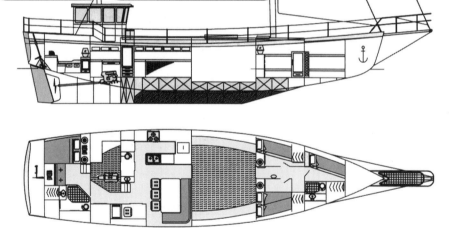
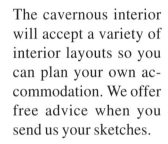

The cavernous interior will accept a variety of interior layouts so you can plan your own accommodation. We offer free advice when you send us your sketches.

If you are considering owning a boat that can earn you some income and double as a live-aboard then the Trader 65 may be the ideal boat for you.

The hull pictured was built by Thomas and Linda Owens for their own use.

LOD	65'-0"	19.80 M
LWL	58'-10"	17.90 M
BEAM	16'-7"	5.10 M
DRAFT	6'-0"	1.80 M
DISPL	100,000 LB	45,360 Kg
BALST.	30,000 LB	13,608 Kg
S/AREA	2,036 S/F	189 S/M

R/C Steel, Copper-Nickel or Aluminum.

Chapter 18
POWERBOAT DESIGNS FOR METAL

Waverunner 28. Coastworker 25/30/35. Waverunner 342. Waverunner 38. Waverunner 44. Waverunner 48. Waverunner 52 Waverunner 55/65

As we get older many of us consider moving across to power ! If you are considering making this transition, albeit for any reason, then you will need to consider the relative merits of the different power boat hulls.

Power boat hulls are divided into three main types, namely Displacement, Semi-displacement and Planing hulls. Each type of hull can have many sub types, which are closer to one or other end of the spectrum. Each type of hull configuration has its benefits and draw backs, your choice may depend on your intended usage and the size of your wallet.

Metal power and sailing catamarans are becoming increasingly popular and although we have not included them here, we do have a small range of these designs. If you are interested in this type of boat, please contact any one of the Bruce Roberts design offices for additional details.

The size of your intended power boat will also be a factor in your choice of hull type; for instance if you are considering a large power boat (large is a relative term) then you will be less likely to choose a full planing hull. Large fast planing hulls require large expensive engines and have a very high fuel usage, and therefore operating costs would also be high. Below I will detail the qualities of the range of power boat hull types.

Let us start at the Displacement end of the range as these were the first to be developed and to go back to the beginning of time; the original log canoe and even the ark (as far as we know) were all displacement hulls.

HEAVY DISPLACEMENT

These heavy displacement hulls include such craft as Tugs and Deep sea Trawlers. If you study these boats in profile, you will notice that the stern rises above waterline. The mid section of the hull is very full and deep in the water. The chine and buttock lines will reveal the full bellied shape usually present in this type of hull. The heavy displacement hull has to be able to carry great loads and in the case of Tugs, be able to get a great grip on the water in order to do its job properly. The "hull speed" of this type of vessel is generally less than that of other types. See explanation below of the term "Hull Speed".

MEDIUM DISPLACEMENT

These hulls include most regular work boats, general fishing boats and the pleasure boats where speeds of 1.34 times the square root of the water line length are sufficient to fulfil their operating requirements. For instance let us consider a 40 ft / 12.19 M, LOA. motor cruiser with a waterline length of 36 ft / 10.97 M, the square root of the waterline is 6 so multiply this by 1.34 and you arrive at a potential speed of just over 8 knots / 14.8 km/h. This is an economical speed for this vessel taking into account power required and fuel used to drive the vessel at "hull speed". Medium displacement vessels can only exceed the 1.34 rule by adding excessive amounts of power. If you already own an engine that has more horsepower than required to fall within the 1.34 calculation, then consider building a longer hull or one that employs the semi-displacement hull characteristics. The term "Hull speed" is generally used to express the potential speed that any hull will achieve without digging in at the stern or using an inordinate amount of fuel. The V at the transom is usually fairly flat with anything from 5 to 10 degrees being the norm.

Once the most economical speed is achieved, it takes a considerable amount of power to make a displacement hull go faster. When this type of hull is over driven, then the stern will drag in the water and usually create a large stern and bow wave. The boat may reach such an extreme bow high, stern down angle, where water could come in over the stern and swamp the vessel.

Displacement hulls should not be driven much in excess of their "hull speed". For vessels ranging in size from 30 ft / 9.1 M to 60 ft / 18.3 M waterline length, you should consider displacement hulls only if your speed requirement is around the 6 to 12 knot mark respectively. For higher speeds consider Semi-displacement or Planing hulls.

One important factor is that Displacement and Semi-displacement hulls are generally considered better 'Sea Boats' and are more suitable for serious off-shore cruising than the planing hull type. As with heavy displacement hulls, medium displacement hulls are not so affected by weight as the semi-displacement and planing hull types.

SEMI-DISPLACEMENT

As the name suggests these hulls fit neatly in between the displacement and the planing hull types. The stern of the Semi-displacement hull is lower and designed to be always below the water. The hull can be round bilge form but is generally of the 'Hard chine' type. These hulls have less fullness than a full displacement hull. The chine line runs aft with a small curve from where it enters the water and on back to the transom. The hull sections are moderately Veed.

The semi-displacement hull will out perform the displacement 'Hull Speed' rules and will accept additional power and convert it to additional speed however there are limits to this benefit. Generally speaking for vessels with 30 ft 9.1 M to 60 ft / 18.3 M waterline length, you should only consider Semi-displacement hulls if your speed requirements do not exceed 12 to 18 knots.

As you have seen with displacement hulls additional power is wasted, however with semi-displacement hulls often the extra power may be utilised to advantage. If you already have access to a certain size of engine; or you already own the engine(s), then this factor may assist you in making the decision as to which type of hull best suits your situation.

As with Displacement hulls, Semi-Displacement hulls can be driven harder, but at the expense of greater fuel consumption and again the stern will tend to dig in at higher speeds. Existing semi-displacement hulls can be made to achieve extra speed with the same horsepower by adding trim tabs or planing wedges at the stern. The trim tabs and the wedges will be fixed after trials are completed to establish the best angle. In no case should you try to improve the performance of your hull in this manner without the assistance of professional advice.

If you are building a Semi-Displacement hull, you should try to keep the weight to reasonable levels. The Semi-Displacement hull is a good weight carrier

but it takes additional power and fuel to get the best out of an over weight hull of this type.

PLANING HULLS

The planing hull is recognised by the straight run of the chine and buttock lines from midships aft. The chine and the bottom of the hull V will generally run parallel to the waterline. The V in section will generally be constant from just aft of midships to the stem. The angle between the baseline and the bottom of the V will be in the range of 12 to 20 degrees at the transom. As with other types of hulls there is a great range of Planing hull variations. Usually there is a planing strake or flat at the chine and often several planing strakes on the bottom of the hull.

Planing hulls, depending on the particular design, can be driven at speeds in excess of 50 knots, however most are designed to cruise at speeds between 20 to 35 knots. Modern computers can accurately estimate the power requirements and speed expectations of all hull types and are especially helpful in the case deciding the power needed for individual planing hulls.

Planing hulls are very popular, they make great pleasure boats if you are prepared to install sufficient power and pay the larger fuel bills. Planing hulls do not like being operated at low speeds; they throw a most unfriendly bow wave. Planing hulls are not the best of sea boats especially in severe conditions. For local and coastal cruising it is worth noting that a planing hull may allow you to get home before the bad weather arrives. On no account select a planing hull if you intend to operate in the canal systems of USA or Europe. These hulls are not suitable if your cruising area is restricted to low speed operation.

Waverunner 48

This boat was designed to be built in Copper Nickel. One of the advantages is that copper nickel has a natural anti-fouling action and therefore does not require any of the familiar coatings that all other types of vessels require to keep the underwater surfaces free from marine growth.

If you are interested in learning more about the use of copper nickel in boats, write to Bruce Roberts and we can supply you with additional information on this material. This boat can also be built in steel or aluminium.

LOA.................................48'-0" 14.63 M
LWL................................43'-3" 13.18 M
BEAM..............................16'-0" 4.88 M
DISPL....................5,763 LB 23,931 KG

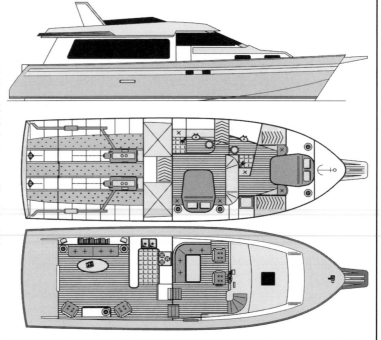

WAVERUNNER 28

The WR28 low profile, motor cruiser features a moderately fast semi-planing hull that when correctly powered will perform best at speeds between 10 and 14 knots. The construction techniques to build this boat in either Aluminium, Steel or Copper-nickel have been kept simple and are ideal for a first time builder. Several of these boats have already been completed and tey have lived up to all expectations.

```
LOD:  .............................................28'-7" / 8.70 M
LWL:  ..............................................25'-0" / 7.60 M
BEAM:  ..........................................10'-2" / 3.10 M
DRAFT:...........................................  3'-0" / 0.90 M
HULL FORM:..................SEMI-DISPLACEMENT
```

This Waverunner 28 was built by Put Veini Ltd in Riga Latvia. This company have built several Bruce Roberts designed steel boats.

WAVERUNNER 342

The WR342 is a planing hull fast cruiser. This boat can be built in Steel or Aluminium. The heavily fitted out steel prototype achieved 23 knots / 42.62 km using twin 200 hp Volvo diesel stern-drives. Many other WR342s have now been competed and the performance reports have all been excellent. This boat handles well under all conditions and makes a fine family boat.

```
LOD:................................ 35'-11" / 11.0 M
LWL:  ...............................................32'-0" / 9.75 M
BEAM:  ............................................12'-3" / 3.73 M
DRAFT:.............................................. 2'-3" /  0.68 M
HULL:.................................................... PLANING
```

This Waverunner 342 was built by Filmar Engineering in the UK and achieved 23 knots with twin 200 HP Volvo diesel stern drives

WAVERUNNER 38

There is a choice of hull types between semi-displacement and planing versions. Over 200 WR38s have been completed to date and the owners report that they are well pleased with the performance and handling characteristics of this design.

This boat is suitable for building in Steel, Copper-nickel or Aluminum or a combination of these metals. Other accomodation lay-outs include an aft cockpit version.

This boat makes a popular hire and self drive charter boat and over 20 of these have been built for this purpose and exported from the UK

```
LOD:  ......................................38'-9" / 11.88 M
LWL:  ......................................34'-6" / 10.05 M
BEAM:  ........................ .............13'-3" / 4.04 M
DRAFT: .......................................3'-6" / 1.07 M
HULL:..................PLANING or SEMI-DISPL
```

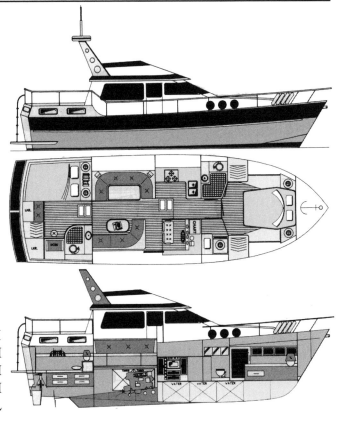

WAVERUNNER 44

The WR 44 like many of our other powerboat designs is offered in two basic versions. You can choose to build either aft cockpit or aft cabin layout. Within these two choices several variations of the accommodation are possible. The different versions are all included in the basic plan and full size pattern package. You can choose between Semi-Displacement or Planing hull. Over 250 examples of this design have been built and are already in service world wide.

The Waverunner 44 has been built in many configirations including Fisheries Patrol vessel in Oman, Drug enforcement patrol boat in USA and of course as a family pleasure cruiser. Ideal for building in steel, aluminium or copper-nickel.

LOD: ....44'-9" / 13.60 M
LWL: ....41'-2" / 12.50 M
BEAM: ....15'-3" / 4.65 M
DRAFT:................................. 3'-3" / 1.00 M
HULL:...................... PLANING OR SEMI-DISPL.

WAVERUNNER 52

This is one of the most popular and versatile large powerboats in our range. The WR52 can be built with aft cockpit or aft cabin layouts. Also included in the plans are Trawler Yacht and Sport Fisherman versions.

Within these four basic configurations, a number of variations are possible. Ideal for building in any of the three metals. There are already over 200 WR52s in service so this is a well proven design. This boat can easily be handled by a couple and it is ideal for charter or family cruising.

LOD: ....51'-9" / 15.77 M
LWL: ....46'-2" / 14.06 M
BEAM:............................ 16'-1" / 4.90 M

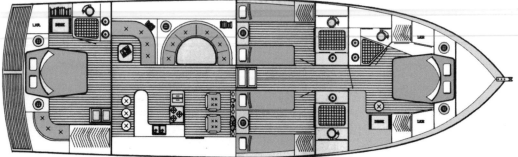

WAVERUNNER 65

VERSION B:

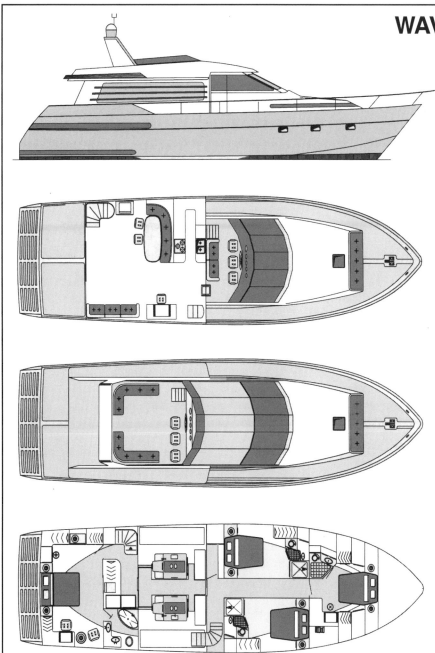

The WR65 has proven to be an incredibly popular design and some time ago we were requested to prepare plans for a pilot house version to be built in fiberglass. Plans for steel or aluminum are available as semi custom plans.

We believe that the WR65 which can be built in steel or aluminum and features a choice of planing or displacement hulls, has a lot to offer. Stock plans and semi-custom versions are available from Bruce Roberts offices.

LOA..... 65'-6" / 20.0 M
LWL.......57'-6" / 17.5 M
BEAM....19'-6" / 5.9 M
DRAFT.......3'-0" / .80 M

If you would like additional information on the Waverunner 65, then you may contact any Bruce Roberts design office for additional information about this vessel.

NOTE:

A 55 FT / 16.76 M version of this design is also available.

Appendix 1
RECOMMENDED READING

BOATBUILDING
by Bruce Roberts-Goodson. Published by Capall Bann Publishing UK. Available in the USA. Recommended if you have not decided which material is best for you. Covers Fiberglass, Steel, Aluminum and Wood/Epoxy building methods, all in considerable detail.

BOATOWNER'S MECHANICAL AND ELECTRICAL MANUAL
by Nigel Calder, Adlard Coles Nautical UK, MacGraw Hill / International Marine USA. How to maintain and repair your boat's essential systems. This is a good book to have on board your boat.

CHOOSING FOR CRUISING
by Bruce Roberts-Goodson. Published by Adlard Coles Nautical, UK. Sheridan House, USA. This book covers all of the aspects of choosing a cruising sailboat and is recommended to those who wish to expand their technical knowledge in sailboat design and associated subjects.

CHOOSING A CRUISING POWERBOAT
(Available mid 1998) by Bruce Roberts-Goodson. Published by Capall Bann Publishing UK and Heron House in USA. This book covers all of the technical aspects of choosing a cruising powerboat and includes offshore Passagemakers (3,000 miles / 4830 km + range) as well as boats suitable for coastal and local cruising.

FIBERGLASS BOATBUILDING
(Available late 1998) by Bruce Roberts-Goodson. Published by Capall Bann Publishing UK and by Heron House in USA. This new book contains all the latest technology on fiberglass boatbuilding including the use of the latest materials and construction techniques. Bruce Roberts-Goodson was a pioneer in the designing and construction of one-off fiberglass sail and powerboats and he shares his extensive knowledge gained over 30 years.

GOUGEON BROTHERS WEST EPOXY SYSTEM
Published by Gougeon Brothers, this book is available from any Bruce Roberts Design office. There is also a German language version of this title. If you are planning to add a timber and plywood deck and or superstructure to your metal boat, then this book will be a great help.

SPRAY - THE ULTIMATE CRUISING BOAT
by Bruce Roberts-Goodson. Published by Adlard Coles Nautical, UK. Sheridan House, USA. Spray was the first boat ever to be sailed singlehanded around the world over 100 years ago. Spray and her skipper Joshua Slocum have become legendary in the annals of small boat sailing; Spray is the mother of all cruising boats. This book covers the original voyage around the world and includes illustrations and photographs many of the over 1,000 replicas and copies of the Spray. Included are details of current and recent past voyages and exploits of those, which sail in the copies of this wonderful boat.

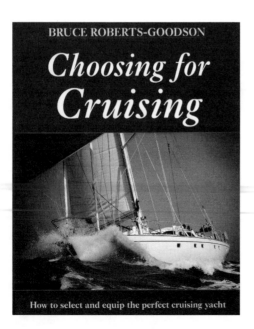

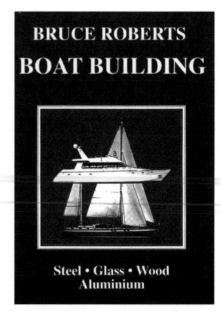

APPENDIX 2
GLOSSARY OF ELECTRICAL TERMS

AC (alternating current) = 220 or 240 Volt (UK, Europe, Australia etc.) or 120 volt (North America) household power, shore power and also is the type of power usually supplied by your generating set. Some Generating sets can supply 12-volt DC power, more on that later.

AH Capacity = The ability of a fully charged battery to deliver a specified amount of electricity at a given rate for a definite period of time. This number may give a false impression because you can not use all of the AH or you will flatten the battery, and the AH capacity of any battery will vary with age and condition, see later in chapter.

Ampere or amp or A = The unit of measure of flow rate of current through a circuit.

Ampere-hour or Amp hour or AH = A unit of measure of the battery's electrical storage capacity, obtained by multiplying the current in amperes by the time in hours of the discharge.

AWG = American wire gauge.

Circuit = An electric circuit is the path of an electric current; a closed circuit has a complete path and an open circuit has a broken or disconnected path.

Current = The rate of flow that is best described by comparing it to a stream of water; the unit of measure is an ampere.

Cycle = One discharge plus one recharge is one battery cycle.

Dip Switch = A series of small switches used for alternate programming in all types of electrical and electronic devices.

Direct current. DC = Power that is stored in any battery or supplied by an alternator or a 12V battery charger.

Discharge or discharging = When a battery is delivering current it is said to be discharging.

Equalise charge = A controlled overcharge of the batteries which brings all cells up to the same voltage.

Gel cell battery = A type of battery, it has the electrolyte in gel form.

Ground = Used in automobiles when the negative battery cable is attached to the body or frame of the car, not recommended or generally used in boats.

ISO = This is a European standard of wire sizes quoted in cross sectional area mm2
LED = Light emitting diode, often used as an indicator light.

Negative = The negative terminal is the point from which electrons flow during discharge.

Ni-cad battery = Nickel cadmium battery, rechargeable and used in small appliances, larger varieties are too expensive for most boats.

Ohm = A unit for measuring electrical resistance.

Positive = opposite to negative.

Volt = The unit of measure for electric potential.

Watt = The unit for measuring electrical power, a measure of the amount of power required by a particular appliance for example a 60 watt light bulb.

Wet cell battery = The type of battery that uses liquid as an electrolyte, you add distilled water to this type of battery.

APPENDIX 3
ELECTRICAL SYSTEMS IN METAL BOATS

Authors note: This appendix was written by Del F. Kahan of Marinetics Corporation of Newport Beach California USA, and is included with his permission.

The information contained here was prepared specifically in response to questions posed by many friends and associates in the marine industry: Naval Architects, Marine Engineers, Production and Plant managers and individuals. All have been apprehensive about the special features, which might be applied to aluminum, or steel hulled vessels for which they are responsible. On several occasions inquiries have been submitted after unfortunate and catastrophic experiences. It can be embarrassing indeed, to have a lovely vessel sink at the dock, suddenly lose bottom paint over a wide area or suffer extensive underwater corrosion.

Generally a metal-hulled vessel differs from one of fiberglass or wood, for the purposes of this text, only with respect to certain special precautions which relate to galvanic corrosion and electrical systems insulation integrity. Basic electrical systems concepts and design procedure should otherwise be identical.

Unless the vessel is to be moored and used in very pure fresh water (an unlikely circumstance in these times) either salt water or fresh water should be considered to be an electrolyte which is capable of accelerating galvanic corrosion - that which is attributed to dis-similar metals in contact, or electrically interconnected.

The designers and builders task, particularly with respect to aluminum hulls, includes selection of an appropriate corrosion resistant alloy for the hull plating, proper welding alloy selection and procedure, and contact insulation with respect to dissimilar materials. Through hulls should be non-metallic or suitably insulated. The propeller shaft should also be insulated from the hull through the use of appropriate non-metallic bearings and coupling insulators. Cathodic protection of the hull through the use of sacrificial anodes such as zinc's may be employed through the classical attachment methods of by means of 'throw-over' zinc's which are connected to the hull only when the vessel is dockside. Frequently it is found that bottom paint lifting problems are simply the result of improper priming and painting procedures and are not at all related to the 'electrolysis bogey-man'. Another phenomenon,

deterioration of the trailing edges and other discontinuities, is frequently found to result from mechanical erosion due to cavitation or water turbulence. The above factors are mentioned here because it is common to blame the ships electrical system for deficiencies, which are totally unrelated.

Stray current corrosion attributable to faulty DC electrical systems installation or to subsequent deterioration; can be prevented through proper system design and installation procedure. With respect to design the author is of the firm conviction (reflecting both analysis and practical experience) that an isolated DC system IS NEITHER ESSENTIAL OR DESIRABLE. Typically, the smaller engines employed utilise single terminal (engine grounded) electrical accessories and the cost to isolate these items, and to maintain that isolation, is difficult to justify. The classical negatively grounded DC system has been proven to be quite acceptable provided that certain simple precautions are adhered to as follows:

1. The negative ground shall be provided at a SINGLE point, the propulsion engine. Note: on a twin screw vessel a hull ground shall be provided at each engine - this will still be considered a single point.

All circuit returns shall by means of suitable insulated conductors, which shall terminate ultimately at the single point.

2. All circuit protection devices (fuses or, preferably, automatic non-self-reset circuit breakers) and control switches shall be located in the positive conductors.

3. DC equipment should, for maximum insulation integrity, be mounted on insulating pads, off the ship ground (hull). This need not apply to engine mounted, thus grounded, accessories such as the engines starting motor, alternator, instrument and warning senders, etc.

All remote pumps, blowers, electronic equipment, etc. should have the cases and metallic mounting ears isolated from ground. The purpose of this procedure is to ensure that the deterioration of the internal insulation will not result in leakage of currents to and through the hull plating.

Should it be deemed desirable to provide a radio-frequency ground NEAR the radio telephone transmitter, rather than to accept the DC single point engine ground for the purpose, a blocking capacitor should be incorporated to confine the ground to RF currents only.

4. All wiring installation shall be made only with the best materials and procedures to insure high quality integrity. Conductors must be carefully bundled and strapped in place and precautions taken to prevent chafe. The latter is particularly important where wire bundles are led around corners, past ribs or gussets and through metallic bulkheads. Liberal utilisation of protective neoprene hose, as a sheath, represents good procedure where hazards exist. Conductors who penetrate metallic bulkheads should be protected by means of plastic grommets or stuffing tubes.

It should be kept in mind that initial installation is not the only consideration. The effects of shock and vibration can cause shifting of improperly secured wiring. In addition, the activities of repair or servicing personnel with respect to other equipment (i.e. engine servicing) can dislodge or damage wiring unless suitable protection has been provided.

The disciplines essential to AC system installation are especially important. All of the principles described above must be conscientiously applied; in addition, special care must be directed toward the AC shore power supply interface.

There are those who promote the use of various forms of so-called 'galvanic isolators' as a solution to the problems of ship's ground connection to the AC grounding conductor (green wire) brought in with the utility shore power connector. Some manufacturers of these devices are conscientious in their attempt to fashion well-designed products of this nature and to reinforce confidence in their product through sophisticated quality control measures. Accordingly, a case can be made for the use of these devices with shore power services brought aboard FIBERGLASS OR WOODEN HULLED VESSELS whose ships ground system is intended to be connected to the AC grounding conductor (i.e. in accordance with ABYC or similar body recommendations). With metal hulled craft the risk of ANY degree of failure or compromise of 'isolation quality' is difficult to accept. By any measure, the most the most acceptable design principle mandates the employment of a high quality ISOLATION TRANSFORMER to ensure that NO common electrical circuit will exist with respect to the shore side utility power system. The best method for connection of the isolation transformer is in accordance with ABYC recommendations.

This Radius chine aluminum Roberts 58 was built in Europe.

APPENDIX 4
USEFUL NAMES AND ADDRESSES

Note: The + in the telephone and fax numbers is where you would insert the number you are required to dial to 'get out' of your home country. The number in brackets for example those calling within the country concerned insert (0).

Ambassador Marine Ltd (UK)
'The Stripper' shaft rope cutters
252 Hursley, Winchester
Hants SO21 2JJ UK
Telephone +44 (0)1962 775405
Fax +44 (0)1962 775 250

ABYC (American Boat and Yacht Council)
Construction standards for small craft
3069 Solomons Island Road,
Edgewater MD 21307 USA
Telephone +1 410 956 1050
Fax +1 410 956 2737

Apollo (USA)
12 volt and 120 volt Generating sets
833 West 17th St, No 3, Costa Mesa Ca 92627 USA
Telephone +1 714 650 1240
Fax +1 714 650 2519

Balmar (USA)
12 V DC high capacity generating sets
27010 12 Th. Ave NW, Stanwood WA 98292
Telephone + 1 360 629 6100
Fax +1 360 629 3210

Bruce Roberts Direct (USA or UK)
The author may be contacted directly via either of the Bruce Roberts Design offices listed for UK and USA. Simply mark the communication 'Bruce Roberts-Goodson, Bruce Roberts Direct'

Bruce Roberts Designs (USA)
Cruising boat plans and custom designs
PO box 1086 Severna Park
MD 21146 USA
Telephone +1 410 349 2743
Fax +1 410 349 2743

Bruce Roberts Designs (UK)
Cruising boat plans and custom designs
'Orchards', School Lane,
Easton, near Woodbridge
Suffolk IP13 0ES
Telephone +44 (0)1728 747 427
Fax +44 (0) 1728 747 663

Copper Development Association (USA)
Information - contact Dale T. Peters VP
260 Madison Avenue, New York NY 10016 USA
Telephone +1 212 251 7214
Fax +1 212 251 7234

Copper Development Association (UK)
Copper-nickel information
Orchard House, Mutton Lane,
Potters Barr, Herts EN6 3AP
Telephone +44 (0)1707 642 769
Fax +44 (0)1707 624 2749

Copper-Nickel Boat Co
Builders of Copper-Nickel boats
Deal Island Rd, Deal Island MD 21821
Telephone + 1 410 784 2292

Copper-nickel Producers in USA

Hussy Copper Ltd. Tel: 1 412 266 8430, 1 800 733 8866. Fax 1 412 857 4243

Olin Brass. Tel: 1 618 258 2000. Fax: 1 618 258 2777

PMX Industries Inc. Tel: 1 319 368 7700, 1 800 531 5468. Fax: 1 319 368 7721

Revere Copper Products Inc. Tel: 1 315 338 2022, 1 800 448 1776. Fax: 1 315 338 2224

Cruising Equipment Company (USA)
(E-Meter and battery monitoring devices and services)
315 Seaview Ave, NW Seattle WA 9807 USA
Fax +1 206 782 4336

Custom Steel Boats
Builders of fine metal hulls
PO Box 148 Merritt NC 28556 USA
Telephone: 1 919 745 7447 Fax 1 745 7066

De Bug tm (USA)
Microorganism fuel filters
Environmental Solutions International
11002 Racoon Ridge Reston VA 22091 USA
Tel: +1 800 411 3284
Fax: +1 703 620 2815

Dickinson Stoves (Canada)
Diesel powered galley and heating stoves
407 - 204 Cayer St, Coquitlam BC V3K 5B1 Canada
Telephone +1 605 525 6444

M.G. Duff Marine Ltd
Zinc and Magnesium anodes
Unit 2 West, 68 Bognor Rd, Chichester,
West Sussex PO19 2NS
Telephone + 44 (0) 1243 533 336
Fax: + 44 (0) 1243 533 422

Ericson Safety Pump Corporation, (USA)
Bilge pumps
435 Roosevelt Blvd., Tarpon Springs, FL 34689 USA
Fax +1 813 934 6890

Terry Erskine Boatbuilder (UK)
Builder of fine steel boats
1 Glendower, Gonvena Hill, Wadebridge PL27 6DQ
Telephone: + 44 (0) 1208 815 862
Mobile 0370 613 914

Float-Pac Pty Ltd (Australia)
Air bags
Unit 4/31 Wentworth St, Greenacre
NSW 2190 Australia
Fax: +61 2 742 5565

Forespar (USA)
Lightning Master and other marine products
22322 Gilberto, Rancho Santa Margarita Ca 926 88
USA
Telephone: +1 714 858 8820
Fax: +1 714 858 0505

Halyard Marine Ltd (UK)
HMI Shaft seal, exhaust systems, engine insulation
Whaddon Business Park, Southampton Rd, Whaddon
Nr Salisbury SP5 3HF
Telephone +44 (0)1722 710 922 Fax +44 (0)710 975

Heart Interface Corporation (USA)
(Battery chargers, inverters and battery monitors).
21440 68th Avenue South, Kent WA 98032 USA
Fax +1 206 872 3412

HFL Industrial and Marine Ltd (UK)
AC Generating sets
HFL House, Lockfield Ave,
Enfield Middlesex EN3 7PX UK
Telephone +44 (0)181 805 9088
Fax +44 (0)181 805 2440

Hypertherm Inc. (USA)
Powermax plasma cutters
Etna Rd, PO box 5010, Hanover, NH 03755 USA
Telephone: +1 603 643 3441
Fax +1 603 643 5352
Toll Free 1 800 643 0030

Lancing Marine (UK)
'Marine diesel engines and rebuild kits etc.'
51 Victoria Rd, Portslade
Sussex BN41 1XY UK
Telephone: +44 (0) 1273 410025
Fax: +44 (0) 1273 430 290

Lestek Manufacturing Inc. (USA)
'Brute' high output alternators
6542 Baker Blvd, Fort Worth Tx 76118 USA
Fax: +1 817 284 2153

Lugger/Northern Lights (USA)
Northern Light generating sets
USA, Telephone +1 206 789 3880
Fax +1 206 782 5455

LVM (UK)
'Aerogen' wind generators and marine pumps
Aerogen house, Old Oak Close, Arlesey,
Bedfordshire, SG15 6XD UK
Telephone +44 (0)1 462 733 336
Fax +44 (0)1 462 730 466

Merlin Equipment (UK)
E-Meter/Heart Link 10
Unit 1 Hithercroft Court, Lupton Road, Wallingford,
Oxfordshire OX10 9BT UK
Fax + 44 (0)1491 824466

Exide Batteries Ltd (UK)
Marine batteries
Gate no. 3, Pontselyn Industrial Estate,
Pontypool, NP4 5DG UK
Telephone +44 (0) 1495 750 075

Mastervolt UK
Heart Inverters, battery monitors, electrical panels
Unit D5, Premier Center , Abbey Park Industrial
Estate, Romsey, Hampshire SO5 19AQ UK
Telephone +44 (0)1794 516 443
Fax +44 (0) 11794 516 453

Marinetics Inc (USA)
Electrical panels
PO Box 2676 Newport Beach Ca 92663
Telephone +1 714 646 8889
Fax +1 714 642 8627

Morglasco Ltd (UK)
Person overboard recovery slings
Bosboa, Mount George Rd, Penelewey, Feock, Truro
Cornwell TR3 6QX UK
Telephone/Fax +44 (0)1872 870 139

Nickel Development Institute
Information on Copper-nickel and stainless steels
214 King Street West, Suite 510 Toronto
Ontario M5H 3S6 Canada.
Telephone +1 416 591 7999
Fax +1 416 591 7987

Nickel Developement Institute
Information on Copper-nickel and stainless steels
European Technical Information Center
The Holloway, Alvechurch, Birmingham B48 7QB
Telephone +44 (0) 1527 584 777
Fax +44 (0) 1527 585 562

Norseman Gibb Ltd (UK)
Norseman fittings
Ollerton Rd, Ordsall, Retford
Notts DN22 7TG UK
Telephone: +44 (0) 1777 706 465
Fax: +44 (0) 1777 860 346
Email Compuserve 10723.2744

Norseman Marine USA Inc (USA)
Masts and Rigging, Norseman fittings (USA)
516 West Las Olas Blvd., Fort Lauderdale
Florida 33312 USA
Telephone: +1 954 467 1407
Fax +1 954 462 3470

Ocean Safety (UK)
Lightweight liferafts
Centurion Industrial Park, Bitterne Rd, West,
Southampton SO18 1UB UK
Telephone +44 (0)1703 333 334
Fax +44 (0)1703 333 360

Porta-Bote (UK)
Folding dinghies
The Barn Snowdrop Cottage, Winchester Rd,
Kings Somborne, Stockbridge, Hants SO20 6NY UK
Tel/Fax + 44 (0) 1794 388046

Put Veini Ltd
Builders of steel boats at a favourable price
PO LV1015 Box 2 Riga, Latvia
Telephone + 371 2 349 543 Fax +371 7 353 831

Rolls Battery Engineering (USA)
Heavy duty deep cycle batteries
8 Proctor St, Salem MA 01970 USA
Telephone +1 508 745 3333

RYA The Royal Yachting Association (UK)
RYA House, Romsey Rd, Eastleigh
Hants SO5O 9YA England UK
Telephone: +44 (0) 1703 629 962
Fax: +44 (0) 1703 629 924

Scanmar International
Self steering windvanes
432 South 1st St, Richmond
CA 94804 USA
Telephone +1 510 215 2010
Fax +1 510 215 5005

Village Marine Tech. (UK)
Watermakers
2000 West 135th St, Gardenia Ca 90249
Fax: +1 310 5383048

Vetus Den Ouden (UK)
Marine equipment, gen. sets, engines, tanks,
ventilators
38 South Hampshire Industrial Park Totton-
Southampton
Hants SO40 3SA
Telephone +44 (0)1703 861 033   Fax +44 (0)1703
663 142

Vetus Den Ouden (Holland)
Marine equipment, gen. sets, engines, tanks,
ventilators
Fokkerstraat 571 3125 BD Schiedam Holland
Telephone +31 10 437 7700 Fax +31 10 415 2634

Vetus Den Ouden (USA)
Marine equipment, gen. sets, engines, tanks,
ventilators
PO Box 8712 Baltimore MD 21240 USA
Telephone + 1 410 712 0740 Fax +1 410 712 0985

APPENDIX 5
GLOSSARY OF BOATBUILDING TERMS

ABAFT: Behind or towards the rear.

ABEAM: A point beside the boat, usually refers to a point relative to the boat such as 'abeam of midships' or abeam of the bow, close abeam, etc.

ABL or ABOVE THE BASELINE: Usually given as a measurement, for example, 'Stem is 6 ft 6 in / 1.98 M 'above the baseline.'

ANGLE: A term to describe 'L' shaped bar.

ARC RADIUS: The radius used to draw an arc of a circle, quoted when discussing 'radius chine' construction.

ATHWARTSHIP: Meaning across the boat, example, 'The webs are mostly athwartship, when located in the keel.'

BACK-CHIPPING: The techniques used to remove unwanted weld metal. Usually undertaken between weld passes. Usually achieved with a chisel or special tool, by hand or using mechanical means. On aluminum welds a power saw may be used with care.

BACKBONE: Another name for the centre line bar that runs most of the length of a hull and could include the stem and the aft centre line bar.

BASELINE OR BL: A line that runs parallel with the DWL / LWL and used on some plans and drawings as a common reference line. The 'baseline' may sometimes be above the hull or as is more usual, the bottom of the keel may act as a 'baseline'.

BATTEN: A long piece of fine grained timber, plastic or may be steel used for fairing purposes. The timber variety are used by loftsman as an aid to drawing the long water-lines and buttocks on the loft floor. Shorter versions are used for drawing the frame sections. Before the advent of computer design, Naval architects used miniature versions called 'splines' for the same purpose.

BEAM: The width of the boat at any given point. Usually given as a measurement at the maximum width of the hull. Beam overall (widest beam) or waterline beam (beam at the waterline).

BEDLOGS: Used when setting up hulls upside down. Can be steel 'I' beams or 6" x 2" / 150 x 100 or similar.

BODY PLAN: Also referred to as 'Stations', or 'Sections', this is the drawing of the hull divided into stations, usually equally spaced and may represent the frames. The waterline length is divided into 10 equal stations and the 90 degree view of these, plus the ones at the bow and stern, are shown on the body plan. The forward stations are shown to the right of the centre line and those aft of the C/L are shown on the left.

BOOT TOP: A decorative stripe painted parallel to and about 6 in / 150 mm above the water-line. This stripe marks the delineation of the topside and bottom paints. It is wise not to paint this line until your boat has been launched and loaded for cruising.

BRACING: Extra bar across or vertically installed on frames as a temporary measure to stiffen them until the hull is completed, stops stringers deforming the frames at an early stage of construction. Used to support frames or other members of the hull during the setting up stage.

BREAK-WATER: This is a vertical bulkhead above the deck, usually located ahead of the wheelhouse. As the name implies the break-water deflects the force of any water or spray that may wash onto or over the fore-deck.

BULKHEAD or BLKD: Abbreviation for the term bulkhead. A bulkhead is any 'wall' in a boat and may run longitudinally or athwartship (fore and aft or across the boat).

BULWARK: Describes any topsides that extend above the main deck. Can be combined with life rails to provide security for the crew when passing along side decks. Usually extends from bow to stern. Can be any height from 4 in / 100 mm to 36 in / 914 mm.

BUTTOCK LINE: These lines divide the hull longitudinally and vertically and when viewed in profile can reveal a considerable amount of information about the shape of the hull. They appear as straight lines in the body and plan views of the hull and as curved lines on the profile view. Used by loftsman as another set of reference lines when lofting a hull full size.

BUTT WELD: A weld used to join two pieces of plate or bar edge to edge. No overlaps!

CAD: Computer assisted drafting.

CAMBER: Used in boat design and construction to denote the amount of 'round' in the deck, cabin top and transom. For decks a common amount of camber is 3/8" / 10 mm for every 1 ft / 305 mm of beam. Sailboat cabin tops tend to have more camber, powerboats with flying bridges tend to have less (this is a heavily trafficked area), pilot houses have more and so forth. If the plans include camber patterns (as ours do) or specify cambers; do not change without consulting the designer.

CAMBER PATTERN: See Camber, patterns are supplied or you need to make your own from measurements supplied with your plans.

CEILING: Longitudinal planking attached to the inside of the frames. In traditional timber boats this inside planking was installed to add strength to the hull. In modern boats the ceiling planks are about 1 1/2" x 3/8" / 35 mm x 10 mm and are intended only as a lining material.

CENTERBOARD: Used in sailboats to reduce draft while reducing leeway. Used in place of a deep keel. See also drop keel.

CENTERLINE or C/L: An imaginary line running down the centre of the vessel, also a drawn line on the plan view and body plan of the designers plans.

CENTER LINE BAR: The bar on edge, that runs long the centre line of a metal boat. The stem is usually part of the centre line bar as is the bar running from the aft end of the keel to the stern. On some power boats, especially planing hulls, the centre line bar runs full length.

CHAIN PLATE: These days seldom used for chain, this is the tang on the hull to which the turnbuckles or rigging screws are attached. Part of the rigging set up on a sailboat.

CHINE: This when used alone generally refers to a 'hard' chine, or abrupt chine of direction between the sides and bottom of the hull. In general terms a chine is the point where the hull bottom and sides meet in a 'chine boat'. A hull can have more than one chine, (double chine), or several chines (multi chine).See also radius chine, see also knuckle.

CHORD: The straight line used to join the end points of an arc.

COLLAR: As the name suggests it can be the lining of a hole through a bulkhead (short length of pipe) so electrical cables or other similar items that penetrate a bulkhead do not chafe on the sharp edges of a raw cut hole.

COMPOUND CURVATURE: A surface that has curvature in more than one direction is said to have 'compound curvature'. A regular round bilge hull have a considerable amount of compound curvature.

COMPUTER LOFTING: Drawing out the boat full size in the computer and then plotting patterns for the frames, stem, keel and deck beams etc. See also Lofting.

CONICAL DEVELOPED or DEVELOPED SURFACE: This is a surface that is part of a cone or several interconnected cones so that a flat sheet of metal or plywood will 'drape' over the surface. Many modern powerboat designs have computer generated developed hull surfaces.

CONSTRUCTION DRAWING: This is a single sheet of drawings, measurements and written instructions that usually forms part of a set of drawings. The construction drawings are usually prepared by the designer but additional drawings may be prepared by the builder, marine electrical engineer or marine plumber.

CURVE OF AREAS: This curve(line) is plotted by the designer from measurements taken from the lines plan. The curve represents the areas of the vessels immersed sections and provides information to the designer about the shape of the hull. The computer now generates this line which was not, and is not, used for lofting.

DEADRISE: This is the change in elevation in relation to the horizontal plane. Most often used to describe the angle of V in the bottom of a powerboat hull. Example, often quoted at the transom, say 18 degrees of V or 18 degrees deadrise, the deadrise in a boats hull usually increases towards the bow.

DECK PLAN: The drawing of the deck, cabin etc., looking down from above.

DECK STRINGER: This is the stringer that intersects the hull and the deck and is used to accept the deck plating and the outboard ends of the deck beams.

DWL or DESIGNED WATERLINE or LWL: The line around the hull where the designer expects, hopes or predicts that the boat will float when completed and launched; stores, half fuel, water and crew should all be aboard when the boat floats on this line.

DEVELOPED SURFACE or DEVELOPABLE SURFACE: Any surface that can be constructed from a flat plate. See also conical surface.

DIAGONAL: Another line used by the designer to fair round bilge lines at the design stage. Not used for lofting.

DISPLACEMENT: The actual weight of the vessel when in 'cruising trim.' The weight of the amount of water displaced by the vessel.

DUCTILE: Easily bent or formed.

DROP KEEL: A ballasted centre board could best describe this item. Often airfoil shaped this ballasted keel is pivoted on a strong pin and can be raised and lowered as required. For safety sake, should be capable of being locked in the down position.

ELEVATION: Engine drawing representing the side view of the boat or other object.

ENGINE BEDS OR BEARERS: The longitudinal bearers or girders on which the engine is mounted usually via flexible mountings.

FAIR LINE or FAIRED SURFACE or FAIRING: A curved line or surface devoid of humps and hollows, fairing is to take some action to achieve this end.

FILLET WELD: The weld placed on the inside intersection where the end of one piece of metal rests at an angle on a flat plate, the weld 'in the corner' is termed a fillet weld.

FLAIR: Used to describe the outward slope of a hull above the waterline. Also used to describe the hollow seen in the bow of some fiberglass powerboats. Example, the boat has a flared bow. Opposite to 'tumblehome.'

FLAT BAR: Metal that is formed or cut into strips for example 1/4" / 6 mm plate that is only 2" / 50 mm to 8" / 205 mm wide, after that it may be called sheet. Flat bar can be any thickness.

FRAME: A structural member, usually on the same plane as a station.

FRAMELESS: Some smaller metal boats are 'frameless' which is really a misnomer as the stringers and chine bars are 'longitudinal framing'.

FREEBOARD: Height of the hull side above the water. Often quoted at various parts of the hull, usually the lowest freeboard is quoted as 'the freeboard.' measurement.

FREEING PORT: An opening in the side of the hull above the deck (usually through a bulwark) to allow the surface water from the deck to flow overboard.

FULL SIZE PATTERNS or FSP: Patterns of the frames, stem, deck beams and other construction members that have been obtained by manual lofting or computer fairing and lofting. Can be supplied on paper or Mylar film. A great aid to getting on with the job and highly recommended by this writer.

GIRTH: A measurement around a curved surface or arc.

GOOD BOATBUILDING PRACTICE: A recognised standard among boatbuilders, that denotes good quality workmanship and the use of good quality materials. As opposed to shoddy practice.

GRID: All straight and parallel lines used by loftsmen to prepare a loft floor for drawing up a set of lines. The grid includes the baseline, waterlines and buttocks.

HALF BREADTH: The distance from any point of the hull to the centre line, when taken horizontally and parallel to the DWL. All symmetrical hulls have the same half breadth for each side.

HEADSTOCK: A length of L angle or timber installed across the frames and used as part of the bracing and setting up procedure.

HEIGHTS: A measurement as in 'heights above baseline.'

HOUSE: As in deck house, dog house or cabin.

I BEAM: A steel section shaped like an I and used in the construction industry. Ideal for use as a setting up base for the frames in hulls that are built upside down.

INBOARD PROFILE: Elevation drawing usually showing one half of the accommodation plan viewed in profile (a slice from bow to stern along the centre line).

INTERCOSTAL: Fore and aft stiffener inserted between frames or deck beams as opposed to a continuous stiffener or stringer.

JIG: An arrangement specially made to hold parts of an object in a certain way until they can be permanently assembled. For example if you were building a number of similar hulls, you may have a building 'Jig' for forming up parts of the hulls or superstructure. A temporary framework as used in frameless construction is a building 'Jig.'

KEEL and BALLAST KEEL: The lowest portion of the hull, may hang well below as in a 'fin keel' or may run almost the full length as in traditional boats like the 'Spray'. There are long keels, three quarter keels. fin keels, bulb keels and wing keels.

KEELSON: The inner keel, usually runs full length of the hull from the stem aft to the transom. More applicable to timber boats but the centre line bar in a metal boat may be thought of as the keelson.

KNUCKLE: A definite change of direction in the hull plating or other surface. In true terms a chine is a knuckle. The change in direction is usually not as abrupt as with a chine, see also chine.

LADDER: As in ships ladder or boat ladder, another term for a set of stairs or steps, usually more vertical than either of the latter.

LAID DECK: A timber planked deck usually installed over a regular deck, for instance over a metal deck. Depending on thickness of the timber planks, this deck can contribute to the strength of the decks and the vessel.

LAYING OUT: To measure and locate a point on a drawing, loft floor or on a boat.

LIGHTENING HOLE: A single hole or a series of circular holes cut in a web or similar beam to reduce the weight without materially reducing the strength. Often arranged to allow the passage of cables and plumbing beneath the sole.

LIMBER HOLE: A hole cut in the bottom of a frame or web or elsewhere to allow the passage of water between frames or webs. In wooden boats a light chain was lead through the series of limber holes so as to be able to clear any rubbish preventing the passage of water to the lowest point of the bilge.

LINES DRAWING or LINES: The original drawing of the hull made by the designer or naval architect that presents the hull in plan view, profile and sectional view (stations). The hull is faired on the drawing board, today in the computer, by using waterlines, buttock lines and stations. From the lines plan the designer 'takes off' a set of 'offsets' that are used by the loftsman, or computer, to draw out the hull full size on the loft floor or by plotting on a printer/plotter.

LOA: Length overall including bowsprits and other appendages.

LOD: Length on deck, this figure is often shown as the LOA, but should not include bowsprits etc.

LOFT FLOOR: An area of floor that has been prepared for drawing out the lines full size. Usually painted 'off white' to allow a clearer view of the various lines to be drawn, seen and identified. A small version of this floor is useful for transferring Mylar or paper full size patterns to a semi-permanent surface.

LOFTING or COMPUTER LOFTING: Drawing out the boat full size on the loft floor so as to provide patterns for the frames, stem, keel and deck beams etc. Today the lofting is more likely to be done in the Computer.

LONGITUDINAL: Fore and aft, for instance a 'longitudinal' when discussing framing of a hull usually referred to a fore and aft stringer.

MARGIN PLATE: This term is used to describe a narrow plate welded inside the hull at the deckline to accept a timber and plywood deck. This plate is located in the same position and would replace the 'deck stringer'.

MIDSHIPS: Around the centre of the hull in the fore and aft plane, for instance 'midships cabin', 'midships steering' or something is located 'midships'.

MIG: An abbreviation for the type of welding more correctly known as METAL INERT GAS welding process.

MULLION: The narrow space or post between windows.

OFFSETS or TABLE OF OFFSETS: The figures or dimensions shown on a lines plan, these are 'offset' from a known point such as a centre line or baseline.

OUTBOARD PROFILE: Side view of the boat as seen from outside.

PAD EYE: A small metal plate welded to a plate or structure with either a eye or hole used to attach a line or chain for lifting plate or other section of the boat.

PASSAGEWAY: Space between bulkheads or joinery used as access, usually fore and aft.

PASSAGEMAKER: A term popularised by Robert P. Beebe meaning a long distance ocean crossing power boat.

PLUG WELDING: Welding through slots or holes for instance when attaching the outside shell of a keel to the inside webs where access from inside is not available. Also used to weld one plate on top of another; not recommended at least for steel, due to potential corrosion problems.

PLUMB-BOB: A pointed weight on a string line used from above a frame or other section to ensure that the frame is truly vertical or 'plumb'.

PORT: To the left, as in port side, left side. Any 'window' in a boat can be termed as a port. Large ports are now usually referred to as windows.

PORTLIGHT: Another boating term for window.

RADIUS CHINE: A radius chine is a chine formed by a known part of a circle where the radius is constant from the stern right through to the bow. Most radius chine boats are designed using complex yacht design computer software. The amount of arc may vary in a radius chine boat, but the radius remains constant. The largest amount of arc is at the stern, tapering right through to the bow.

SCALE: Ratio of size relative to actual size, for example, 1/2" = 1'-0" means one half inch on the drawing equals one foot on the boat. In drawings prepared the metric scale, 1 = 50 would mean that one on the drawing equals 50 on the actual boat.

SCANTLINGS: Sizes and dimensions of materials used to build the boat. The thickness and other dimensions shown on the 'list of materials' are the scantlings.

SEA-COCK: According to one version of 'Word Perfect' this was an offensive term! In boating language it means a tap or valve used to shut off the flow of water to and from hull. Drains, inlet pipes and other pipes that pierce the hull surface, should all be fitted with a 'sea-cock'.

SHAFT HORSEPOWER: The horsepower actually available at the propeller.

SHEER or SHEERLINE: Top of the hull viewed in profile.

SHELL: The outer skin of the hull, as in 'shell plating'.

SHOAL DRAFT: A boat with shallow draft is said to be a 'shoal draft vessel'.

SHROUD: A side stay or wire support for the mast on any boat.

SPANISH WINDLASS: A loop of rope or wire that is twisted with a stick or rod to 'draw in' one surface or section to another.

STAY: Fore and aft wire supporting the mast, as in fore stay or backstay.

STANCHION: The posts around the edge of the deck are known as stanchions.

STARBOARD or STBD: Left hand side of the boat.

STATION or STN: Usually there are 10 stations, slices through the hull side to side, dividing up the waterline.

STEM: The vertical forward end of the boat when viewed in profile.

STERN: Aft end of the boat, as in Counter stern (long overhanging stern), Transom stern (squared off after end of the hull), Canoe stern (when the aft end of the hull comes to a point similar to that at the bow)

STIFFENER: Frames, stringers and chine bars are all stiffeners. A stiffener supports an area of the hull from inside and breaks up areas of hull shell into smaller stiffened or supported areas.

STRINGER: Fore and aft stiffener as in hull or deck stringer.

STRAKE: A stiffener or stringer on the outside of the hull. Traditional timber boats often have strakes on the outside to add additional strength. Work boats have strakes to protect the hull against fishing gear etc. Modern planing hulls have 'Planing strakes' to assist them in reaching and maintaining the planing attitude.

STRONGBACK: A jig used to set up the frames during the initial setting up of the hull.

STUFFING BOX: A packing gland used to keep the water from entering the hull from the stern or rudder tube.

T BAR: As the term indicates, this is a bar shaped like a T and used for transverse frames, deck beams and other structural members in a metal boat.

TANG: Usually refers to a point on the mast where the rigging is attached. Usually a strap or flat bar. Can be used elsewhere on the boat.

TEMPER: Heat treatment of metals to change the mechanical qualities for example to make a metal more or less ductile.

TEMPLATE: A pattern of any object. A plate template is a pattern that is made off the framework of the hull and then transferred to the plate before cutting to shape and installing on the hull.

TIG or TUNGSTEN INERT GAS: A welding process suitable for most metals, uses a non-consumable electrode and a shielding gas.

TRANSOM: Correctly describes a form of stern on the hull. Transom stern is a squared off stern. Reverse transom is as seen on many modern sailboats.

TRANSVERSE: Across the boat at 90 degrees to the centre line of the boat.

TUMBLEHOME: Used to describe a hull where the sheer has less beam than a lower point on the hull.

WATERLINE or WL: The fore and aft plane of the hull relative to the line where the topsides meet the water, or where the vessel floats. Load waterline is the line where the vessel floats. Designed waterline is where the designer hopes it will float. On a lines drawing , waterlines are drawn at regular intervals above and below the waterline.

WATERTIGHT: A hull or other part of the boat that will not allow the passage of water.

WHEEL: A boating term for the propeller.

"S" is for SAFETY. This is my final piece of advice. No matter what operation you undertake when building and maintaining your metal boat always remember "SAFETY FIRST". Equip yourself with the correct safety equipment appropriate for the job in hand. Thank you Mr M. Bastion of Devon UK for the photo to illustrate this point.